Traces of the Ramayana and Mahabharata in Javanese and Malay Literature

The **ISEAS – Yusof Ishak Institute** (formerly Institute of Southeast Asian Studies) is an autonomous organization established in 1968. It is a regional centre dedicated to the study of socio-political, security, and economic trends and developments in Southeast Asia and its wider geostrategic and economic environment. The Institute's research programmes are grouped under Regional Economic Studies (RES), Regional Strategic and Political Studies (RSPS), and Regional Social and Cultural Studies (RSCS). The Institute is also home to the ASEAN Studies Centre (ASC), the Nalanda-Sriwijaya Centre (NSC), and the Singapore APEC Study Centre.

ISEAS Publishing, an established academic press, has issued more than 2,000 books and journals. It is the largest scholarly publisher of research about Southeast Asia from within the region. ISEAS Publishing works with many other academic and trade publishers and distributors to disseminate important research and analyses from and about Southeast Asia to the rest of the world.

Traces of the Ramayana and Mahabharata in Javanese and Malay Literature

EDITED BY

DING CHOO MING
WILLEM VAN DER MOLEN

ISEAS YUSOF ISHAK INSTITUTE

First published in Singapore in 2018 by
ISEAS Publishing
30 Heng Mui Keng Terrace
Singapore 119614

E-mail: publish@iseas.edu.sg
Website: bookshop.iseas.edu.sg

ISEAS Library Cataloguing-in-Publication Data

Traces of the Ramayana and Mahabharata in Javanese and Malay Literature / edited by Ding Choo Ming and Willem van der Molen.
1. Vālmīki. Rāmāyaṇa.
2. Mahābhārata.
3. Malay literature.
4. Javanese literature.
I. Ding, Choo Ming.
II. Molen, W. van der (Willem), 1952–
PL5170 T75 2018

ISBN 978-981-4786-57-7 (soft cover)
ISBN 978-981-4786-58-4 (E-book PDF)

Cover illustration: wooden statue of a scribe. Collectie Stichting Nationaal Museum van Wereldculturen. Coll. nr. TM-809-112.

Typeset by International Typesetters Pte Ltd
Printed in Singapore by Mainland Press Pte Ltd

CONTENTS

Abbreviations vi

About the Contributors vii

1. Introduction 1
   Willem van der Molen

2. The Rāmāyaṇa in Java and Bali: Chapters from its Literary History 5
   Stuart Robson

3. Abimanyu Gugur: The Death of Abimanyu in Classical and Modern Indonesian and Malay Literature 30
   Harry Aveling

4. Drona's Betrayal and Bima's Brutality: Javanaiserie in Malay Culture 58
   Bernard Arps

5. Ramayana and Mahabharata in Hikayat Misa Taman Jayeng Kusuma 99
   Gijs L. Koster

6. The Death of Śalya: Balinese Textual and Iconographic Representations of the Kakawin Bhāratayuddha 137
   Helen Creese

7. The Illustrated Aṣṭabrata in Pakualaman Manuscript Art 180
   Edwin P. Wieringa

Index 217

ABBREVIATIONS

AJ	Anno Javanico (Javanese Era)
BhK	Bhaṭṭikāvya
BKI	*Bijdragen tot de Taal-, Land- en Volkenkunde*, published by the Koninklijk Instituut voor Taal-, Land en Volkenkunde, Leiden
BP	Balai Pustaka
BY	Bhāratayuddha (Supomo 1993)
Cod. Or.	Codex Orientalis of the Leiden University Library
HKS	Hooykaas-Ketut Sangka Collection
HMTJK	Hikayat Misa Taman Jayeng Kusuma
K	Gedong Kirtya, Singaraja
KITLV	Koninklijk Instituut voor Taal-, Land- en Volkenkunde, Leiden
LOr	Codex Orientalis, Leiden University Library
OJR	Old Javanese Rāmāyaṇa
RGCK	Raden Galuh Candera Kirana
RIK	Raden Inu Kertapati
RY	Rāmāyaṇa
VKI	Verhandelingen van het Koninklijk Instituut voor Taal-, Land- en Volkenkunde, Leiden

ABOUT THE CONTRIBUTORS

Bernard Arps is fascinated by performative and mediated worldmaking, particularly in religious contexts in Southeast Asia. Currently Professor of Indonesian and Javanese Language and Culture at Leiden University, his most recent book is *Tall Tree, Nest of the Wind: The Javanese Shadow-Play Dewa Ruci Performed by Ki Anom Soeroto; A Study in Performance Philology* (2016).

Harry Aveling PhD (NUS) DCA (UTS) holds an adjunct appointment as a Professor in the School of Languages, Literatures, Cultures and Linguistics at Monash University, Melbourne, Australia. He has translated extensively from Indonesian and Malay literature and received the Anugerah Perkembangan Sastera in 1991 for his commitment to the international understanding of Malay literature.

Helen Creese is Associate Professor in Indonesian in the School of Languages and Cultures at the University of Queensland. She has published extensively on Old Javanese literature, particularly on the Balinese *kakawin* tradition, as well as on later Balinese literature and history. Her most recent book is *Bali in the Early Nineteenth Century: The Ethnographic Accounts of Pierre Dubois* (2016).

Ding Choo Ming is Professor Emeritus of Malay Literature at the National University of Malaysia. He is the author of a handbook on Malay philology (*Kajian manuskrip Melayu: Masalah, kritikan dan cadangan*, 2003), and edited, together with Zalina Abdul Aziz, *Bridging* *the Past and the Present: A Festschrift Honouring Muhammad Haji Salleh* (2015), besides publishing on Malay literature in the Riau Islands, especially the pantun and local knowledge in the Malay world.

Gijs L. Koster is an independent scholar who has lived in Portugal since 2003. After taking his PhD (Leiden University, 1993) he has taught Malay-Indonesian and comparative literature (University Sains Malaysia, Universitas Indonesia), Indonesian language and Southeast Asian culture (University of Porto) and history of China (University of the Minho, Braga). Resulting from a Portuguese government scholarship (2003–9) he has among others published a chapter "Popular and Court Visions of the Portuguese in the Traditional Narratives of the Malay World", in Jorge Santos Alves, *Portugal and Indonesia: The Political and Diplomatic Relations (1500–1974)*, Vol II. (Instituto de Macau: Macau, 2013), pp. 209–325. His current research is concerned with Malay Panji romances..

Willem van der Molen is Adjunct Professor of Philology and Old Javanese at the University of Indonesia, Depok, and Senior Researcher at the Royal Netherlands Institute of Southeast Asian and Caribbean Studies in Leiden. His major interest of research concerns the story of Rama and Sita in Old Javanese and Javanese literature. Recently, he published a history of Javanese literature (2016). He is co-editor of the Tokyo-based series "Javanese Studies".

Stuart Robson is currently an Adjunct Professor of Indonesian Studies in the School of Languages, Literatures, Cultures and Linguistics at Monash University in Melbourne. He was born in Sydney in 1941, spent many years in Leiden, and taught Indonesian at Monash (1991–2001). He specialized in Javanese, including Old and Middle Javanese, and has contributed a number of translations in this field. With a special interest in lexicography, he assisted with P.J. Zoetmulder's *Old Javanese–English Dictionary* (1982), and compiled a Javanese–English dictionary (2002). He also wrote a textbook of Indonesian (*Basic Indonesian*, 2010) and of Javanese (*Javanese Grammar for Students*, 3rd ed. 2014).

Edwin P. Wieringa is Professor of Indonesian Philology and Islamic Studies at the University of Cologne. Among his most recent publications is a bilingual (German and Indonesian) exhibition catalogue of Indonesian manuscripts at the Berlin State Library (with T. Hanstein), *SchriftSprache; Aksara dan bahasa. Ausstellungskatalog; Katalog pameran* (2015).

1

INTRODUCTION

Willem van der Molen

The written literatures of Malay and Javanese have a long history — more than one thousand years in the case of Javanese. During this long period the outward appearance of the book changed beyond recognition, themes occupying the minds of the authors and their audiences were adapted to new ideologies, long established literary conventions gave way to completely different ones, and the languages concerned, subject to constant renewal like any natural language, went through successive stages that became more and more incomprehensible with increasing distance in time.

These and other factors contributed to old texts falling into oblivion and new ones rising to popularity. A constant element amidst change, resisting the threat of oblivion, was the Ramayana and Mahabharata. Having arrived early in the history of Javanese literature, both epics found expression in various forms during the long period of Indian influence. The epics remained after the Indianized culture to which they belonged waned and disappeared. Continuing to manifest themselves in all sorts of shapes, their presence was not undermined by the advance of Islam in Java, nor was it by the more recent influence of Western culture. Information on the history of Malay literature, though providing less detail, shows a similar picture.

The chapters collected in *Traces of the Ramayana and Mahabharata in Javanese and Malay Literature* go beyond mapping epic presence. They show what happened during transmission, adaptation and borrowing, and offer hypotheses on the underlying motives. The authors scrutinize a couple of selected texts and pictorial representations and — again or for the first time — address old questions and raise new ones, going back and forth in time, connecting Javanese and Malay and even Balinese literature.

The author with whom the volume opens, Stuart Robson, gives an overall view of the history of one text, the story of Rama and Sita, from the Old Javanese Ramayana of the ninth century up to the Serat Rama and Rama Keling written in the seventeenth and eighteenth centuries. Quite extraordinarily, the intervals between copies (partly hypothetical, partly based on real examples) appear to coincide with important moments in the history of Javanese culture. Taking Teeuw's theory on literary history and on translation as his starting point, the author is able to explain continued Javanese interest in the story from the wider social context as it developed over almost one millennium.

Harry Aveling in the third chapter considers an even longer stretch of time of almost two millennia. He takes a closer look at the "Death of Abimanyu", a story from the Mahabharata, which he follows in its treatment in four different periods in four different literatures: the Sanskrit original (traditionally ascribed to the beginning of the Western calendar), the Old Javanese version of 1157, the undated Classical Malay rendering, and the Modern Indonesian short story "Nostalgia" of 1987 by Danarto. The four versions propound fundamentally different ideals. While Abimanyu in all renderings is a great hero, the Sanskrit text stresses the ksatriya-dharma, the heroic ideal of the nobleman. The Old Javanese exaltation of the poetic beauty of death, on the other hand, brings us to the "tantrism of the battlefield", as it was called by Zoetmulder. The Classical Malay text returns to the ideal of the nobleman, not in the old Sanskrit sense but the Malay way, applying the Malay norm of a good name. "Nostalgia" with its pantheistic overtones holds up a completely different ideal again, in the phrasing of one of its antagonists: "There is a more noble human destiny and that is to vanish from history."

A famous story about Bima, one of the main heroes of the Mahabharata, is that of his quest for the water of life. Many versions of this story exist in Javanese. In his discussion of a Malay version, Bernard Arps in Chapter 4 presents an alternative for the usual way we see the phenomenon of borrowing: he invites us to imagine the presence of Javanese elements in Malay literature not as something lent by Javanese culture or selected by Malay authors, but as a deliberate creation on the part of the Malay authors. This procedure, apart from expressing admiration, at the same time leaves room for dealing with certain aspects considered problematic for a Muslim society, such as magic and sorcery: they are projected onto the Javanese, although they are as much alive among the Malays themselves.

Gijs Koster in his contribution (Chapter 5) addresses a Malay Panji story, one of the stories that revolve around the love between Raden Panji, the Prince of Koripan, and Princess Candra Kirana of Daha. Originally Javanese, these stories also found their way into Malay and other literatures of Southeast Asia. How the Malay stories relate exactly to the Javanese stories has still to be cleared up, but they are by no means direct translations. Koster shows that elements from the Mahabharata and Ramayana – most probably taken from New Javanese and Malay adaptations – together with disparate elements from other texts were deployed to foreground the fictionality of the story discussed by him.

In Chapter 6, Helen Creese's contribution offers an excursion into the realm of Balinese literature and pictorial representation. Created in the nineteenth century, the works discussed belong to a Balinese tradition of continued interest in the Mahabharata and Ramayana. They refer to the episode of the final war with which the Mahabharata concludes. This episode is the subject of one poem in Old Javanese in particular, the twelfth-century Baratayuda, which has been held in high esteem in Bali until now. In addition to the Sanskrit text, and clearly created by the twelfth-century Javanese poet, the Baratayuda contains a passage about one of the army commanders and his wife. In the text it is given a name of its own. Scholars of Old Javanese like to refer to it as a poem in its own right. It is remarkable that it is precisely this passage that inspired the products of later Balinese authors and artists.

Edwin Wieringa in the last chapter likewise turns to the field of pictorial art. The drawings discussed by him illustrate three nineteenth- to early twentieth-century manuscripts of the Asṭabrata. The Asṭabrata is a well-known text in Javanese on royal behaviour, ultimately deriving from the Old Javanese Ramayana. The title refers to the eight (*asṭa*) exemplary Hindu deities who are portrayed in the manuscripts. Wieringa is interested to know how the language of silhouette and wording relate. Iconography is a highly developed branch of knowledge in Java, both at the general level of categories and at the specific level of individuals. However, in the case of the Asṭabrata manuscripts the characteristic features were applied too loosely to bring out a systematic relationship between the two languages.

The six chapters of *Traces of Ramayana and Mahabharata in Javanese and Malay Literature* grew out from papers presented at a conference on the Indian epics in these two literatures, held in 2014 at the ISEAS – Yusof Ishak Institute in Singapore. The initiative for the conference was taken by Professor Ding Choo Ming from the Universiti Kebangsaan Malaysia, at that time a Visiting Senior Fellow at the ISEAS – Yusof Ishak Institute. Keen to bring the worlds of Javanese and Malay studies together, he successfully created the conditions for mutually profitable discussions that led to the present volume. After having been host to the conference of 2014, the Institute also took responsibility for publishing the results. I wish to thank both Professor Ding and the Institute for their commitment to this project.

2

THE RĀMĀYAṆA IN JAVA AND BALI: Chapters from its Literary History

Stuart Robson

Taking as foundation an article by Professor A. Teeuw from 1986, this chapter aims to look at the questions of literary history, translation and transformation, as they apply to the theme of the Rāmāyaṇa, ranging from the Old Javanese Rāmāyaṇa in Java and Bali to the Serat Rama and Rama Keling in Java. The chapter takes socio-cultural setting into consideration, and concludes that much more basic philological work is needed before any satisfactory results can be produced.

Keywords: Old Javanese; Rāmāyaṇa; literary history; translation and transformation; structural analysis; transmission; manuscripts.

Introduction

Beyond the narrow circle of specialists, even among scholars of Southeast Asia, the very existence of a literature in a language called Old Javanese may come as a surprise, and so one should not automatically expect to find an appreciation of its special qualities. Yet it is undoubtedly part of the heritage of the people of Java and Bali who created it, and hence more generally of all Indonesians, constituting an element of their national culture.

At the same time, however, it has often been non-Indonesians who have taken an interest in Old Javanese, beginning with Dutch scholars in the colonial period, and continuing with others in various countries in the post-independence era. Such international attention suggests that the products of Old Javanese literature are by no means the exclusive possession of any one group, but are capable of taking their place among the treasures of world literature, which can be enjoyed by readers of any background. This is then the present writer's point of view.

The scholars who first came to the academic study of Old Javanese (as distinct from the traditional indigenous study) approached it from their understanding of the cultural history of the region, with its obvious links to Indian civilization — after all, the script used for writing and many of the themes could be traced to Indian origins. A knowledge of Sanskrit is understandably useful for reading Old Javanese. However, the spirit and the inspiration of many of these literary works, prose and poetry, is also plainly indigenous, so that we should not make the mistake of denying the Old Javanese authors due credit for their remarkable achievements.

These remarks apply to the Rāmāyaṇa as well, of course. Here we are confronted with a famous product of Indian literature, which has been transplanted and recreated in a new setting, namely Java in the early Hindu period. As a result we propose to treat the Javanese Rāmāyaṇa as an *independent work of literature*, acknowledging its Indian sources and yet claiming a special place among the literary products of Java and Bali, worthy of study in its own right. This is a brief statement of our starting point in the review of its literary history.

Translation

An article by Professor E.M. Uhlenbeck published in 1975 placed the Old Javanese Rāmāyaṇa "on the agenda" once again, drawing attention to it as a remarkable piece of literature deserving of further close study, including translation which, he says, is usually done with most success into one's own mother tongue (Uhlenbeck 1975, p. 213).

Next an important paper published by Professor A. Teeuw in 1986, with the title "Translation, Transformation and Indonesian Literary History", provided what might be called a theoretical foundation for a further discussion of the case of the Rāmāyaṇa. The 1980s formed an optimistic period in Indonesian literary studies in Leiden, and considerable progress was made with work such as this.

Teeuw begins by asking what "literary history" is, and distinguishes no fewer than four approaches in European studies: looking at it as "part and parcel of cultural history"; or featuring a periodization according to the major periods of national history; or a mere chronological enumeration of the main works; or the study of the origins of the literary motifs and themes. We can probably recognize various examples of these in the fields of Malay and Javanese literature.

He then observes a gradual shift in emphasis from the historical to the structural, so that a work came to be looked at for its own sake, analysed in its own right, "apart from information about its author, his biography or intentions, and also apart from its socio-historical relevance" (Teeuw 1986, p. 191). This was a weakness, he says, "as the emphasis on the autonomy of the text inevitably isolated the work from its literary context", and it also "consciously isolated the work from its socio-cultural context; in this way literature was denied its social function and relevance" (Teeuw 1986, p. 192).

Teeuw states the problem as "how to integrate what is valuable in the structuralist approach, that is, the attention for the text as a coherent, meaningful, structural whole, into a historical approach which synchronically and diachronically deals with literature as a system and which puts the literary work at the centre, without detaching it from its socio-cultural setting". There are thus at least six major aspects of the literary work that have to be taken into account, namely:

1. The literary work as a linguistic structure;
2. The literary work in its synchronic setting;
3. The literary work in its diachronic setting;
4. The literary work and the reader;
5. The literary work in its social context; and
6. The literary work as a work of art. (Teeuw 1986, p. 192)

With regard to literature in any Indonesian language, this is a pretty tall order. However, for Malay Vladimir Braginsky's monumental *The Heritage of Traditional Malay Literature* (2004) is a fine example of what can be achieved in terms of the above points, even though he calls it just a "historical survey" and not a history. One of the main problems was, and still is, the lack of texts published according to proper philological principles (Robson 1988): how can we possibly talk about texts or their literary history, when they are simply not available on the shelf for us to read, enjoy and evaluate?

Teeuw points to the importance of foreign texts for the development of Indonesian literatures; in the past Dutch scholars tended to trace the origins of texts to Sanskrit, Arabic and Persian originals. The main questions, as Teeuw formulates them, are:

1. Why was a particular text chosen for translation or transformation in an Indonesian language?
2. What happened to the text in the process of translation?
3. What did such a translation do to Indonesian literature?
4. What did Indonesian literature do with such a text? (Teeuw 1986, p. 194)

Teeuw takes as an example F. Vodička's study (1976) of the Czech translation by Jungmann in 1805 of the French text *Atala* by Chateaubriand, which, it is argued, is the spark which led to the rise of Czech as a national language in the nineteenth century. He then moves on to four examples from Indonesia, namely the Old Javanese Rāmāyaṇa, the Malay *hikayat*, the Malay *syair*, and the modern Indonesian novel. It is the first of these that we now have to examine in a little more detail.

The best account of the origins of the Old Javanese Rāmāyaṇa (OJR) is still the article by Vinod Khanna and Malini Saran, "The Rāmāyaṇa Kakawin: A Product of Sanskrit Scholarship and Independent Literary Genius" (1993), and the present remarks draw heavily on this article.

A suggestion made by H.B. Sarkar as early as 1934, and developed by C. Hooykaas in 1955, is that the OJR had an Indian prototype, and this was not the Vālmīki Rāmāyaṇa but the Bhaṭṭikāvya (BhK, alias

Rāvaṇavadha, "Death of Rāvaṇa", by Bhaṭṭi). However, a detailed comparison by Khanna and Saran shows that the author was familiar with both these sources, and followed them to varying degrees in different places: the first part follows the BhK closely, then this is abandoned for Vālmīki, and then there is a return to the BhK. To make it even more complicated, there are parts that are an independent creation, and there are also two passages where the author is basing himself on two more Sanskrit classics, namely the Bhagavadgītā and the Manusmṛti (alias Mānavadharmaśāstra). In any case Vālmīki provided the bulk of the plot. But the last section, consisting of part of Sarga 24, Sarga 25 and Sarga 26, is quite different from the Sanskrit epic, and is probably by a different author, according to Zoetmulder (Zoetmulder 1974, p. 230).

It remains a mystery why the author should have started out to translate or paraphrase the BhK, which happens to be an extremely abstruse Sanskrit work and which has as its aim to illustrate the full gamut of artificial literary figures — whereas the Old Javanese work is generally a model of simplicity and elegance. The Old Javanese author was apparently aiming primarily to tell a story; hence the nature of the text is basically narrative, and the style may have been adapted to the needs of an audience, who perceived the work aurally, rather than visually, on a written page. Within the story, there is ample scope for descriptions of nature, and we also find lengthy passages containing instruction on statecraft (as will be mentioned below).

The OJR is the earliest extant example of its kind. On the one hand it is inspired by the Sanskrit *kāvya* ("artificial court epic"), in that it uses a large number of metres constructed on the same principle as Sanskrit metres, namely "quantity" (that is, the distinction between long and short syllables, in Sanskrit called "heavy" and "light"), and on the other hand the language is clearly a member of the Austronesian family, and the mature conventions suggest a long use for literary purposes. In the subsequent course of Hindu-Javanese history, and after that in (Hindu) Bali, the same metrical system would continue to be used for the genre of poetry termed *kakawin*.

The precise dating of the OJR is a subject of debate. It is likely that it was written in the second half of the ninth century, with the final part dating from around 900–930, bearing in mind, of course, that such a long work will have taken some years to complete. And add to this the complicating political factor of the well-known shift in the centre of the Hindu-Javanese kingdom from Central to East Java, which took place at precisely this time, namely the end of the ninth century up to about 930. It is probable that this geographical shift had important consequences for the fate of the literary work.

In this way, we have here an example of how an act of translation and transformation led to the creation of a genre, the Old Javanese *kakawin*, and ushered in a series of independent compositions, which themselves would be important for Javanese literary history.

Thought-World

Bearing in mind the dating for the OJR suggested above, it becomes apparent that it was created in the same environment as other, more concrete, witnesses — cultural expressions which can be assumed to have been inspired by the same set of ideas, which we call Hindu-Javanese civilization. One thinks immediately of the monumental remains still to be seen in several localities in Central Java, such as the temples at Prambanan and Borobudur. These buildings obviously had a special purpose and function within the thought-world of the people who erected them. There are other products as well, sometimes neglected, such as sculpture, bronze and gold jewellery. All these together are evidence of the existence of a highly sophisticated and aesthetically advanced civilization in Java in the ninth century. This then is the context in which we have to imagine the author, or authors, of the OJR at work composing their epic story.

The text itself is evidence of what the author wanted to say — it is after all the result of his effort and thought. What is he saying? Does he have a message? In order to discover this we have to examine the text closely from beginning to end, treating it as an integrated whole. It is telling us the story of Rāma and Sītā, the conflict with Rāwaṇa, and the resolution of the strife through Rāma's final victory. So it is "just a story"? Numerous passages in the text, taking the form of long speeches by the main characters, point us in the direction of another layer of meaning, namely the duty of royalty to maintain and restore the welfare of the world. This was clearly a very important subject. Some passages are for example where:

> Rāma instructs his brother Bharata on how to rule in his place (Sarga 3.53–84);
> Wibhīṣaṇa advises his brother Rāwaṇa on good policy (Sarga 13.40–96); or
> Rāma instructs Wibhīṣaṇa on how to rule as the new king of Lĕngkā (Sarga 24.48–86).

The last-mentioned would become famous in later times as the Aṣṭabrata ("Eight Rules of Life"), and has been traced back to Chapter IX of the Sanskrit Manusmṛti. It is thus small wonder that scholars in modern Bali value the OJR as a source of edifying instruction on such subjects.

But it may be possible to take the investigation to an even deeper level. Where is the story *as a whole* taking us, apart from the passages of instruction? The answer to this question is to be found where the story has reached its climax, that is, when Rāma has achieved his victory over Rāwaṇa, and Sītā's purity has been established. This juncture comes at Sarga 24.200–201, where none other than the Supreme Lord, Parameśwara, intervenes in visible form and declares to Rāma:

> You are indeed the god Wiṣṇu, and your best-beloved Sītā, she is Śrī herself — undivided, of one soul, pure and faithful [...] Fulfil the purpose for which you were born [...] The welfare of the world, this must be nurtured. That will be the fruit of your victory.

The audience has been conducted through the whole succession of events — the abduction of Sītā, the misery of separation, the search and mobilization of the monkey allies, the building of the causeway and preparations for war, the clashes between the many heroic warriors, right up to the huge final battle and the death of Rāwaṇa. So now the world is coming to life again and is being restored to a flourishing condition through the action of this exemplary ruler. But the additional fact that we now have to understand is that this king only achieves his aim because he is a channel (sometimes unconscious!) of divine power: he is an incarnation of the god Wiṣṇu. And the point is also made clear that Rāma and Sītā are a couple, working together in unity, as Wiṣṇu and his consort Śrī.

The theme of the divine nature of Rāma had already been announced by a troupe of sages in the sky in Sarga 21.126–147, in a long passage addressed to Rāma which has been traced to a Sanskrit source, the Bhagavadgītā Chapter X, the crucial difference being that in the latter case Arjuna is being addressed by Kṛṣṇa.

In this way we have already moved toward addressing some of the points raised by Teeuw regarding structural analysis and literary history, in particular the socio-cultural setting of the work. We observe that:

1. The institution of kingship is central; it is all about kings, as the pivot of society. This suggests that the audience who heard the story were also imbued with this conception of the structure of society, and probably had their own slot within that;
2. The function (duty, *dharma*) of the king as a Kṣatriya was to fight and maintain the "welfare of the world", to defend and promote order and prosperity, and we can even postulate that the demonic order so prominent in the story is intended to embody the opposite condition, namely chaos and destruction; and finally,
3. The gods are seen as ever-present, sometimes visible and sometimes not, but always ready to intervene at critical times and to exert their superior power when needed.

Before moving forward, we need to look back for a moment and reflect on another kind of telling of the Rāmāyaṇa theme, namely the one to be seen at Prambanan (Loro Jonggrang). This takes the form of narrative reliefs, sculpted on the walls of the Śiwa and Brahma temples in this complex. The construction is dated to the mid-ninth century, so this places the reliefs in approximately the same period as the text as handed down in manuscript form. On this basis one might have expected the two forms to match, but this is apparently not the case, as was established by W. Stutterheim in 1925 (English translation 1989). Although both are definitely a Rāmāyaṇa, they differ in detail. The Prambanan version is not identical with Vālmīki, and also does not correspond with the Bhaṭṭikāvya, but is thought to have some resemblance to the Malay Hikayat Seri Rama. However, this is something that needs to be investigated in more detail. In any case at least two versions of the Rāmāyaṇa were current at this time in Central Java. The one which formed the basis of the reliefs was not necessarily an oral one, but could also have been a written text (Jordaan 1996). But it clearly could not have been the Hikayat Seri Rama as we have it today, as this is much later, a product of the early Islamic period (Robson 2002, p. 14); the form of the names in the Malay work makes a Tamil origin very likely, although not the literary version of Kamban.[1]

Another important piece of literature that should be introduced here is the Old Javanese Uttarakāṇḍa,[2] a prose work which mentions the name of King Dharmawangśa, and hence can be dated to the same era as other Old Javanese prose works, the parwa, namely the end of the tenth century. The Wirāṭaparwa is dated precisely to 996 (Supomo 1972, p. 264). The title indicates that it is the "last book", that is, it comes at the close of the Rāmāyaṇa tale, following Rāma's return to Ayodhyā, when the sage Agastya relates the "prehistory" of the conflict between Rāma and Rāwaṇa. It is a later addition to the Vālmīki Rāmāyaṇa, and formed the basis of an Old Javanese kakawin from the Majapahit period, the Arjunawijaya (Supomo, ed. 1977), as well as a group of *wayang* stories focusing on the figure of Arjuna Sasrabahu.

Transmission

Having been created at a certain point of time, in order to be handed down to the present day, and to be available for us to read now, a text such as the Rāmāyaṇa has to be transmitted by means of the physical vehicle of manuscripts. It can reasonably be assumed that in the period concerned such manuscripts took the form of lontar leaves — certainly not bark paper, stone or copper plates. According to one estimate, based on dated colophons attached to other works, the necessary recopying of a manuscript might have been carried out at intervals of approximately 150 years.

Now our argument becomes more speculative. How many times would the OJR have had to be recopied in the course of its textual history? Using 150 years as a basis, and assuming that the original was completed in 900, then recopying might have taken place in the following periods:

1. In 1050, that is, in East Java, in or soon after the reign of King Erlangga;
2. In 1200, that is, in the Kadiri period, famous for the composition of the major examples of the *kakawin* genre;
3. In 1350, that is, in the middle of the Majapahit period, also known for several important works;
4. In 1500, in Bali, in the Gelgel-Klungkung period, noted for its literary activity;
5. In 1650, also in Bali; and
6. In 1800, in Bali or Lombok — which brings us into the modern era.

This rough calculation suggests recopying about six times, three times in Java and three times in Bali, at junctures which happen to coincide with periods of literary activity, which may have included efforts to preserve works handed down from the past, for the purpose of conservation and study. However, as kindly pointed out by Willem van der Molen (personal communication), this is merely one scenario; it is also possible, even likely, that someone wishing to possess the work might order a copy at any time in its "life", not necessarily at the end. This could result in even more recopyings.

One clear fixed point in the sequence is formed by the depiction of scenes from the Rāmāyaṇa on the walls of Candi Panataran (then called Palah), on the main temple. Regarding dating, the "dated temple" bears the year AD 1369 (and there are other dates elsewhere in the complex), so these reliefs can confidently be placed in the second half of the fourteenth century, in agreement with recopying number 3 according to the above reconstruction.

While the connection of these reliefs with the Rāmāyaṇa is undoubted, they do not depict the whole story by any means. From a study of the scenes found here, it becomes apparent that the figure of Hanuman is prominent, much more so than the supposed hero Rāma, leading to the conclusion that in the belief system of the people of that time Hanuman has assumed a special role, which Kieven calls one of a "mediator endowed with magical powers" (Kieven 2011).[3]

This clearly demonstrates that with the passage of several centuries and a changed socio-cultural environment it was possible for the significance of the theme to be viewed in an entirely new light. Anticipating the next stage in our discussion, we should note the remarks made by Vickers on the figure of Anoman (Hanuman) as seen in Balinese painting: Anoman, in common with Bima, is able to fly and is associated with power:

> Anoman literally has world-destroying potential, and his links with such powers, and with Siwa, illustrate the same kind of power that Stutterheim links to Bima [...] As Hildred Geertz has shown, the pervasiveness of forms of power outside those perceived by the senses is a major Balinese preoccupation. (Vickers 2011, p. 129)

Finally, Klokke (2006) refers to the appearance of statues of Anoman in the Majapahit period.

With the waning of the Majapahit period, the account is taken over by the island of Bali, and the continuity of literary tradition is embodied in the figure of Nirartha, Ida Wau Rauh, and described in the Dwijendratattwa and Babad Brahmana, as set out by Rubinstein (2000, pp. 72–97). Although the dating is not, and cannot be, precise, we find here a record of remarkable original literary activity in sixteenth-century Bali.

On the eve of the modern period, the last link in the chain of transmission is formed by manuscripts still in existence and now kept in catalogued collections. Restricting ourselves just to specimens which happen to be complete (rare in the case of such a long work!), by way of example we find in the collection of the Leiden University Library the following:

> Cod. Or. 2201, dated Śaka 1729 (= AD 1807), and
> Cod. Or. 2202, dated Śaka 1706 (= AD 1794) (Pigeaud 1968, p. 83).

However,

> Cod. Or. 4436 and 4438 have no colophons mentioned by Pigeaud (1968, p. 217), while Creese (2011, p. 118) for 4436 lists a date 06-09-1807, and Śaka 1735 (= 1813) for 4438.

So there is either an omission or an error on somebody's part here. In any case, the dates found come close to the year 1800 suggested above for the last recopying of the OJR.

Creese has reviewed the available manuscripts of the OJR (Creese 2011, pp. 99–100) found in Bali, and remarks that three (very) fragmentary specimens are found in the Lombok collection, taken from Cakranegara at the time of the Dutch expedition of 1894; these are:

> Cod. Or. 5094, dated by Creese 5-06-1828 (Pigeaud 1968, p. 264);
> Cod. Or. 5262 (Pigeaud 1968, pp. 293–94); and
> Cod. Or. 5384 (Pigeaud 1968, p. 310).

This shows that manuscripts of the OJR existed not only in Bali but also in Lombok. Creese writes that

> [...] just as elsewhere in South and Southeast Asia, in Bali too, there is no single '*Rāmāyaṇa*' but instead a number of distinct literary, visual and performing arts representations that have each contributed to the creativity that underpins the vitality of *Rāmāyaṇa* traditions broadly considered. (Creese 2011, p. 93)

The core theme of the OJR does not seem to have spawned new creations in Bali, however. Instead there is a proliferation of materials taken from the Uttarakāṇḍa, leading to the composition of a number of new kakawins, forming what Creese terms "a *Rāmāyaṇa* corpus". Among these works are the Hariśraya A (Wulandari, ed. 2001) and Hariśraya B. These are worth mentioning as they are, with others, proof of the close study of the lexicon of the OJR on the part of Balinese authors, who then deliberately imitated its vocabulary in their new compositions.

Meanwhile, Back in Java

Naturally one wonders what later became of the OJR in the area where it was created, Java. Here again we observe a transition, although of a somewhat different nature from the transition from Majapahit to Bali. In Java, as well as the geographical and chronological factors to be considered, there was another, equally important one, namely the transition from a Hindu realm to an Islamic one. In view of the significance of the socio-cultural milieu of our literary work, one might predict some interesting shifts in its nature. We are now moving from Old Javanese to what can be called Modern Javanese, and from a Hindu to an Islamic period.

McDonald has considered the processes of transmission, and discusses whether there is evidence of continuity or not. She writes, "In terms of retaining the spirit of the text, there is no evidence of a thoroughgoing Islamisation of Old Javanese material, although there are certain adjustments, to be sure, among the Modern Javanese versions" (McDonald 1986, p. 11), giving examples from the texts to show how they were adjusted. Also: "[…] the Modern Javanese poems cannot be viewed as 'Islamised' versions of classical themes that were familiar via theatrical media" (McDonald 1986, p. 14), and "The Javanese tradition manuscripts […] are tangible evidence of the written transmission of Indic-Javanese literary themes and principles of statecraft and ethics that date from an early period of Javanese history" (McDonald 1986, p. 19). How does this apply specifically to the transmission of the Rāmāyaṇa?

A cursory survey of the manuscript catalogues provides some interesting results. For example, the Cod. Or. 1790, titled Rama Kawi, a manuscript of some 736 pages, in one leather-bound volume and written in "quadratic kraton script" in Surakarta, bears the date AJ 1709, that is, AD 1782 (Pigeaud 1968, p. 26). This places it in the reign of Sunan Pakubuwana IV (ruled 1788–1820). The text is in Old Javanese, then known as Kawi; but its origins or antecedents were unfortunately not recorded.

This was the *babon* (original) of the next manuscript in the list, Cod. Or. 1791, called Rama Jarwa, in 763 pages, also from Surakarta and in the same kind of script, but without a date. Pigeaud (1968, p. 26) says that this *jarwa* (explanatory) text is "the Old Javanese Ramayana rendered into modern Javanese, but still in (quasi) Old Javanese metres (called kawi miring)". There are more such examples[4] which do not need to be described in detail here, showing considerable activity in the preservation, transmission and adaptation of the story in the setting of the court. However, two more curious items can be mentioned, firstly a Madurese version of the Rama, said to be almost the same as the Javanese (Vreede 1892, pp. 8–9), and secondly a summary of the Vālmīki Rāmāyaṇa made by the Englishmen William Carey and Joshua Marshman on the instructions of Sunan Pakubuwana VII (1830–58) in Surakarta, and translated into Javanese prose by the famous C.F. Winter in two volumes, now Cod. Or. 1834 (Pigeaud 1968, p. 39) — so should we conclude that Winter knew English?

Questions arise in one's mind regarding the route that the Rāmāyaṇa may have taken, after, one assumes, having been read and preserved in the area of Majapahit up to the end of the fifteenth century (and the transition from Majapahit to the sultanate of Demak in the early sixteenth century), and then emerging once more, not in East Java but far away in the interior of Central Java some three centuries later. One has to bear in mind, however, that the regions of Pajang and Mataram were indeed parts of the Majapahit kingdom in the fourteenth century: King Hayam Wuruk is reported as having travelled as far as Pajang (part of the present Surakarta) on one of his royal tours in 1353 (see Deśawarṇana 17.6a).

The evidence of the Merapi-Merbabu manuscript collection may provide a breakthrough, as it shows that a wide range of Old Javanese works had been kept in a hermitage on Mount Merbabu for centuries, and these included the Rāmāyaṇa (Wiryamartana and Van der Molen 2001, p. 55). Another familiar kakawin title is the Arjunawiwāha (palm-leaf MS 181), which according to the critical study by Wiryamartana (1990, pp. 264–71) formed the basis of the Serat Wiwaha Jarwa by Sunan Pakubuwana III (1749–1788). "If the translation was made somewhere in the Mount Merbabu area, then the contribution of the area to the literary life of the Solonese kraton was even greater than was hitherto believed" (Wiryamartana and Van der Molen 2001, p. 54). More detailed studies of these textual links are needed before a clearer picture can be gained, but at least we have an idea of how the way was paved for the next transformation of the text into the Modern Javanese metrical system of *tembang macapat.*

The result was the Serat Rama, attributed to Yasadipura, as Pigeaud writes, "very much admired by contemporaries and subsequent generations for its literary qualities. For a long time it was considered as the masterpiece of Surakarta renaissance literature" (Pigeaud 1967, p. 240). As Poerbatjaraka says, it is very difficult to decide whether we are looking at Kyai Yasadipura I or Yasadipura II here (Poerbatjaraka 1952, p. 134); he is critical of the author's lack of understanding of the original language, which led to mere guesswork — understandable as he had nothing else to work with than his sharp mind and experience of similar works. Probably it should be stressed that a literal rendering was not the main aim; he aimed to create a literary work that conformed to ideals of beauty, and in the *tembang macapat* the aspect of musicality is at least as important as the verbal layer.

The Serat Rama of Yasadipura was printed a number of times, beginning with the edition by C.F. Winter in 1846–47, reprinted in 1875, 1878 and 1884. An edition in three volumes with a preface by J. Kats was published by Balai Pustaka in 1925. However, Poerbatjaraka points out that before the Serat Rama was published by C.F. Winter somebody else (or Winter himself?) had inserted a number of additional lines not found in earlier versions (Poerbatjaraka 1952, pp. 136–37). Hence the textual history of this work remains to be clarified.

Can we conclude that the significance of the work is solely aesthetic? Probably not. Pigeaud has some insightful observations which are worth quoting at length. He writes:

> [...] the pujanggas (poets) of the Surakarta renaissance made poetic versions of the Old Javanese *kakawin*s in the poetic idiom of their own time. These modern epic poems exercised an important influence in the development of nineteenth century Javanese literary style, and they were much imitated. Makers of wayang theatre plays borrowed plots and names of heroes and heroines from them, and they were repeatedly printed by local printers in Java. The popularity of modern Javanese versions of the old *kakawin*s of Indian inspiration, and the spread of wayang plays connected with them, determined the aspect of nineteenth century Javanese literature as retrospective, full of admiration for an imaginary past. Probably the rather languorous disposition observed in several nineteenth century romances, invariably turning on episodes of old epics, was partly caused by a dissatisfaction with actual circumstances in the poets' surroundings in Central Java, where modern European economic and social order was in the ascendant, and no less by a nostalgic yearning after ancient glory and splendour. (Pigeaud 1967, p. 239)

Pigeaud is right in associating the literary works with the *wayang* theatre,[5] and probably the *wayang wong* should be included in this. McDonald has made a comparison between the *kakawin* subject-matter and the Serat Rama, showing a redistribution of the episodes, a change in the nature and function of the descriptive passages, a greater use of direct speech, and an extended interest in characterization and certain character types (McDonald 1981, p. 28), which brings us much closer to the structure and nature of a *wayang lakon*.

Regarding the impetus for the so-called Renaissance of Javanese literature, there has been debate as to whether the apparent increase in output was due to the comparative time of peace following the Treaty of Giyanti in 1755, which enforced a division of the kingdom into two parts, Surakarta and Yogyakarta. On the other hand McDonald writes,

> Conditions in the Surakarta court were considerably altered after 1755, with divided loyalties among the court elite, the notion of equal sovereignty, and the emergence of a vital neighbouring force [...] If the values of kingship, statecraft, autonomy, and knightly allegiance as contained in the *Serat Rama* were still deemed relevant and ideal, the commission to render the *Rāmāyaṇa* into popular verse may have presented Yasadipura with the quandary of how to reconcile the ethical tenor of the epics with the reality of the social and political situation. (McDonald 1981, p. 27)

She continues,

> The emphasis on the ideals may have been an expression of Yasadipura's personal disappointment with the disintegration of the Surakarta court and the inability of the ruler to engender or maintain knightly allegiance. Alternatively, the commission to recast the work may imply a royal directive to present the ethics in a lucid manner with a familiar story frame to a disenchanted or vacillating *kraton* elite. (McDonald 1981, p. 28)

And finally,

> The re-renderings of the *Rāmāyaṇa* and *Mahābhārata*-based *kakawins* indicate that despite the intervention of Islam and the literary expansion into *Panji*, *Damarwulan*, and *Menak* stories, the epics were still seen as

> highly appropriate vehicles for the ethics common to Islam and Hinduism, a basic prudence with respect to social form and moral behaviour, and the transmission of classical ideas of loyalty to the state and the principles of statecraft. (McDonald 1981, p. 31)

Ricklefs discusses at length in what sense, if any, there really was a "renaissance", a conscious rewriting of the literature, by looking at the dates attached to manuscripts, and states, "the late eighteenth and early nineteenth centuries witnessed the writing of some of the greatest works of modern Javanese literature now known" (Ricklefs 1974, p. 225). Having taken the dates into consideration, he concludes,

> When all this literary evidence is compared with the political developments in the last decade of the old century (A.J. 1690–1700/A.D. 1764–1774), the conclusion seems unavoidable that the changing century meant a very great deal [...] Those years witnessed the regularization and legitimation of the divided kingdom after two decades of doubt about the permanence of the division [...] the long-standing if now peripheral involvement of the Dutch in Central Javanese politics had led the major Javanese princes to conclude that a military resolution of the division was unlikely to succeed. (Ricklefs 1974, p. 226)

Pigeaud viewed the literary production against the background of encroaching European influence in the period concerned, and this would undoubtedly have been felt at the courts and more generally across the countryside. This was a time of change, perceived as a threat or challenge to Javanese culture and society. It is striking that the works of renaissance literature under consideration here, as well as the *wayang* theatre, show no influence of Islam whatever, although this was certainly gaining ground at the time. Would it be going too far to surmise that a purely Hindu past, depicted as so glorious, was presented precisely as a reaction to an excessive pressure from Islam, which was also felt to be foreign? In either case we can postulate that the significance of a work such as the Serat Rama can be seen as an assertion of Javanese identity and an expression of the unique values attaching to this. We note that the literary works are products of the Javanese court, precisely the site where the deprivation of political power would have been felt most acutely in the colonial period.[6]

A Pasisir Variant

To complete the account of the stories of Rāma found in Java and surrounding areas, we need to step back to a slightly earlier phase than the Surakarta period, and look at a group of works which Pigeaud (1967, p. 243) gathers under the general heading of "Popular Rama Tales". He writes,

> […] Rama tales not in accordance with the *kakawin* tradition do not appear in written literature of the pre-Islamic period, but they do appear in the Islamic Pasisir literature of the sixteenth and seventeenth centuries. The Sĕrat Kaṇḍa contains extensive Rama tales which were used as models by makers of wayang tales. In East Java and the Pasisir districts, Rama epics related with the Sĕrat Kaṇḍa tales, probably written in the seventeenth and eighteenth centuries, were popular. From East Java they spread to Bali and Lombok. Inter-relationship between these Rama tales, belonging to Javanese Pasisir literature, and similar tales in Malay, the interinsular medium of communication of the seventeenth and eighteenth centuries, is evident.

Many tales of Rāma written in East Java were called Rama Kling (Kĕling). Pigeaud points out that Kĕling was an old name for a district in the Brantas delta (Pigeaud 1967, pp. 243–44), probably the same as Kahuripan, but another explanation is that here it alludes to South India, as the name is used in this sense in various texts (Zoetmulder 1982, p. 843). A considerable number of manuscripts are listed under this heading, for example Cod. Or. 2047, consisting of 546 pages, written in *macapat* verse on Javanese paper (*glugu*), and bearing the date AJ 1748, that is, AD 1820 (Pigeaud 1968, p. 63). The story is said to be closer to the Malay, but also to deviate from this in many details (Vreede 1892, p. 8). A comparative study has not yet been undertaken.

Examples have also been found in Lombok, such as Cod. Or. 3780 or Cod. Or. 3803, both in verse and written on palm leaves. Cod. Or. 4449 is a specimen from Bali. Juynboll (1911, pp. 67–68), describing this manuscript, indicates that the script is Balinese but the language is Modern Javanese with an occasional Balinese word; he states that this version does not derive from the Old Javanese, but has as its source the Tamil Ramayana, and where it deviates from the Old Javanese epic it agrees with the Malay Hikayat Seri Rama and the Madurese Rama. The mention of Tamil is not substantiated, but it is tempting to link it with the name Kĕling mentioned above.

Marrison (1992, p. 22) says, "It seems probable that at one time some Hindu-Javanese poems were known to the Sasaks. Engelenberg's collection, which is mostly from East Lombok, contains manuscripts of *Angling Darma* (E.20), *Ramayana* (E.26), *Panji Jayalengkara* (E.27) and *Tantri* (E.47)" (Engelenberg 1907). The term "Hindu-Javanese" used here is interesting, but probably can also be explained with reference to the origin of these works from the Pasisir area of East Java, perhaps more specifically Surabaya, where in the sixteenth century Javanese literature inherited from Majapahit flourished for a short time, before being affected by the establishment of Islam in this region.[7] There was a clear contact from the north coast of Java eastwards to Bali and as far as Lombok, accounting for the numerous works in the Javanese language still to be found there (Marrison 1992). This is a chapter of cultural and literary history needing to be studied in more depth.

Concluding Reflections

Reviewing some of the points made by Teeuw (see above), we can now offer some conclusions. The term "literary history" suggests tracing a trajectory over an extended period of time. Certainly in the case of the RY we can speak of a long life of the work, having been preserved for well over a thousand years. It was an incredible achievement for the copyists who set to work copying the whole story onto fresh palm leaves, letter by tiny letter, and making so few errors that we are still able to read the results of their efforts in an almost perfect form (Van der Molen 2015).

The genre of the *kakawin* which the OJR ushered in has likewise displayed a remarkable stability, having been practised right up to the twentieth century in Bali.

In both cases, why would the authors and scholars have been so dedicated to the enterprise? This tells us something about the veneration in which the text was held. It was a valuable artefact by virtue of its various qualities: as a work of art, as teaching, and as an expression of the nature of the relation between mankind and the world of the divine. This applies to the Hindu societies of early Java and of modern Bali.

The language which formed the vehicle of the message was "poetic", in the sense of being elevated above the mundane and removed from the sphere of earthly affairs, as is appropriate for carrying exalted messages about heroic and supernatural actors.

In this way, the history is extended every time the text is recited, studied, copied or republished.

Can the term "translation" be used properly in the case of the RY? Translation may entail a range of activities, from a literal or "faithful" reproduction to an adaptation, transformation or recreation, depending on the imperatives impinging on the author in his own mind, or imposed by his king or sponsor. The author of the RY certainly followed the BhK for a major part of his work, but the result is so utterly different from the original — not necessarily because he misunderstood it, but because the aims of the works themselves were worlds apart. The author was addressing an audience in and around the court who were used to listening to stories — hence the simple sentence structures; the listeners were open to the moral lessons to be learned from hearing about the great, the good and the evil, and they joined in the joys and sufferings of the characters. Who could not sympathize with Rāma and Sītā's sadness in separation, or be moved by the injustice of Sītā's rejection, or the fierce defence by her faithful companion Trijaṭā? These results are not achieved by mechanical translation of a foreign source, but somehow flow from the consciousness of an author in tune with his audience.

Apart from the Sanskrit to Old Javanese "translation" in the case of the RY, the transformation of the Old Javanese (Kawi) text into a *jarwa* version, and then into the *macapat* verses of the Serat Rama is even less a matter of translation in the strict sense, because of the loss of a close knowledge of Old Javanese in the intervening centuries which made a recreation necessary. The story continued to be important, and probably also its moral lessons, but the level of verbal and musical beauty made appreciation on a new and different plane possible, as was highly valued among court circles in Surakarta. Again we can imagine the audience, from the Sunan down, enjoying the archaic and noble language replete with its alliterations and assonances, carefully structured to fulfil the requirements of the appropriate metrical and melodic patterns.

The *macapat* verse-forms were also the vehicle of the poetical versions of the tales of Rama circulating in the Pasisir, but we have to visualize quite a different socio-cultural setting there.[8] The trading centres of the North Coast of Java were open to influences reaching Java from outside, almost always via the Malay world, and hence probably answering to a different set of aesthetic values compared to the inland courts. If a Malay story formed a model here (and that still has to be proved), then not only the plot and characters may have been different, but also the ideas underlying their actions and driving the story forward, in keeping with the values upheld in the relevant parts of society that formed the audience.

Probably the concepts of translation and transformation can again be invoked in the case of the production of Rāma stories in performance, in particular in the *wayang* theatre. The *wayang* is interesting as it is also an imaginative reconstruction of a Hindu past, peopled by kings and heroes, sages, gods and demons, who move in a magical world and embody ideals and ideas, manipulated by the dalang in such a way as to strike a chord in the hearts of his audience in the contemporary world. The dalang is master not only of the verbal art, but also of the musical vehicle which carries the performance, and all the philosophical and ethical teachings that have to be incorporated and passed on to the audience.

Considerations of the theory and practice of Translation Studies have obviously moved on since Teeuw wrote on the subject in 1986, and a very recent comment comes from Ricci, who offers some relevant observations on translation into Javanese, and the ways in which the text may have been reformulated in the process. For *macapat* verse, this involved making it "poetically Javanese", referring not only to the form but also to "mood and tone" (Ricci 2014, p. 92).[9]

As a general conclusion, again and again one notes the difficulty of writing anything approaching a satisfactory history of literature, in this case more specifically of the Rāmāyaṇa in Java, due to a lack of materials, either scholarly discussions or, more crucially, the basic philological spadework of editing and explaining the texts involved. Hundreds and hundreds of manuscripts are languishing neglected in the dim vaults of the Leiden University Library (not to mention the collections in Jakarta, Surakarta and Yogyakarta), longing to be visited by a wandering student and read for the undoubted gems that lie concealed in their pages.

NOTES

1. A feeling for the style of Kamban can be gained via the English translation of the Ayodhya canto by C. Rajagopalachari (1970).
2. A full edition of this work is not available, but a large portion was published by Zoetmulder (1958), who also provides a summary (Zoetmulder 1974, pp. 83–87).
3. For illustrations, see Bernet Kempers (1959), plates 278–81 and pp. 92–93.
4. With reference to the Dewaruci, Poerbatjaraka (1940, p. 40) claims that the *macapat* version preceded the *sekar ageng*. In a footnote he says that after a cursory comparison he has the same impression with regard to the *Rama sekar ageng*. I am grateful to Willem van der Molen for drawing my attention to this.
5. Although the *wayang* theatre is not a central topic here, it is interesting to note that according to Kats (1923, pp. 88–89) only eighteen lakons derive from the Rama cycle, while there are 147 from the Mahābhārata cycle (Kats 1923, pp. 89–98). This data comes from the Mangkunagaran tradition.
6. A similar interpretation has been offered in the case of the Wédhatama (Robson 1990, pp. 17–18) and the Tripama (Robson 1999, pp. 43–44).
7. See Robson (1980), pp. 295–99, describing the Serat Arok, which provides details of the literature of this area.
8. Pigeaud used the term "popular" (above), without defining it further.
9. I am grateful to Harry Aveling for having drawn my attention to this contribution to the discussion of translation.

REFERENCES

Bernet Kempers, A.J. *Ancient Indonesian Art*. Amsterdam: Van der Peet, 1959.

Braginsky, Vladimir. *The Heritage of Traditional Malay Literature: A Historical Survey of Genres, Writings and Literary Views*. Leiden: KITLV Press, 2004. VKI 214.

Creese, Helen. "*Rāmāyaṇa* Traditions in Bali". In *From Laṅkā Eastwards: The Rāmāyaṇa in the Literature and Visual Arts of Indonesia*, edited by Andrea Acri, Helen Creese, and Arlo Griffiths. Leiden: KITLV Press, 2011. VKI 247, pp. 93–118.

Engelenberg, A.J.N. "Inventaris van de door den Heer A.J.N. Engelenberg, Assistent Resident van Midden-Celebes, aan het Genootschap in bruikleen afgestane handschriften afkomstig van het eiland Lombok". Batavia: *Notulen van het Bataviaasch Genootschap*, 1907, 45.4.

Hooykaas, C. *The Old-Javanese Rāmāyaṇa Kakawin with Special Reference to the Problem of Interpolation in Kakawins.* 's-Gravenhage: Nijhoff, 1955. VKI 16.

Jordaan, Roy E., ed. *In Praise of Prambanan: Dutch Essays on the Loro Jonggrang Temple Complex.* Leiden: KITLV Press, 1996. KITLV Translation Series 26.

Juynboll, H.H. *Supplement op den catalogus van de Javaansche en Madoereesche handschriften der Leidsche Universiteits-Bibliotheek.* Deel II. Leiden: Brill, 1911.

Kats, J. *Het Javaansche Tooneel*; *I Wajang Poerwa.* Weltevreden: Volkslectuur, 1923.

Khanna, Vinod and Malini Saran. "The Rāmāyaṇa Kakawin: A Product of Sanskrit Scholarship and Independent Literary Genius". *BKI* 149 (1993): 226–49.

Kieven, Lydia. "Hanuman, the Flying Monkey: The Symbolism of the Rāmāyaṇa Reliefs at the Main Temple of Caṇḍi Panataran". In *From Laṅkā Eastwards: The Rāmāyaṇa in the Literature and Visual Arts of Indonesia*, edited by Andrea Acri, Helen Creese, and Arlo Griffiths. Leiden: KITLV Press, 2011. VKI 247, pp. 209–32.

Klokke, Marijke J., ed. *Narrative Sculpture and Literary Traditions in South and Southeast Asia.* Leiden, Boston, Köln: Brill, 2000.

———. "Hanuman in the Art of East Java". In *Archaeology: Indonesian Perspective. R.J. Soejono's Festschrift*, edited by Truman Simanjuntak et al. Jakarta: LIPI Press, 2006, pp. 391–405.

Levin, Cecilia. "The Rāmāyaṇa, Rāmakathā and Loro Jonggrang". In *Narrative Sculpture and Literary Traditions in South and Southeast Asia*, edited by Marijke J. Klokke. Leiden, Boston, Köln: Brill, 2000, pp. 59–72.

Marrison, Geoffrey E. *The Literature of the Sasak of Lombok: A Survey of Javanese and Sasak Texts.* Parts I and II. [Hull]: Centre for South-East Asian Studies, University of Hull, 1992.

McDonald, Barbara. "The Serat Rama of Yasadipura: Some Structural Determinants in Tembang Macapat". *Indonesia Circle* 9.26 (1981): 25–32.

———. *Old Javanese Literature in Eighteenth-century Java: A Consideration of the Process of Transmission.* Clayton: Centre of Southeast Asian Studies, Monash University, 1986. Working Paper 41.

Molen, Willem van der (Romanized edition by). *H. Kern Rāmāyaṇa: The Story of Rāma and Sītā in Old Javanese.* Tokyo: Tokyo University of Foreign Studies, 2015. Javanese Studies 1.

Pigeaud, Th.G.Th. *Literature of Java: Catalogue Raisonné of Javanese Manuscripts in the Library of the University of Leiden and Other Public Collections in the*

Netherlands. Volume I, Synopsis of Javanese literature AD 900–1900. The Hague: Nijhoff, 1967.

———. *Literature of Java: Catalogue Raisonné of Javanese Manuscripts in the Library of the University of Leiden and Other Public Collections in the Netherlands.* Volume II, Descriptive lists of Javanese manuscripts. Leiden: Leiden University Library, 1968.

Poerbatjaraka. "Déwa-Roetji". *Djåwå* 20 (1940): 1–51.

———. *Kapustakan Djawi*. Djakarta, Amsterdam: Djambatan, 1952.

Rajagopalachari, C. *The Ayodhya Canto of the Ramayana as told by Kamban*. New Delhi: Sahitya Akademi, 1970.

Ricci, Ronit. "Response". *Translation Studies* 7 (2014): 90–93.

Ricklefs, M.C. *Jogjakarta under Sultan Mangkubumi 1749–1792: A History of the Division of Java.* London: Oxford University Press, 1974. London Oriental Series 30.

Robson, Stuart. "The Serat Arok". *Archipel* 20 (1980): 281–301.

———. *Principles of Indonesian Philology*. Dordrecht Holland-Providence USA: Foris, 1988. KITLV Working Papers 1.

———. *The Wedhatama: An English Translation.* Leiden: KITLV Press, 1990. KITLV Working Papers 4.

———. "The Tripama: A Didactic Poem of Mangkunagara IV". *Indonesia and the Malay World* 27.77 (1999): 34–45.

———. *From Malay to Indonesian: The Genesis of a National Language.* Clayton: Monash Asia Institute, Monash University, Victoria, Australia: Centre of Southeast Asian Studies, 2002. Working Paper 118.

Rubinstein, Raechelle. *Beyond the Realm of the Senses: The Balinese Ritual of Kakawin Composition.* Leiden: KITLV Press, 2000. VKI 181.

Stutterheim, Willem. *Rama-Legenden und Rama-Reliefs in Indonesien*. München: Müller, 1925. Two volumes.

———. *Rāma-legends and Rāma-reliefs in Indonesia*. New Delhi: Indira Gandhi National Centre for the Arts, 1989. Abhinav Publications. Translated by C.D. Paliwal and R.P. Jain.

Supomo, S. "On the Date of the Old Javanese Wirataparwa". In *Studies in Indo-Asian Art and Culture. Vol. 1: Commemoration Volume on the 69th Birthday of Acharya Raghu Vira*, edited by Perala Ratnam. New Delhi: International Academy of Indian Culture, 1972. Śata-piṭaka Series 95, pp. 261–66.

———. *Arjunawijaya: A Kakawin of Mpu Tantular*. The Hague: Nijhoff, 1977. KITLV Bibliotheca Indonesica 14. Two volumes.

Teeuw, A. "Translation, Transformation and Indonesian Literary History". In *Cultural Contact and Textual Interpretation: Papers from the Fourth European Colloquium on Malay and Indonesian Studies, held in Leiden in 1983*, edited by C.D. Grijns and S.O. Robson. Dordrecht Holland/Cinnaminson USA: Foris, 1986. VKI 115, pp. 190–203.

Uhlenbeck, E.M. "De interpretatie van de Oud-Javaanse Rāmāyaṇa-Kakawin. Enige algemene beschouwingen en gezichtspunten". *BKI* 131 (1975): 195–213.

Vickers, Adrian. "The Old Javanese Kapiparwa and a Recent Balinese Painting". In *From Laṅkā Eastwards: The Rāmāyaṇa in the Literature and Visual Arts of Indonesia*, edited by Andrea Acri, Helen Creese, and Arlo Griffiths. Leiden: KITLV Press, 2011. VKI 247, pp. 119–30.

Vreede, A.C. *Catalogus van de Javaansche en Madoereesche handschriften der Leidsche Universiteits-Bibliotheek.* Leiden: Brill, 1892.

Wiryamartana, I. Kuntara. *Arjunawiwāha: Transformasi teks Jawa Kuna lewat tanggapan dan penciptaan di lingkungan sastra Jawa.* [Yogyakarta:] Duta Wacana University Press, 1990.

Wiryamartana, I. Kuntara and W. van der Molen. "The Merapi-Merbabu Manuscripts: A Neglected Collection". *BKI* 157 (2001): 51–64.

Wulandari, K.A. "Hariśraya (A): A Balinese Kakawin". M.A. thesis, Australian National University, 2001.

Zoetmulder, P.J. *Sĕkar Sumawur* I. Djakarta: Obor, 1958.

———. *Kalangwan: A Survey of Old Javanese Literature.* The Hague: Nijhoff, 1974. KITLV Translation Series 16.

Zoetmulder, P.J. with the collaboration of S.O. Robson. *Old Javanese-English Dictionary.* 's-Gravenhage: Nijhoff, 1982. KITLV.

3

ABIMANYU GUGUR: The Death of Abimanyu in Classical and Modern Indonesian and Malay Literature

Harry Aveling

In Indian mythology, Abimanyu is the teenage son of Arjuna and Subadra. He has learned from his father how to break through the enemy line in battle but, unfortunately, not how to get out again. Abimanyu's tragic death is told in the Mahabharata (the "Adi Parwa" and the "Drona Parwa"), and was later retold in many vernacular versions from South and Southeast Asia — often with additional details, such as his marriage to Siti Sundari, which is absent from the Mahabharata and the Sanskrit tradition in general. This chapter will compare the accounts of his death in the Javanese Kakawin Bharatayuddha, the Malay Hikayat Pandawa Lima and the contemporary Indonesian short story "Nostalgia" by Danarto. The comparisons will describe the ways in which the story and the ideology framing the meaning of Abimanyu's death shift between these various accounts.

Keywords: Abimanyu; Mahabharata; Bharata Yuddha; Hikayat Pandawa Lima; Danarto.

Introduction

Abhimanyu replied:
'I will fight for the victory of my fathers
and pierce the splendid strategy of Drona.

My father Arjuna
taught me the secret of penetrating this array
but I do not know how to come out of it
should an emergency arise.'

(Mahabharata VII: 35.18–19,
trans. P. Lal 2007: 190)

It has been said that there are many Ramayanas, both in India and abroad, and "each reflects the social location and ideology of those who have appropriated it" (Richman 1991, p. 4). The same is, of course, true of the Mahabharata. There are many Mahabharatas and its multiple stories are variously read, recited, acted, danced, sculptured, filmed, drawn, and possibly recreated in many other ways as well, all reflecting the values and aesthetics of the time and place in which they are recreated. Sutjipto's Indonesian translation of the Old Javanese Kakawin Bharatayuddha describes the story of fratricidal violence as "*cerita yang mengerikan ini*", this horrifying story (Sutjipto Wirjosuparto 1968, p. 360). Few sections of the epic are as horrifying as the death in battle of Abimanyu, the young son of Arjuna and Subadra.[1] As Dritarastra comments: "How terrible/ is this war-code called Ksatriya-dharma/ that makes power-hungry men kill a small boy!"[2] In this chapter, I would like to show how this episode has been handled in three Southeast Asian texts: the Old Javanese Kakawin Bharatayuddha (1157–1159 CE), the medieval Malay Hikayat Pandawa Lima (possibly thirteenth to fourteenth centuries, but no doubt also regularly revised by copyists, see Griffith (1976), p. 75 and Brakel (1980), pp. 153–60 for a discussion of dates), and the modern short story entitled "Nostalgia" (1987) by the contemporary Indonesian author, Danarto. Each of these four versions tells the story in a different way for a vastly different audience. Each sets the young warrior's death within a very different ideological framework:

not only warrior-dharma, but also tantric conceptions of beauty in love and death, the virtue of dying with a good name, and a contemporary Javanese understanding of spiritual self-transcendence.

The Indian Background to Tales of the Death of Abimanyu

The story of Abimanyu originates from Indian mythology, most clearly from the Mahabharata. Let us begin first with the original tale as an initial way of orienting ourselves for our discussion of the later Southeast Asian versions.

The story of Abimanyu is foreshadowed in Chapter 67 of the first book of the Mahabharata, the "Adi Parwa", as follows:

> And he who was known as the mighty Varchas, the son of Soma, became Abhimanyu of wonderful deeds, the son of Arjuna. And before his incarnation, O king, the god Soma had said these words to the celestials, 'I cannot give (part with) my son. He is dearer to me than life itself. Let this be the compact and let it be not transgressed. The destruction of the Asuras on earth is the work of the celestials, and, therefore, it is our work as well. Let this Varchas, therefore, go thither, but let him not stay there long. Nara, whose companion is Narayana, will be born as Indra's son and indeed, will be known as Arjuna, the mighty son of Pandu. This boy of mine shall be his son and become a mighty car-warrior in his boyhood. And let him, ye best of immortals, stay on earth for sixteen years. And when he attaineth to his sixteenth year, the battle shall take place in which all who are born of your portions shall achieve the destruction of mighty warriors. But a certain encounter shall take place without both Nara and Narayana (taking any part in it). And, indeed, your portions, ye celestials, shall fight, having made that disposition of the forces which is known by the name of the *Chakra-vyuha*. And my son shall compel all foes to retreat before him. The boy of mighty arms having penetrated the impenetrable array, shall range within it fearlessly and send a fourth part of the hostile force, in the course of half a day, unto the regions of the king of the dead. Then when numberless heroes and mighty car-warriors will return to the charge towards the close of the day, my boy of mighty arms, shall reappear before me. And he shall beget one heroic son in his line, who shall continue the almost extinct Bharata race.' Hearing these words of Soma, the dwellers in heaven replied, 'So be it.'

And then all together applauded and worshipped (Soma) the king of stars. (Kishari 1883–96, pp. 143–44)

Despite the length of the passage, it focuses on only two events in the life of Abimanyu. One is his death in battle. The other is the birth of his son, Pariksit, offspring of his marriage to Uttara (Indonesian: Utari), the daughter of Wirata with whom the five Pandawa have taken refuge during the final year of their exile. The story of the marriage is told in Sections 71 and 72 of Book 4, the "Wirata Parwa". As Arti Dhand (2008, p. 46) notes, "sex and violence" are the two themes that provide an essential counterpoint to the ascetic world-renouncing other tendency of the Mahabharata. The wedding is described in grand detail but only a few verses are devoted to the couple themselves. The princess is "decked in every ornament and resembling the daughter of the great Indra himself". Abimanyu is praised by Arjuna, his father, in these terms: "Surpassing all in knowledge of weapons, resembling a celestial youth in beauty, my son, the mighty-armed Abhimanyu is the favourite nephew of Vasudeva, the wielder of the discus. He, O king, is fit to be thy son-in-law and the husband of thy daughter."

Books 6 to 9 describe the great and final battle at Kuruksetra. The violence of Abimanyu's death receives much greater treatment than the previous description of his marriage. In Book 6 of the Mahabharata, the "Bhisma Parwa", Abimanyu takes his first steps in the war and here too his appearance in the text is limited to a few verses on each occasion. Although he is presented as already being a mighty warrior, he always fights in the protective company of his father, Arjuna (6.55, 94), and his uncle Bima (6.63, 69).

This minor focus changes in the next book, the "Drona Parwa". Book 7 contains five parts: the Dronabhisheka Parwa (the appointment of Drona as commander-in-chief of the Kuru army, 1-30), the Abhimanyu-vadha Parwa (the death of Abimanyu, 31-84), Jayadratha-vadha Parwa (the death of Jayadrata, 85-151), Ghatotkacha-vadha Parwa (the death of Ghatotkacha, 152–83), and finally the Drona-vadha Parwa (the death of Drona, 184–203). These are small, self-contained episodes, which include hymns or set pieces praising such objects as horses or banners, and consist to a high degree (70 per cent) of formulaic lines (McGrath 2011, p. 48). One scene is allocated for each death.[3]

After some preliminary narrative preparation in which both Arjuna and Bima are drawn to the fringes of the battle, Section 35 begins with the Pandawa troops facing an onslaught from the Kurawa led by Drona. Yudistira pleads with Abimanyu to pierce the enemy's *cakra-vyuha*, "the circular battle-array", as he is one of only four warriors with this knowledge. Abimanyu accepts the request, stating: "I will fight for the victory of my fathers/ and pierce the splendid strategy of Drona.// My father Arjuna/ taught me the secret of penetrating this array/ but I do not know how to come out of it/ should an emergency arise.//" (35.18–19).[4] Yudistira assures Abimanyu that he and the other Pandawa troops will be close behind him: "From our side/ you will be reinforced by brilliant bowmen/ who are like perfected mortals/ or like Rudras and Maruts/ who are the equal of Adityas and Vasus/ who are like fire itself" (35.30). Despite the concerns of his driver Sumitra, Abimanyu again all too confidently boasts of his own abilities and then charges at the enemy line, slaughtering the enemy on a vast scale.

In response, Duryodana attacks Abimanyu, but he has to be rescued by Aswatama, Kripa, Karna and other Kurawa heroes, who then attack Abimanyu once more, filling his body with arrows. Yet again, Drona's troops are forced to retreat. Dursasana vows to kill Abimanyu, but is himself overcome and carried unconscious from the field of battle by his charioteer. Intent on killing Drona, Abimanyu at last "smashed through the ring of horses and elephants and soldiers" (41.7). Only Jayadrata now dares to stand and face him. He blocks the Pandawas when they come to help Abimanyu, "like an elephant dominating a flat area" (42.7), his strength the result of a boon given to him by Siva (43.16–19). Without the support of his comrades, Abimanyu nevertheless continues to massacre the enemy.

Finally, however, he is completely surrounded and killed by the massed forces of Drona, Kripa, Karna, Drauni-Asvataman, Brihadbala, and Hrdika's son, Kritavarman (47.4), but only after he has been successively deprived of his bow, the Gandharva bow which Arjuna had won by his asceticism (45.21–22) (by Karna), horses, "maya producing" chariot (45.21) and sword (Drona), shield (Karna), chariot wheel and club. In accordance with Drona's treacherous advice: "Hit him from behind/ after somehow making him turn his back [...]" (48.30), the final blow is delivered as Abimanyu lies on the ground. Thus, "The Kuru-glory-enhancing son of Duhsasana [...] brought his mace down/ on Abhimanyu's head as he struggled to rise" (49.13).[5] The fight is unfair in many ways — at least six men against one, continuing to fight an unarmed man, killing him by a blow to the back of his head as he lies on the ground. "They ganged up and killed him", Sanjaya straightforwardly and sorrowfully tells Dritarastra (49.14). The deed is universally condemned by the kings and others who have witnessed it, saying: "This is not dharma:/ six maha-chariot-heroes of Dhrtarasta/ led by Drona and Karna/ slaughter a lone hero!" (49.22).

Yudistira must now tell Arjuna what has happened at his instigation when the father returns from his distant part of the battle. The Righteous King is overcome by guilt. "He was only a boy", Yudistira laments, "We should have given him delicious food./ We should have given him soft beds and ornaments./ Instead we sent him into the thick of the battle." Yudistira is afraid that: "Arjuna will show his wrath-filled grief/ and we will burn in the shame of our deed" (51.16–18). Nevertheless, as he laments the rashness of his actions, Yudistira is suddenly visited by the great rishi, Krishna-Dwaipayana (Ganguli)/Vyasa (Lal), who provides him with a first major religious-moral perspective on the events. Vyasa tells him a long series of stories, beginning with the creation of Death and of its physical and moral inevitability in human life, as revealed through the deaths of many young princes: Raja Akampana (section 54), Raja Suhotra (56), Raja Paurava (57), Sibi (58), Rama, son of Dasarata (59) ... sixteen kings in all (71.1).

There is also a second and more immediate religious-moral perspective, contained in Vyasa's final assurance to Yudistira:

> As for Abhimanyu
> he was brave and had finished his life-mission
> for he fell fighting on the battlefield
> after killing thousands of his enemies.
>
> Your son Abhimanyu
> attained the eternal realm that is achieved only
> by those who observe brahmacarya
> and perform the yajna.

Learned men
always seek to achieve heaven by pious deeds
but the heaven-dwellers have no desire to
return to earth.

It is not possible
to see any reason why Abhimanyu should want
to return to earth. He is happy in heaven. (71.12–15)

Vyasa's message is supported by Krishna, who agrees that: "Death is inevitable/ for the never-retreating Ksatriya hero. Abhimanyu has attained the realm of the virtuous" (72.72). The righteous death of a warrior, true "ksatriya-dharma" to use Dritarastra's words, carries its own spiritual reward.[6]

What is ksatriya-dharma, whose reward is heaven (54.54–55)? One way to answer this question is to turn back to the Bhagavad Gita (Bisma Parwa, 25–42), where it is emphasized at the start of the war that each caste has its own innate, specific and binding set of social duties, its own *dharma*. The works of a warrior, a *ksatriya*, are described as: "a heroic mind, inner fire, constancy, resourcefulness, courage in battle, generosity and noble leadership" (18.43). Such duties are inescapable; they should never be abandoned (18.48). The person who "finds joy in his work", Krishna teaches Arjuna, "will pass to a region supreme which is beyond earthly action" (18.45–49). Abimanyu has indeed "gone to heaven". His enemies, on the other hand, it may also be deduced from this passage, have displayed the characteristics of "a man who is born for hell", namely: "deceitfulness, insolence and self-conceit, anger and harshness and ignorance" (16.4). Their behaviour is condemned as *adharma*: "this is", most definitely, "not dharma", as we have heard "the king and others" say, even granted that "in all work there may be imperfection, even as in all fire there is smoke" (18.48).[7]

There is a third position, a less obvious and dissenting perspective on Abimanyu's death, which is a parent's and particularly a woman's perspective. The story concludes with Arjuna's sorrow at the absence of his son (72.7–68), which spurs him to vow further violence, and also with Subadra's pitiful lament for her son, in the presence of Utari and Draupadi (78.1–38). She grieves for the loss to herself and her daughter-in-law of a child and a husband and prays for his journey in the after-life. The prayers are positive — "May you attain the goal [...]" that is attained by ascetics, warriors, kings, faithful sons and husbands, virtuous men and women (78.24–38). But she is also angry with those who did not protect him (Arjuna, Bima, the Vrsni heroes, and others [78.12–13]), and more than a little despondent about the meaning of life itself:

O my heroic son, you were to me
  a treasure seen
and lost in a dream.
  Hai! Life's a fleeting bubble. (78.17)

Despite Arjuna and Krishna's insistence that Abimanyu has died a noble death, a warrior's death, which ensures him a place in heaven (77.11–26), Subadra can only agree with the wise who "find death mysterious", especially when Krishna is powerless to protect those dear to him (78.23). It is a meaningless, pathetic death that cannot be justified.

The Death of Abimanyu in the Old Javanese Bharatayuddha

The original 18 *parwa* of the Mahabharata were perhaps first translated into Old Javanese at the end of tenth century (Zoetmulder 1974, p. 96). Zoetmulder suggests that: "The *parwa*s are adaptations in prose of parts of the Sanskrit epics and show their immediate dependence by Sanskrit quotations from the original, scattered throughout the text" (Zoetmulder 1974, p. 68).

Today only nine of the eighteen books remain in Old Javanese: Books 1, 2, 4, 5, 6, and 15 to 18. Presumably the intention was to translate the whole text (they are all listed in the Old Javanese "Adi Parwa" and their verses counted, Phalgunadi 1990, pp. 20–25) but whether the other books were lost (as Berg thought), or never translated at all (as Pigeaud and Zoetmulder thought), is unknown (Supomo 1993, p. 5). The marriage of Abimanyu and Utari is told in the "Wirata Parwa", Book 4, 82–97, and retold in the classical poetic kakawin Abhimanyu Wiwaha ("Abimanyu's wedding"), a possibly very late text (eighteenth century according to Creese 2004, p. 261) but nevertheless a close reworking of the Old Javanese prose version (Zoetmulder 1974, p. 385). The original Old Javanese description of the death of Abimanyu, Book 7 "Drona Parwa", which is unavailable to us today, occurs in poetic form in the Kakawin Bharatayuddha. The retelling was described by Raffles as "the most popular and celebrated poem in the (Javanese) language" (cited in Supomo 1993, p. 45).[8]

The Kakawin Bharatayuddha consists of 52 cantos and 489 stanzas. Its completion required two authors. The composition was begun on 6 September 1157 under the patronage of King Jayabaya of Kadiri (Daha), East Java. The first part ("to the episode of Salya becoming commander of the army", canto 33 onwards) was composed by mpu Sedah (1.6–7, 52.13). The remaining part was written by mpu Panuluh (50.10–13) and finished in September 1159, under Sri Sarveswara. As Supomo (1993) has argued, "the narrative of the *Bharatayuddha*, from the beginning to end, generally follows the sequence of the episodes of the war as recounted in the *Mahabharata*", although in a greatly reduced form (p. 21), such that "all non-essential episodes and digressions were eliminated" (p. 29). Supomo believes that the "ultimate source" of Part Three of the narrative of the *Bharatayuddha*, the description of the war, is "the Dronaparvan which belongs to the Northern recension, either its Bengali or Devanagari version" (29, also 37). Nevertheless, he also points out that there is a considerable portion of passages, more than 200 stanzas, "which have no comparable parts in the *Mahabharata*", and were added "to transform a mere *carita*, 'story', into a *kalangwan*, or work of poetry" (29).

These additional elements of aesthetic import particularly relate to the descriptions of nature and tales of romantic passion, including the stories of the immolation of Siti Sundari, and of the final hours together of Salya and his wife Satyawati. In Supomo's opinion, the most significant departure in the Bharatayuddha from the Mahabharata is, in fact, this introduction of women into the battle scenes. He notes that: "we often find that after the death of certain heroes, there are scenes where the women take the centre stage: King Wirata and his queen mourn for the death of their three sons, Uttara, Sankha and Sweta (12.1–4); Subhadra mourns for her son Abimanyu (14.3); Utari and Siti Sundari lament over the death of their husband, Abimanyu (14.4–5; 15.4–18); Hidimbi over her son Ghatotkaca (19.13–19); Satyawati over her husband Salya (44.15–18); Sugandhika over her mistress Satyawati (45.6–8); and Dropadi over the death of her five sons and all her relatives (50.18–19)" (Supomo 1993, p. 33). This is not quite as remarkable as Supomo supposes. As Kevin McGrath writes: "In the hypothetical origins of epic song it is arguably the women who stand in the first place distributing the kirti, the 'fame' that constitutes this medium: at the death of a hero it is women, who — as kin relations, mothers, wives, sisters or daughters — sing the laments praising the deceased and extolling their deeds, beauty, and sagacity. It is these laments that later develop into epic poetry" (McGrath 2011, pp. 17–18).

"Nevertheless", Supomo (1993, p. 33) continues, "except for Subhadra (MB 7.55) and Dropadi (MB 10.11), the lamentations of the other women have no counterparts in the *Mahabharata* [...]". Supomo, in fact, insists: "The names of Ksitisundari and Satyawati do not occur in the *Mahabharata* nor, as far as I know, in any other Sanskrit work" (1993, p. 33).[9]

The story of Abimanyu's death covers barely a dozen verses in the Kakawin Bharatayuddha. The development of the narrative agrees with the Mahabharata account: Drona has arranged for Arjuna and Bima to be engaged in distant parts of the battlefield (13.19–21); the Kaurawa order their troops in the discus battle array (13.23); Abimanyu admits that "although he knew how to attack and penetrate it, he had not yet mastered the withdrawal tactic" (13.23);[10] and Jayadrata is able "to block the advance of the Pandawas, like the shutting of a mighty door" (13.26).

Surprisingly, the description of Abimanyu's fighting is not only violent but also highly sexualized, in a manner that today might even be considered sadistic:

> His assault could be compared to the performance of a youth deflowering a maiden, the quivering of his sharp arrows resembling her frowning eyebrows. When he saw the arrow wounds on his chest, he thought that they were scratches from the maiden's nails, and he mistook the clamour of the elephants, horses and chariots for her moaning. (13.29, trans. Supomo)

This may also be compared with the subsequent, and contradictory, erotic statement that:

> How could he, who was as handsome as the God of love, survive, for he had never been scratched by a lovely lady in the bed-chamber — he had not even been slashed by her sharp-pointed eyebrows, which would melt the heart of the lovesick. Those who overwhelmed Abhimanyu in battle, moreover, were equally valiant. This was why he was always invoked by the maidens, as they moaned in sorrow and gazed with longing to the sky. (13.34, trans. Supomo)

Abimanyu is more a representation of youthful passion than a mature warrior. The reality, of course, is that Abimanyu has not one but two wives. Great detail is provided in the following chapters of the self-immolation of his first wife, Siti Sundari, and potentially that of his second wife, Utari, who is only saved because she is in an advanced stage of pregnancy (Chapters 14 and 15). Although it is difficult to write a history of *wayang*, it is possible that the nature of his death may bear an unspoken link to the *lakon* in which Abimanyu lies to Utari before their wedding, claiming that he is still a virgin, even though he is, in fact, already married to Siti Sundari. "If I am not telling the truth", he assures Utari, "may I die with a body filled with arrows".[11] He is not telling the truth and this is exactly how he dies.

Again surprisingly, the inevitable death is also presented as a poetic achievement. Supomo translates the final line of 13.35 as: "Overwhelmed by the enemy, he was on the point of death, but truly his death was as beautiful as the search for sweetness [of honey]."[12] Sutjipto goes further in his translation: "Enough, he died and was buried in the battle, but the beauty of his death represented an attempt to find beauty."[13] It is again not obvious why this death should be finally presented overall in such poetic terms.

One possible explanation of these puzzles of eroticism and the artistic beauty of death may come from Zoetmulder's discussion of the mystical dimensions of literary creation, "*religio poetae*", the dedication of the *kakawin* form to the poetic worship of "a god of beauty". Such a god is invisible but still takes many forms: the deity resides in nature, in "feminine grace and charm", and: "For the ksatriya the same god may be a god of chivalry and valour in battle; for the scholar and the sage a god of higher wisdom" (Zoetmulder 1974, p. 175). Abimanyu's death may be a compound image of the "tantrism" of the battlefield (Zoetmulder 1974, p. 206), uniting sexuality, poetry and death in battle in the one act of beautiful and profoundly emotional tantric ritual self-transcendence.[14]

The Death of Abimanyu in the Malay Hikayat Pandawa Lima

The wives of Abimanyu play their fullest role in the Hikayat Pandawa Lima. The story of the abduction of Siti Sundari (Dewi Satya Sundari) by Abimanyu (Bimanyu), which is not included in the Bharatayuddha but is present in the Ghatotkacasraya, is told in considerable detail in the Hikayat Pandawa Lima (Khalid Hussain 1964, pp. 18–53).

Abimanyu is fully twelve years old at this time (Khalid Hussain 1964, p. 19). His subsequent marriage to Utari (Dewi Utari), told in the Abhimanyu Wiwaha, is also present, although it is given far fewer pages than his first marriage (Khalid Hussain 1964, pp. 59–62). The second marriage is facilitated by Betara Krishna, who sardonically comments in response to the reservations of the pious Maharaja Darmawangsa (Yudistira): "There is nothing wrong with that. Many men have ten or twenty wives. Let me go and discuss this with King Mangaspati."[15] Arjuna (Sang Rajuna), too, readily agrees to the marriage, despite Mangaspati's fears that he might not (in the Mahabharata, Utari was originally offered to Arjuna), and the king notes with delight that: "This is an appropriate marriage; they are both young and equally attractive."[16] Only Siti Sundari is displeased but Abimanyu is quickly able to win her around, thanks to a spell he has been given by Arjuna (Khalid Hussain 1964, p. 61). Unlike the Javanese version, there are no self-destructive oaths taken in the *hikayat*: the stories are principally told for their immediate romantic interest.

By way of contrast with these romantic stories, Abimanyu's death plays only a small part in the *hikayat* (Khalid Hussain 1964, pp. 110–14). The episode begins in a manner with which we are familiar. Dangyang Drona has lured Sang Rajuna and Sang Bima away from the main battlefield. He has arranged his army into the "*Cakra Anggar*" formation, confident that no one but Arjuna would be able to resist it. Shocked, Darmawangsa asks his leading generals — Sakula and Sadewa, Sang Seta Jaman, Sang Setyaki and Maharaja Gatotkaca — if they are able to pierce the line but they make no reply. Finally, Abimanyu himself volunteers that he can break into the enemy formation, although he does not know how to get out again: "My Lord, I can push my way through Dangyang Drona's strategic circle called 'Cakra Bayu' and I can enter it. But I do not know how to come back through it."[17]

From this point on, however, the story develops in some significantly different directions from the previous accounts. Abimanyu breaks through the line — accompanied not by Sumitra but by Semar, normally a clown figure in Javanese *wayang*. At Drona's orders, Maharaja Jaya Drata closes the space through which Abimanyu has entered, "he immediately closed like a door [or, a gate]".[18] Abimanyu kills Maharaja Salya's brother and seriously wounds Duryudana's son, Laksamana Kumara (a rival for Siti Sundari in some versions of that story). In revenge, Duryudana launches a vicious counterattack but succeeds only in killing Semar (who has loyally stayed with his young master, despite Abimanyu's urging him to retreat). Remarkably, Karna has pity on Abimanyu and does not kill him. He urges the boy to leave the field of battle, but Abimanyu forthrightly refuses, keen to protect his own good name and afraid that he will be considered a coward: "Then Abimanyu alone of all the men did not want to retreat from his enemies and he said, 'If I die let me die with the name of a man. If I die with the name of an evil man, would I not be ashamed, my Lord?'."[19] Karna then compassionately fires an arrow that breaks Abimanyu's (magical) bow. Taking his disc, Abimanyu chases after Duryudana, only to be hit by a shower of arrows from the Kurawa, a number of which pierce his ears and his head from front to back and back to front.

The erotic overtones of the Kakawin Bharatayuddha, to which the Hikayat Pandawa Lima owes much, are present but softened to present a more modest image of female adornment:

> He was like a man engaged in amorous play as he received the unbroken shower of arrows. Abimanyu did not feel the tips of the arrows hit him because he behaved like a man looking at a beautiful woman. The arrows clinging to his body were like a woman's waist-band. His reddening

> wounds were like a bath of red *kesumba* flowers sprinkled with lime and the wounds around his neck were like two chains of a necklace. The wounds on his body shone like shoulder ornaments and the blood spurting on his chest was like the essence of a perfume. The marks of the wounds on his hands were like wristlets of brilliant precious stones and the wounds on his arms were like wedding bracelets. That was how he felt. As for Abimanyu's role in the war, everyone praised him, just as we find depicted in the story of Betara Merta marrying Dewi Pertiwi.[20]

Abimanyu is not killed by the "six maha-chariot-heroes of Dhrtarasta/ led by Drona and Karna" (Drona Parwa, 49.22) but by a single arrow wound (Khalid Hussain 1964, p. 113). Still maintaining the difference from earlier accounts, once Abimanyu is dying it is again Karna who prevents Jaya Darata from delivering a final blow to Abimanyu's head. In fact, Karna weeps as he holds his nephew's body and kisses it, saying regretfully: "Oh my son, had I known that you did not want to retreat, I would never have broken your bow."[21] Abimanyu's final death is described in this way: "as a perfect death which will establish his name as a man in the field of battle".[22] The lamentations of Abimanyu's wives are very briefly dealt with in a few paragraphs and the women are presented as much as daughters as wives — "Dewi Satya Sundari the daughter of Maharja Baladewa and Dewi Utari the daughter of Maharaja Mangaspati."[23] This is a trivial sense of the concept of name.

The reason for the brevity of the lamentations may be explained by a passage from almost the end of the Hikayat Pandawa Lima. The author (or a later copyist) even further abbreviates the story of the entry of the wives of the various heroes into the heavenly realms by merely saying:

> This erroneous Javanese story says that their deaths were most perfect. After all the wives of the Pandawa had thrown themselves into the fire, King Yudistira walked to heaven with all the kings and their wives. I will not tell about this any more because the story is absolutely wrong, although you, sirs, will know more than I do. I will not prolong the scene (*lelakun*)[24] because I am running out of paper and my ink is dry and my pen is broken, so there is no more opportunity to do so.[25]

These may be the weary musings of a different age but clearly the writer considers a heaven won by self-immolation to be *sesat* — "erroneous", or "religious deviant" — and *salah*, wrong. He is prepared to refer to it but only because his listeners know better.

The same may be more broadly true of the reworking of the rest of what was once a Hindu manuscript in an increasingly Muslim and culturally Malay context. However, the use of the term "*nama*" (reputation) provides a crucial cultural validation of the perfection of Abimanyu's death. Note the two passages: "*Jikalau beta mati sekali pun dengan nama laki-laki. Jikalau dengan nama yang jahat tiadakah malu tuanku*" (Khalid Hussain 1964, pp. 112–13) and "*Maka Sang Bimanyu pun matilah sempurna nama laki-laki beroleh kenamaan di tengah medan*" (Khalid Hussain 1964, p. 114). There are no less than five aspects to "name" contained here:

1. a name must be earned (*beroleh kenamaan*);
2. the name of a man is praised for the courageous performance of his duties (*nama laki-laki*);
3. it is equally possible to receive an evil name (*nama yang jahat*);
4. such a name, good or evil, is confirmed at the hour of death and survives thereafter;
5. an evil name is a matter of profound shame (*malu*).

Milner (1982) argues that "name" was of crucial importance in a hierarchical Malay society where power, authority and prestige were all determined by one's closeness to the ruler. He sees the term as combining a reference to one's title, social rank and reputation: "men have", he argues, "only one kind of identity or personal worth and that is a social one" (Milner 1982, p. 100). Yet it is clear from the Hikayat Pandawa Lima that this is not an automatic correlation: no matter what one's rank, one may earn a good name, equally one may earn an evil name.

Exactly the same choices are present in the Hikayat Hang Tuah. As their battle begins, Hang Jebat describes Hang Tuah as "*hulubalang besar lagi ternama*", "a great and renowned warrior" (Kassim Ahmad 1975, p. 339). Hang Jebat himself is referred to throughout the event of his rebellion as "*si Jebat derhaka*", "the contemptuous traitor Jebat" (beginning on page 321). If he had hoped his actions might be justified "so that my name would be famous in every kingdom",[26] then unfortunately the reverse is the case. Jebat is made to accept this personal choice for evil and even to boast of it: "The reason that I have done these things is so that I should acquire a name of utmost evil; as the Malay proverb says 'decay spreads to the whole onion from its stem'; my name as a traitor and as an evil person must be perfect."[27] Hang Tuah replies to this perverted statement by placing it within a wider and more positive frame:

> What you say is true, but we servants of the king should weigh every act very carefully; as the old people say: "it is better to die with a good name than to live with an evil name, so that one can enter into the company of heaven."[28]

His good name assured, Abimanyu enters heaven, but as a loyal Malay warrior should and not as a pagan might as a matter of the fulfilment of his caste duties seeking heaven.

'Nostalgia': a Modern Indonesian Retelling

At first glance, Danarto's world would seem to be a long way from the courtly Malay world of the Hikayat Pandawa Lima that is built on fame and position in a courtly hierarchy. Danarto was born on June 27, 1941, in Mojowetan, Sragen, Central Java. His father was Jakio Harjodinomo, a senior iron worker in a sugar factory; his mother was Siti Aminah, a small batik trader in a local market. He was educated in a somewhat haphazard way at elementary and junior high schools in Sragen, at a senior high school in Solo, and at the Indonesian Institute of the Arts (ASRI), majoring in Art (1958–61). At college, he helped edit the children's magazine *Si Kuncang* (1958–61) and was a member of Sanggarbambu ("Bamboo Monastery"), a group of artists, actors, musicians and dancers in Yogyakarta. He worked creating domestic and public sculptures and reliefs in Jakarta and West Java during the 1960s, designing posters at the Jakarta Arts Centre, Taman Ismail Marzuki Jakarta (1969–71), and finally as a lecturer at the Jakarta Academy of Fine Arts from 1973 to the mid-1990s. He has left Indonesia briefly on a number of occasions:

as chief designer of the Indonesian cultural group at Expo ’70 in Osaka; a fellow of the International Writing Program, Iowa, in 1976; as an actor and set-designer with the choreographer and dancer Sardono during a tour of Europe and Asia in 1978; participant in the International Poetry Festival, Rotterdam, 1983; a pilgrim to Mecca in 1983; recipient of the Southeast Asia Write award in Bangkok in 1986; and writer-in-residence at the University of Kyoto 1990–91.

Religiously, Danarto was raised in a Javanese *abangan* environment, part Hindu and only potentially part Muslim, where there was no obvious access to religious scholars or *pesantren* schools. His father was fond of reading books on mysticism after returning home from work each day. His father read these books in Javanese and often in the Javanese script, but Danarto also remembers the names of Al-Ghazali and Agus Salim, and of two writers prominently associated with the Theosophical movement, C.W. Leadbeater and Krishnamurti. He did not learn to pray in the Muslim manner until he was twenty-seven years old and then only with the guidance of a book, *Tuntunan Salat*. The result was an immediate and profoundly mystical experience:

> When I first recited the takbir “Allahu Akbar” the whole area seemed to respond with the same expression: Allahu Akbar, Allahu Akbar. So, it was as though thousands of people were responding. That went on for a week. At that time I was praying alone at home. And that was my first religious experience [...] And my sufistic short stories came from that too [...]’[29]

In this same interview, Danarto has also described his stories as being “comfortable with the Islamic idea of pantheism (*wahdat al-wujud*)”.[30] Th. Sri Rahayu Prihatmi argues that: “All of Danarto’s short stories are filled with mysticism or Javanese spirituality mixed with Islam and are coloured by a pantheistic outlook.”[31] Most commonly they are considered to be “surrealistic” and, more recently, even “magical realist”. However we categorize them, there can be no doubting the originality of Danarto’s approach to the writing of literature.

“Nostalgia” (the title is in English) was written within two years of Danarto’s overwhelming mystical experience. It begins with a scene not found in any other version of the story. The sun is setting. Abimanyu is resting in his tent, as torrents of blood spread across the floor, and he is visited by a frog. He does not know who the frog is but conjectures that it might be Batara Surya, the sun god, Batara Indera, the supreme god, or Batara Bayu, the wind god. The frog does not know who it is either. It insists that its body is very different from that of a human being, but its soul ("*nyawa, roh, jiwa, dan sukma*", Danarto 1987, p. 91) is the same. Indeed, "All creatures are God's representatives on earth, whether they be human, animal, plant or object."[32] The frog reminds Abimanyu of the deaths of two great heroes — Seta (Sweta) and Bisma, assuring Abimanyu that he too will soon be "a great hero, boasted of and remembered for as long as history lasts".[33] But, he insists, "there is a more noble human destiny and that is to vanish from history."[34]

A traditional Hindu metaphysics of reincarnation that can only be ended by an escape from the cycle of birth and suffering lies behind the frog's assertion:

> Seta and Bisma and all of us are on a long journey. Far. Far. Very far. We will die and live again and die again and live again. We are following an amazing evolutionary path. Like that, like that, like that over and over again. What is it all for? To perfect happiness. Until one day, who knows how many million years of journeying hence, we will reach His lap. His heart. We will be still but moving. Calm but clanging with the business of work. Multiple but one. We are eternal in our essence. Human beings are eternal in their nature. Animals are eternal. Plants are eternal. Things are eternal.[35]

As Danarto presents the idea, human beings do not cease to be at this final stage, they do not simply merge completely with the Divine. Their destiny is to continue to live in a particular way: to live without ego. This is, in fact, the purpose for which human beings are born: "to continually confront the natural world".[36] One is not born to be a philosopher, a statesman, an artist, or anything else. It is only when one: "embraces a complete knowledge of the world, of the essence of creation, of the being of God", that one can then consider fulfilling such roles[37] — otherwise, the frog assures Abimanyu, they are merely a burden (*beban*). One has the "dharma" of being human, being a warrior is subordinate to that; "warrior dharma" is not an automatic process and one should not wish for it.

The frog encourages Abimanyu to search for the meaning of his own existence, before his discourse is interrupted by the entrance of "Sri Batara Kresna". It is Krishna (not Yudistira) who brings the decision of the council that the youth will lead the battle the next morning, then quickly leaves, praising the frog as he does so: "Abimanyu is now being purified; complete knowledge floods his soul, thanks to you, audacious frog!"[38]

Danarto describes the battle in brutal but highly focused detail. The Kurawa are led by Jayajatra and it is he who destroys Abimanyu's chariot (his powerful lance is disguised as an ordinary soldier).[39] Abimanyu commandeers a horse and chases after the Kurawa, continuing to cause enormous damage to the enemy troops. He appears to have killed Jayajatra, is isolated in the middle of his enemies, continues to fight, then, suddenly, he is hit by a general shower of arrows and falls to the ground. Upright, he begins to walk, his eyes fixed determinedly ahead of him.

A second interlude follows, in which an unnamed soldier, speaking in the first person, confirms that Abimanyu is "sipping the Absolute Essence",[40] as he dies. The interlude gives way to a further long scene in which a woman pours out her feelings for Abimanyu, following the third perspective on his death in the Mahabharata. The woman is not Siti Sundari, not Utari, neither of whom appears in the story, but his mother Sembadra. She engages in a bitter argument with Arjuna and Krishna. Sembadra is determined that her son should live, insisting that: "if the Bharatayudha is a problem belonging to the gods, then they should have created their own warriors out of clay and not have dragged my beloved son into the cauldron of war."[41] The men are determined that Abimanyu should die a hero and that it is his destiny (*kodrat*) to do so. It is the same gendered argument that we find in another of Danarto's short stories, "Godlob" (Danarto 1987, pp. 1–9) and indeed in the feminine subtext of the Mahabharata: men need heroes, women need their husbands and sons. Unlike the young man in the earlier story, Abimanyu is able to intervene in his parents' argument: "Don't argue about me", he tells them. "I am not. But in my non-being I find my real meaning: God. I am eternal."[42] It is the fulfilment of the frog's mission, grumbles Krishna. This confrontation of reality and unreality, being and non-being, is not found in other accounts of Abimanyu's death but is obviously completely consistent with Danarto's pantheistic worldview.

The final act of the drama has arrived. Leading the soldiers from both armies forward, Abimanyu declares that they are now faced with a greater problem than that of playing their appointed roles in society. He insists that: "Our problem is the universe", he tells them. "We must pass though the world. Like a baby in the womb, from not knowing anything, back to not knowing anything. From not-being back to not-being. But it is particularly in our not-being that we become what we really are: Being. We are not, only God is."[43] He offers a brief statement of negativity — "I am not life and not death. I am beyond life and death. I am eternal ... I am not happiness or suffering. I am beyond them. I am eternal."[44] Then he moves to a highly poetic and extremely paradoxical statement of affirmation that can only be compared with Krishna's self-revelation in the seventh, ninth and tenth chapters of the *Bhagavad Gita*:

> I am Kurusetra, the Pandawa and the Kurawa. I am the strategy-planners, the army, the heroes and the cowards, all become one, without space or limitation, like water mixed with mud. I approve of war, I oppose war, everything explodes in my soul. Oh, my soul that faints at the sight of blood. Oh, my spirit that walks hand in hand with death. I am Brahma, Shiva, Vishnu united as one in the clenched fist of my hand ...
>
> I am the guest who knocks at the door, I am the door, I am the knock, I am the host, yes, I am the greeting, I am the separation and I am the memory.
>
> Remembering Kurusetra is like diving to the deepest bottom of the ocean, the very deepest bottom: its people, its weapons, its tents, its provisions, its animals, its plains, its bright sparkling rivers flowing in all directions.
>
> Yes, I am the soldiers, the camps, rice, daggers, death.[45]

Or as al-Hallaj, one of Danarto's favorite mystical authors, very succinctly said: "*Ana al-haqq*", "I am the Truth".

Conclusion

Danarto's is the latest in a long series of retellings of the story of the death of Abimanyu. The story shifts and grows with each new reworking.

How Abimanyu learnt the secret of breaking through the *cakra vyuha* while he was still in the womb, and from whom — Arjuna or Krishna — is not part of any of these stories. His marriage to Siti Sundari and her subsequent self-immolation take different emphases. Compared to the story of Siti Sundari, the story of Utari is and is not of importance. In the *wayang* version, his lie to her inescapably determines the manner of his death but there is no way of showing that this story was known to the author of the Kakawin Bharatayuddha. More commonly, his marriage to Utari largely matters for the conception of Pariksit as a way of continuing the Pandawa line long afterwards, once the Pandawa have been brutally murdered by Aswatama. Who finally killed Abimanyu is uncertain — the six warriors including his uncle Karna, "Dursasana's son", Lesmana Mandrakumara (whom he cheated of Siti Sundari), Jayadrata, no one in particular, these are all possibilities. "Abimanyu gugur" is a story that stuns the mind in its heroism, treachery, pathos, and its variety. It is, however, a story whose unity exists only in retrospect, in the mind of those who know "the whole story" and not in any text.

Danarto provides yet another framework to the Abimanyu story. His approach is highly compatible with abstract philosophical Hindu principles of eternal and all-pervading spirit, birth and rebirth, egoless social service, and self-transcendence through self-knowledge. This is not a framework that is applicable to the Hikayat Pandawa Lima. It would be inaccurate to say that this framework has been written out of the *hikayat,* for it is not present in the Kakawin Bharatayuddha or the seventh book of the Mahabharata either, which have other understandings of Hinduism.

Each of these four texts develops its own understanding of the tragic and cruel death of the young warrior in accordance with the values of its own day. All accepted that sex and violence are natural parts of life but also that they must be constrained within moral and other limits relating to space, time and the appropriate agents for such actions (Arti Dhand 2008, pp. 46–49). The Drona Parwa spoke of the duty of a warrior and the promised reward for those who observed their martial duties, *ksatriya dharma*. The Kakawin Bharatayuddha emphasized the spiritual beauty of love, poetry and death on the battlefield and in the bedroom, poetic *tantra*, while the Hikayat Pandawa Lima preferred the Malay values of earning a virtuous public reputation, fulfilling one's public roles in a proper manner, of avoiding disgrace, and of dying with dignity. The Islamicized *hikayat* provides the most radical shift in the values of the story. Danarto's story too is Islamic but it shares little in common with any of these other versions. In their own individual manner all these changing values have enabled the story to survive its passage from India to Southeast Asia, from Hinduism to Islam, and then to the modern world, as a series of narrators, editors and copyists have struggled to produce an aesthetic and ideologically acceptable literary work for their new audiences.

The comparatively recent copyist of the Hikayat Pandawa Lima concludes in a series of verses directed at those readers who might hire the book to read for themselves, ending:

> Because I do not have a lot of ideas
> if I am wrong, please do not scold me.
> If there are wrong letters
> please correct them with the proper signs[46]

In the company of scholars of Classical Malay literature, I ask for the same pardon.

NOTES

I would like to acknowledge assistance received in the preparation of this chapter from Associate Professor Greg Bailey (La Trobe University), Dr Adam Bowles (University of Queensland), Associate Professor Helen Creese (University of Queensland), and Professor Stuart Robson (Monash University).

1. Please note that in order to maintain some consistency throughout this very preliminary survey of extremely diverse materials, the spelling of most names, except in direct English quotations, will be regularized in accordance with the common contemporary Indonesian/Malay forms — hence Abimanyu, Bima, Duryudana, Dursasana, Siti Sundari, etc.
2. Mahabharata VII.33:23, trans. P. Lal (2007), p. 190.
3. There are a number of different Sanskrit texts and English translations of the Mahabharata. I will mainly follow the Lal modern "transcreation" of the

Drona Parwa and the online Ganguli version for the other books. The more poetic Lal text draws on a wide range of Sanskrit texts; it also numbers the verses, which Ganguli does not.

4. To my understanding, the widely known story of Abimanyu learning (half of) the mantra to break through the enemy's lines while still in Subadra's womb is not to be found in the Mahabharata and does not occur in any of the later Southeast Asian versions discussed here. Drona Parwa 35.19 merely indicates that "My father Arjuna taught me the secret of penetrating this array." Arjuna is equally insistent in 72.24: "I did not teach him how to get out of the cakra-formation." The word which Lal translates as "secret" is *yoga* (personal communication from Adam Bowles, University of Queensland, 29 January 2014).
5. Dursasana's son is known simply by his patronymic Daushasani.
6. In the Swargarohana Parwa 5.18–20, Abimanyu enters the moon in his previous form of Varcas.
7. These translations follow Mascaro (1970). Other egregious examples of unfair fighting in the War include the death of Bisma (by Arjuna's hiding behind Srikandi), that of Drona (by the lie that Aswatama was dead), the death of Jayadrata (through Krishna's hiding of the sun), the death of Karna (unarmed and not fighting), the death of Duryodana (by a blow on the thigh), and Aswatama's destruction of the sleeping Pandawa. Neither side can claim absolute purity in the final assessment.
8. There are some ninety surviving manuscripts of the Kakawin Bharata Yuddha but only approximately seventy of the Ramayana and about fifty of the Arjunawiwaha (Supomo 1993, p. 41).
9. However, Siti Sundari is widely known in the folklore of South India, where she is called Vatsala or Shashirekha. A Malayalam work, the *Sundarisvayamvaram Tullal*, tells of the abduction of Siti Sundari by Abimanyu with the assistance of his cousin Gatotkaca, the offspring of Bima and the *raksasi* Hidimbi, in exactly the same way as the Kakawin Ghatotkacasraya (Ghatotkaca to the Rescue) does. Significantly, mpu Panuluh, the second author of the Kakawin Bharata Yuddha, is also credited with the authorship of this latter *kakawin*, possibly between 1194 to c. 1205, although the story itself does not appear in the Kakawin Bharata Yuddha (possibly because the events occurred before the War began). See "Summary of *Sundarisvayamvaram* (Marriage of Sundari) *Tullal*", available at <http:// Mahabharata-resources.org/variations/sundarisvayamvaram-tullal-summary-html> (accessed 18 December 2013). A preliminary search of the web indicates the enormous popularity in Andhra Pradesh of the story as a source for extremely large numbers of ballads, stories and *harikatha*, as well as films and even comic books (see no. 61 in the Amar Chitra Katha series, *Ghatotkacha*, Bombay 1977). It is, logically, possible that the story may have come to India from Southeast Asia.

10. Suggesting here too a learned skill and not a pre-birth boon.
11. This tragic self-cursing is told in many accounts of the *wayang* story, including Kats (1984), pp. 404–6.
12. Braginsky (2004), p. 150 suggests that "a sea of honey" is "a traditional symbol of amorous passion in Malay and Javanese literature" and compares it with the image of "the sea of blood", which he describes as "a symbol of war and death". Here the two images would seem to be one.
13. "Cukuplah, ia telah mati dan terkubur dalam pertempuran, tetapi keindahan dari kematiannya berbentuk usaha untuk mencari keindahan" (Sutjipto 1968, p. 229).
14. It sould be noted that the theme of righteous warrior dharma also occurs later in BY 51.9: "those who fight righteously in accordance with the Law will return to heaven" (Supomo 1993, p. 252), "siapa yang dalam medan pertempuran secara jujur berpegangan kepada dharma akan bertempat tinggal di sorga" (Sutjipto 1968, p. 351). The one verse summary of the whole of the Bhagavad Gita in verse BY 10.13, simply forbids a warrior to leave the field of battle, thus ignoring the major thrust of the original text.
15. "Apatah salahnya, tiadakah orang berbini sepuluh duapuluh. Biarlah beta sendiri pergi mendapatkan Maharaja Mangaspati" (Khalid Hussain 1964, p. 60).
16. "Baiklah Satya Utari dudukkan Sang Bimanyu, berkenanlah kepadanya. Lagi pun Sang Bimanyu orang muda, patutlah dengan Dewi Satya Utari sama muda baik paras" (Khalid Hussain 1964, p. 61).
17. "Tuanku patek dapat menempoh ikat perang Dangyang Drona itu yang bernama 'Cakra Bayu' tetapi dapat patek memasoki juga. Undor-nya patek tiada tahu" (Khalid Hussain 1964, p. 111). Again there is no reference to him having learnt this strategy while still in the womb.
18. "maka segera ditutupnya yang seperti pintu bangunnya" (Khalid Hussain 1964, p. 112).
19. "Maka Sang Bimanyu pun satu laki-laki tiada mahu undor daripada lawannya seraya katanya, 'Jikalau beta mati sekali pun dengan nama laki-laki. Jikalau dengan nama yang jahat tiadakah malu tuanku'" (Khalid Hussain 1964, pp. 112–13).
20. "Hatta kalakian seperti orang bermain lakunya kena panah itu tiada bersela lagi kena ujung panah itu pun tiada diperasakannya oleh Sang Bimanyu dan lakunya seperti laku laki-laki melihat perempuan yang baik parasnya. Demikianlah anak panah lekat pada tubuhnya seperti pengilas perempuan yang baik rupanya. Demikianlah segala lukanya itu bermerah-merahan seperti kesumba kena limau dan luka pada lehernya seperti orang bertali leher dua pengikat. Demikianlah luka kepada sekalian tubuhnya itu seperti orang berkilat bahu dan darah yang terpercik itu seperti urap-urap sari kepada dadanya. Demikianlah kepada pengarasnya Sang Bimanyu luka kepada tangannya itu seperti orang bergelang permata sagah murka dan luka kepada lengannya itu seperti orang berpinta bernikah. Demikianlah rasanya. Maka Sang Bimanyu pada segala

perang itu sekaliannya memuji-muji dia seperti dapat digambarkan seperti laku Batara Merta sedang kawin dengan Dewi Pertiwi itu" (Khalid Hussain 1964, p. 113). My translation is influenced by Braginsky (2004), p. 150. Contrary to Braginsky, however, the reference in the last sentence is probably to the rape by the god Harimurti (Vishnu) of the earth goddess, Pratiwi, described in the Bhomantaka 2.7, and not to "the god of love Kama" (Robson, personal communication, 14 January 2014).

21. "Wah anakku. Jikalau tahu akan engkau tiada mahu undur, kira apakah aku memanah panahmu" (Khalid Hussain 1964, p. 114).
22. "Maka Sang Bimanyu pun matilah sempurna nama laki-laki beroleh kenamaan di tengah medan" (Khalid Hussain 1964, p. 114).
23. "Dewi Satya Sundari seorang namanya, anak Maharaja Baladewa dan Dewi Utari seorang namanya, anak Maharaja Mangaspati" (Khalid Hussain 1964, p. 114).
24. The suggestion that this is a lelakun of a Javanese story may mean that the long narrative passages are Malay versions of originally Javanese shadow plays rather than translations of actual kakawin texts.
25. "Maka cerita Jawa yang sesat ini dikatanya amat sempurnalah kematiannya itu. Setelah sudah segala isteri Pandawa belalah, maka Maharaja Darmawangsa pun berjalanlah ke kayangan dengan segala Maharaja dan segala isterinya. Maka tiadalah tersebut lagi perkataan itu kerana terlalu salah ceritanya, melainkan segala tuan-tuan juga yang lebih tahu. Tiadalah hamba panjangkan lelakun lagi kerana kertas pun sudah kurang dan dawat pun sudah kering dan kalam pun sudah patah, tiadalah sempat lagi" (Khalid Hussain 1964, p. 246).
26. "supaya namaku masyur pada segala negeri" (Kassim Ahmad 1975, p. 339).
27. "Sebab pun kuperbuat demikian ini, sepala-pala nama jahat jangan kepalang, seperti pantun Melayu, rosak bawang ditimpa jambaknya; maka sempurnalah nama derhaka dan nama jahat" (Kassim Ahmad 1975, p. 343).
28. "Sungguh seperti katamu itu, tetapi akan kita diperhamba raja ini hendaklah pada barang sesuatu pekerjaan itu bicarakan sangat-sangat, seperti kata orang tua: 'Baik mati dengan nama yang baik, jangan hidup dengan nama jahat; supaya masuk syurga jemah'" (Kassim Ahmad 1975, p. 343).
29. "Ketika saya pertama kali mengucap takbir: 'Allahu Akbar', seluruh kawasan itu seolah-olah menyahut dengan ucapan yang sama: Allahu Akbar, Allahu Akbar. Jadi seperti ada sambutan dan dalam jumlah ribuan orang. Itu berlangsung sampai satu minggu. Ketika itu saya salat sendiri di rumah. Dan itulah pengalaman spiritual saya yang pertama kali [...] Dari situlah muncul cerpen-cerpen sufistik saya [...]". Details in this paragraph are taken from Danarto: "Awalnya, saya salat berbahasa Jawa", available at <http://islamlib.com/?site=1&aid=723&cat=content&cid=12&title=awalnya-saya-salat-berbahasa-jawa> (accessed 31 December 2013). For a detailed discussion of Danarto's religious background, see Siti Sundari Tjitrosubono et al. (1985), pp. 8–12.

30. A year later, in 1968, Danarto had a similar experience, again in Bandung, in which: "Saya melihat Tuhan ada di mana-mana; kucing yang Tuhan, ayam yang Tuhan, dan lain-lain. Jadi dari situlah saya merasa cocok dengan paham wahdatul wujud. Jadi sebetulnya di dunia ini tidak ada yang lain kecuali Tuhan. Dari situlah mengalir terus cerpen-cerpen saya", "I saw that God was everywhere; the cat was God, the hens were God, and so was everything else. It was from there that I began to feel comfortable with the Islamic idea of pantheism. So really there is nothing in this world except for God. My short stories flow from that."
31. "Cerpen-cerpen Danarto [...] semua bernafaskan mistik atau kebatinan Jawa bercampur Islam dan diwarnai oleh pandangan panteisme" (Th. Sri Rahayu Prihatmi 1989, p. 32).
32. "Maka, semua makhluk adalah wakil Tuhan di bumi: apakah ia manusia, hewan, tumbuh-tumbuhan atau benda-benda" (Danarto 1987, p. 91).
33. "pahlawan besar yang dibanggakan yang akan dikenang sepanjang sejarah" (Danarto 1987, pp. 93–94).
34. "manusia utama adalah yang mampu melenyap dari sejarah" (Danarto 1987, p. 94).
35. "Seta dan Bisma dan kita semua kan melakukan perjalanan yang jauh, jauh dan jauh sekali. Betapa dahsyatnya evolusi yang wajib kita jalani. Begitu, begitu, Untuk apa itu semuanya? Untuk menyempurnakan kebahagaiaan. Hingga pada suatu saat nanti entah berapa juta tahun kita dalam perjalanan ini, kita akan sampai di haribaanNya. Di jantungNya. Kita akan diam tapi bergerak. Tenteram tetapi gaduh oleh kesibukan kerja. Banyak tetapi Esa. Kita adalah kekal pada hakikatnya. Manusia adalah kekal pada kodratnya. Binatang adalah kekal. Tumbuh-tumbuhan adalah kekal. Dan benda-benda adalah kekal" (Danarto 1987, p. 94).
36. "Manusia lahir seharusnya ia terus berhadapan dengan alam semesta" (Danarto 1987, p. 94).
37. "Memeluk suatu pengetahuan semesta, tentang hakikat penciptaan, tentang ketuhanan" (Danarto 1987, p. 94).
38. "Abimanyu kini mengalami pembasuhan hebat dalam dirinya dan dengan derasnya pengetahuan semesta masuk ke dalam sukmanya. O, katak yang lancang!" (Danarto 1987, p. 95).
39. At the very start of the Hikayat Pandawa Lima, Maharaja Darmawangsa loses his kingdom because Maharaja Duryudana orders Arya Manggala to transform himself into the gambling board (*papan*) and Pateh Sangkuni becomes the dice (*pareh*) (Khalid Hussain 1964, p. 1). Such transformations are far from "postmodern".
40. "menghirup Zat mutlak" (Danarto 1987, p. 99).
41. "Kalau memang persoalan Bharatayudha adalah persoalan dewa-dewa, saya harap mereka mencipta pahlawannya dari tanah liat. Jangan pernah mereka

menyeret-nyeret anakku yang kucintai ke dalam kancah peperangan ini" (Danarto 1987, p. 101).

42. "Janganlah persoalkan saya. Abimanyu itu tidak ada. Tetapi justru di dalam ketiadaanku, aku memperoleh arti yang sebenarnya: Tuhan. Akulah kekekalan" (Danarto 1987, p. 103).
43. "Persoalan semesta. Marilah kita mengarungi alam semesta. Seperti bayi dalam kandungan, dari tidak tahu apa-apa, kembali ke tidak tahu apa-apa. Dari tidak ada kembali ke tidak ada. Tetapi justru dalam ketidakadaan kita ini, kita menjadi yang sebenarnya: Yang ada. Kita itu tidak ada, hanya Tuhanlah yang ada" (Danarto 1987, pp. 103–4).
44. "Aku bukan hidup dan bukan mati. Akulah di atas hidup dan mati. Akulah kekekalan ... Aku bukan kebahagiaan atau penderitaan. Aku di atasnya. Akulah kekekalan" (Danarto 1987, p. 104).
45. "Akulah Kurusetra, Pandawa, dan Kurawa. Akulah perancang perang, bala tentara, pahlawan dan pengecut bertumpu menjadi satu, tak berjarak tak berbingkai, seperti air dengan lumpur. Aku setuju perang, aku menentang perang, semua meledak dalam sukmaku. O, rohku yang nanar melihat darah. O, nyawaku yang bergandengan dengan maut. Akulah Brahma, Siwa, Wisnu di dalam kepalan tanganku menyatu ...

    Akulah tamu yang mengetuk pintu, akulah pintu, akulah ketukan itu, akulah tuan rumah, ya, akulah tegur sapa, akulah perpisahan dan akulah kenangan.

    Dan kenangan pada Kurusetra adalah seperti menyelam dalam lautan yang terdalam ke dasarnya, ke dasar-dasarnya: pada manusianya, pada senjata, pada kemah, pada perbekalan, pada binatang-binatangnya, pada tanah datarannya, pada sungai-sungai jernih yang mengalir di sana-sini.

    Ya, akulah prajurit, kemah, nasi, keris, maut" (Danarto 1987, pp. 104–5).
46. *Karena hamba kurang pendapat*
    Jikalau salah jangan diumpat
    Jikalau ada huruf yang ghalat
    Tuan-tuan tambahi dengan isyarat (Khalid Hussain 1964, p. 248).

REFERENCES

Arti Dhand. *Woman as Fire, Woman as Sage: Sexual Ideology in the Mahabharata.* Albany: State University of New York Press, 2008.

Brakel, L. "Two Indian Epics in the Malay Archipel". *Archipel* 20 (1980): 143–60.

Braginsky, V. *The Heritage of Traditional Malay Literature.* Singapore: Institute of Southeast Asian Studies, 2004.

Creese, H. *Women of the Kakawin World.* Armonk, NY: Sharpe, 2004.

Danarto. "Nostalgia". In *Godlob.* Jakarta: Grafitipers, 1987. 2nd ed., pp. 90–105.

Griffith, H. "Salyawadha – the Death of Salya". Canberra: Department of Indonesian Languages and Literatures, Australian National University, 1976. Honours sub-thesis.

Kassim Ahmad, ed. *Hikayat Hang Tuah*. Kuala Lumpur: Dewan Bahasa dan Pustaka, 1975.

Kats, J. *De wajang poerwa: Een vorm van Javaans toneel.* Dordrecht etc.: Foris, 1984. 2nd ed., intr. by J.J. Ras and H.A. Poeze. Indonesische herdrukken.

Khalid Hussain, ed. *Hikayat Pandawa Lima*. Kuala Lumpur: Dewan Bahasa dan Pustaka, 1964.

Kishari Mohan Ganguli, trans. *The Mahabharata.* Calcutta: Bharata Press, 1883–96. Eighteen volumes. P.C. Roy ed. Available at <http://www.sacred-texts.com/hin/maha/index.htm>.

Lal, P., trans. *The Mahabharata of Vyasa. Book 7: The Complete Drona Parva.* Calcutta: Writers Workshop, 2007.

Mascaro, J., trans. *The Bhagavad Gita.* London: Rider, 1970.

McGrath, K. *Jaya: Performance in Epic Mahabharata*. Boston: Ilex Foundation, 2011.

Milner, A.C. *Kerajaan: Malay Political Culture on the Eve of Colonial Rule.* Tucson: University of Arizona Press, 1982.

Phalgunadi, I.G.P. *The Indonesian Mahābhārata: Ādiparwa, the First Book.* New Delhi: International Academy of Indian Culture and Aditya Prakashan, 1990. Śata-piṭaka Series 360.

Richman, P., ed. *Many Ramayanas: The Diversity of a Narrative Tradition in South India.* Berkeley: University of California Press, 1991.

Siti Sundari Tjitrosubono et al. *Memahami cerpen-cerpen Danarto.* Jakarta: Pusat Pembinaan dan Pembangunan Bahasa, 1985.

Supomo, S., ed. *Bharatayuddha: An Old Javanese Poem and its Indian Sources*. New Delhi: International Academy of Indian Culture and Aditya Prakashan, 1993. Śata-piṭaka Series 373.

Sutjipto Wirjosuparto, ed. *Kakawin Bharata-Yuddha*. Djakarta: Bhratara, 1968.

Th. Sri Rahayu Prihatmi. *Fantasi dalam kedua kumpulan cerpen Danarto. Dialog antara dunia nyata dan tidak nyata.* Jakarta: Balai Pustaka, 1989.

Zoetmulder, P.J. *Kalangwan: A Survey of Old Javanese Literature*. The Hague: Nijhoff, 1974. KITLV Translation Series 16.

4

DRONA'S BETRAYAL AND BIMA'S BRUTALITY: Javanaiserie in Malay Culture

Bernard Arps

The presence of elements explicitly identified as "Javanese" or "from Java" in traditional Malay literature and performance — settings, characters, objects, idioms, stories, texts, even entire genres like the renditions of Mahabharata story-matter — has mostly been ascribed to the putative prestige of the historical civilization of Java. Here I explore another point of view. Focusing on religiosity and ethics in a hikayat with Mahabharata stories, I propose the notion of javanaiserie, the creation of texts, performances, and other cultural artefacts designed to be considered Javanese. Javanaiserie has proven alluring in Malay contexts. Rather than as a matter of influence I suggest regarding javanaiserie as an active process of worldmaking, the creation of a reality that is culturally at once close to and distinct from an audience's everyday lifeworld, a reality that can be both elegant and evil, appealing as well as appalling.

Keywords: Malay Mahabharata, *hikayat*, religiosity, javanaiserie, worldmaking.

The "Javanese" Presence in Malay Literature and Performance

It has long been noted by scholars that traditional literature and performance in Malay, as once practised throughout the archipelago, in an area ranging from the island of Java itself, particularly Batavia, up to Kedah and Kelantan in Malaysia, contains elements with explicit and strong Javanese associations. Settings, characters, objects, idioms, stories, texts, even entire genres are explicitly identified as "Javanese" or "from Java". Certain Malay prose and verse narratives (*hikayat* and *syair*) are set at medieval Javanese courts, with Javanese protagonists. These works mostly tell stories about Prince Ino Kertapati (Panji) and his close relatives. Some are labelled as translations from the Javanese language or said to have been performed by narrators in or from Java. An often-discussed example is the Hikayat Andaken Penurat, but there are numerous others (Robson 1969, pp. 7–8; Koster 1997, pp. 55–56; Braginsky 2004, p. 159). There are also, of course, Malay texts with only a few episodes set in Java and with Javanese characters more as antagonists, including the celebrated Sejarah Melayu and Hikayat Hang Tuah. A genre of shadow-play named "Javanese" (*wayang Jawa*) used to be performed in a variety of Kelantan Malay with Panji and Pandawa narratives — stories about the heroes of the Mahabharata — for its repertoire (Sweeney 1972, pp. 3–25). Other texts may appear not to have a Javanese connection at first because they can be categorized, as Braginsky does, as "[t]ales about heroes of Sanskrit epics and *purana*" (Braginsky 2004, p. 143), yet Malay audiences identified some of them as Javanese (see for instance Hussain 1992, p. 280). As philological comparison has shown — and to be fair to Braginsky I should stress that he was perfectly aware of this and discusses it in his monumental study — among them are renditions of Old Javanese texts (Wieringa 2007, pp. 19–20; Brakel 1980).

In his discussion of the Javanese presence, Robson even refers to works like Hikayat Pandawa Lima and Hikayat Galuh Digantung collectively as "Malayo-Javanese literature" (1992, p. 27), as Winstedt had done earlier (1991, pp. 30, 35, 36). To explain this presence Robson notes that in the fifteenth and sixteenth centuries Java had greater political and economic power than the Malay-speaking lands. He argues that this caused a "spread" or "flow" of culture from the former to the latter, involving texts that pictured the superior literary and dramatic refinement of Java (Robson 1992).

Robson cites Overbeck as one of the first scholars to examine the Javanese presence in detail. Overbeck has a more specific theory, which, he stresses, is "for the time being totally unproven" (and which he never got to verify). He hypothesized that Panji and Pandawa narratives were written in Malay in Java as political propaganda and exported to regions over which Java claimed sovereignty or with which it maintained friendly ties (Overbeck 1938, pp. 305, 309; Robson 1992, p. 28). Robson considers it unlikely that these texts were, as Overbeck suggested, authored by Javanese, but he does support the possibility that "Malays came to Java, became familiar with its arts and culture (perhaps over a period of generations), and then propagated them in their home country" (Robson 1992, p. 37). Braginsky, in turn, finds Robson's ideas convincing (2004, p. 199).

Overbeck made his hypothesis public in an extended review of a survey of Malay literature, Hooykaas's *Over Maleise Literatuur*, first published in 1937, written for use in a colonial secondary school for Indonesians and students of Indology in the Netherlands. Far more accessible and influential in Malay studies at large has been Winstedt's counterpart, *A History of Malay Literature*, which came out in 1939. Winstedt categorizes Malay literature according to major sources of influence in approximate chronological order and treats "the Javanese element" as part of this literary-historical periodization. In an incisive discussion, introducing a study intended to put Malay orality and "schematic composition" on the scholarly agenda, Sweeney points out with devastating dryness that "the model is particularly unsuited to what we know of Malay literature" (1987, p. 26) and makes short work of it with well-chosen examples. To mention one: a *wayang* performance today, "undeniably a product of the *present*", would have to be assigned to Winstedt's Hindu period (Sweeney 1987, p. 26).

With Overbeck and Sweeney as notable exceptions, the authors of these studies (and too many others to allow further discussion) tend to account for the Javanese presence in Malay texts as a matter of influence received. To be sure, they did not think of it as passive adoption. The Javanese influence was selectively processed. Robson suggests that "in some cases relative fidelity may have been called for, while in others the 'translation' may have been a reshaping of material familiar in Javanese in accordance with the demands and tastes of a Malay audience, with plenty of room for adaptation" (1992, p. 36). But the process is seen as reception-led. Such a perspective asks to be complemented and enriched by observation from another vantage point, one that shows texts as components of literary *activity*.

These works are in varieties of the Malay language. Authors, performers and audiences mastered such varieties and some of them may at times have called themselves Malays. They may have been writing, performing, reading, and listening in environments regarded as Malay.[1] The questions arise what these Javanese-flavoured texts and performances were *designed to do* in their cultural contexts, and — not quite the same — what they actually *did* in those contexts once they had begun to circulate. It is obvious that "the Javanese element" played a role in this, but what role? In abstract terms one may say that in composing, hearing, and reading these texts and performances, their authors, performers, and audiences immersed themselves in diegeses (worlds, universes, realities) that had something decidedly Javanese about them.[2] Though fleetingly, these textual diegeses were part of a bigger diegesis, these people's lifeworlds. The artefacts that were these texts and performances circulated in and across communities, as did the diegeses they helped call into being. From this perspective, as Overbeck and Sweeney sensed, "the Javanese element" is not about receiving influence but about having it, not about reflecting a Javanese past but about making a Malay present.

The Malay "Nawaruci" According to Scholarship

It is from this perspective that I want to consider these narratives here. My empirical focus is on one episode in one "Javanese" work in Malay, an episode that is particularly suitable for consideration under this aspect because it tells a story known in Java (and Bali) in a range of narrative inflections, but recounts it with a plot resolution and thematic emphases that differ substantially from all other known versions.

The narrative of Bima's arduous quest for the purifying water at the direction of his teacher Drona, Bima's meeting with a deity in the ocean, and the enlightenment he receives when he has entered the deity's body is one of the classics of Javanophone literature and drama. Many versions exist, under such titles as Nawaruci (after the deity's name in certain literary versions, known from Bali, in Old Javanese), Dewa Ruci (his name in another Old and most Modern Javanese literary and dramatic renditions), and Bima Suci ("Bima Purified", a long-standing alternative title in Modern Javanese). The story, not known from South Asia, has been attested in Java since the mid-fifteenth century. Renditions continue to be produced, in written, spoken and dramatic form, and statues and *wayang*-style paintings of key scenes are on display in public places and homes across Java and Bali.

One of the reasons for this story's longevity has been its multiple religious interpretability. Multiple, that is, in certain respects, because in an important way its interpretation is constant. The doctrinal backgrounds are variable. The story has been framed in Shivaite, Buddhist, Islamic, Javanist, Christian and New Age terms, and interpretations of it in a nationalistic vein also exist. The reinterpretation often entails changes to the narrative. But that it is somehow a religious and, more specifically, a mystical story is evident across all interpretive transformations. The story always recounts the protagonist Bima (who may bear other names), the second of the five Pandawa brothers, questing for an enigmatic kind of water and sometimes other matters, having to overcome hindrances that are easily taken as symbolic, encountering a mysterious and knowledgeable personage in the ocean, entering paradoxically that personage's body which turns out to contain boundless space, and attaining some kind of deep insight there. The very structure of the narrative, thematizing as it does enigma and a series of trials over the course of a quest that ends in understanding, suggests a mystico-religious *modus interpretandi*.

At least, this is so in the story's known Old and Modern Javanese, Balinese, Madurese, and Sundanese manifestations. It was reported almost a century and a half ago that versions in Malay exist as well (Van der Tuuk 1879, pp. 512–13; 1881, pp. 53–54). These have not exactly basked in the limelight of scholarship. Unlike several of their

Javanese counterparts, they have not entered the literary canon. They have an obscure position in an area of Malayophone literature, *wayang* mythology, that Malays have long regarded with suspicion for religious reasons. Still as it happens, questions about the cultural context of the Malay narrative have received attention from the few scholars who did mention it. They tended to examine it as part of the multilingual corpus of stories about Bima's enlightenment, however, more than as a specimen of Malay writing or storytelling. This helps to explain the pronounced emphasis they have put on what the text is not and does not do, rather than what it is and does.

Ever since Van der Tuuk made the suggestion (1881, pp. 53–54), the Malay rendition is assumed to be based on the version in Old Javanese known to scholarship as Nawaruci. This version, it was proposed fifty years later, was probably written in Bali in or before 1613 (Prijohoetomo 1934, pp. 13, 21). The teachings of Nawaruci to Bima amount to an elaborate survey of Shivaite religious dogmatics (Prijohoetomo 1934, pp. 1–2). But, as Poerbatjaraka put it when he published the only edition and translation of a Malay rendition so far, "of Nawaruci's teachings nothing remains in the Malay version, because the Malays were concerned to give the 'story', not the teachings" (Poerbatjaraka 1940, p. 38, my translation from the Dutch).

Poerbatjaraka called the text he published (incompletely, as we shall see) "the Malay version" while in fact there are several related ones. Van der Tuuk had implied as much (1879, pp. 491, 513 note 4), as had Juynboll in his catalogue of the Malay manuscripts in Leiden University Library (Juynboll 1899, pp. 56, 61). These Malay versions are striking exceptions to the tendency mentioned above as regards the play between interpretive constancy and changeability of the story. The main title under which the story was long known in Javanese, "Bima Purified" (Bima Suci), is grossly inapplicable to the Malay versions — in spite of the fact that in these versions, too, Bima's quest is motivated by the desire to have a body that is pure (*suci*). The only teaching remotely worthy of the name that he receives from the deity concerns a magical spell and the quest yields no purification or enlightenment whatsoever. This is all the more striking because the preceding narrative does build the expectation that something extraordinary is about to happen.[3]

Poerbatjaraka attributed this anticlimax to "the Malays" and their concerns. Gonda went a step further. He noted that "Buddhist" teachings were contained in the Old Javanese version which he regarded as the oldest ("dating back to the period between 1400 and 1600"), a versified telling that has only partly survived and that was the main object of Poerbatjaraka's philological attention in his 1940 article. Gonda explained the lack of such teachings in the Malay text as a result of adaptation to changed cultural circumstances: "The originally Buddhist elements of the Javanese version were in the course of time eliminated, obviously to make the work [...] acceptable to the Moslems", Javanese and Malay (Gonda 1976, p. 216).

> In Java this story is regarded as an account of profound religious mystery, as a source of "the knowledge of perfection", i.e. as a guide to the ultimate union of the soul with God, in the Malay version it is almost devoid of that deeper sense: here Drona, the *guru* of the epic heroes, in sending Bhīma out for the water of life contrives the other's destruction; Bhīma is, however, resuscitated by Navaruci, who incites him to take revenge on Drona and gives him a magical weapon (Gonda 1976, p. 216).

Clearly, then, the Malay versions are not about Bima's purification, let alone his mystical enlightenment. Nor is Bima's entering of the deity's body recounted, while this is a crucial juncture in other tellings, including the prose Nawaruci (Prijohoetomo 1934, pp. 58–59), the Old Javanese verse rendition (Poerbatjaraka 1940, pp. 22–23), the numerous Modern Javanese versions connected more or less closely with the narrative poem attributed to Yasadipura I, which was written in Surakarta around 1790, and the dozens of *wayang* and other dramatic renditions from the early nineteenth century onwards that I have studied.[4]

Leaving aside Gonda's generalization about "the" Javanese version, sudden or gradual de-doctrinization in order to render the text more acceptable to Muslims is not the only process that has made the Malay versions what they are. Religious bowdlerization may have had a share, but if it did it was not, and could not be, successful. The outcome was hardly a story that agrees with Islamic sensibilities. The crucial personage of the deity was retained, and although he does not impart Buddhist or Shivaite doctrine, he does teach Bima a spell that allows him to walk on water. Other elements like the destruction that Gonda mentions and the recurring fear of blemish and misfortune, sparked by malice, also disagreed with normative Islam. Moreover, although Poerbatjaraka creates the impression that his text is complete when at the end of his Dutch translation he states "Thus far runs the story of the Malay Dewa Ruci" (1940, p. 37), it simply is not.

From What the Story Is Not, to What It Is

If one is interested in the significance of the Malay renditions in their contexts of use it makes sense to examine not only what the story does not or no longer contain, but also what it does contain. Poerbatjaraka's representation is inaccurate. When we go back to the manuscripts, it transpires that the episode is much longer than he states. Poerbatjaraka duly acknowledges that the text in the manuscript he used, Cod. Or. 3240 in Leiden University Library, begins *in medias res* whereas another manuscript also contains a preceding narrative (Poerbatjaraka 1940, p. 35). His source of information here is Van der Tuuk's succinct synopsis of the entire episode (1879, pp. 512–14). Van der Tuuk had used manuscript ML 15, now in the National Library of Indonesia, which was written in Batavia in 1861 (Bijleveld [s.a.], p. 13). Upon scrutiny the episode itself turns out to be quite different in these two manuscripts, and overall they contain partly different episodes while corresponding episodes sometimes come in a different order. Poerbatjaraka remains silent about how the story continues in either version after Bima, incited by the deity, begins to beat Drona.

I will devote the remainder of this chapter to three matters that call for clarification. The Malay versions of the story of Bima's quest for the purifying water do not constitute an independent work or even a discrete part of a longer work. They are one episode in a series. This is so in all four manuscripts that I know to contain the story. It is so in the 1861 Batavian manuscript ML 15 summarized by Van der Tuuk (1879).[5] It is so in Cod. Or. 3240, from which Poerbatjaraka took his partial text. Date and provenance of this manuscript are unknown (Wieringa 2007, pp. 97–100), though it is clearly early nineteenth century or earlier. It is also the case in Cod. Or. 3377, written in 1875 and part of a lending library by 1884 (Wieringa 2007, pp. 340–44). This contains a version resembling Jakarta ML 15 but partly far more elaborate,[6] It is also in a fourth manuscript, Raffles Malay 21 in the Royal Asiatic Society, London. This manuscript will be my main source. Its text is very close to that of the incomplete manuscript Or. 3240. Like earlier commentators I focus on the story of Bima's quest, but in its entirety and not at the exclusion of its narrative context. In Raffles Malay 21 and Or. 3240 the protagonist of the episode is not Bima but rather the Pandawa brothers collectively in their interaction with their Korawa cousins, particularly their eldest cousin Duryodana and the chancellor (*patih*), Sangkuni. I will summarize the episode and discuss its intertextual relations in the next two sections.

The second issue to be examined is the role that religious notions evidently do play in this Malay version in spite of the lack of doctrinal instruction. I will survey the kinds of religiosity that are thematized verbally or narratively in Raffles Malay 21. In the concluding section I try to shed light on the third issue, the story's significance in its contexts of use (as I phrased it earlier), based on the text, other scholars' research into the social life of Malay-language texts, and ethnographic and historical studies of the image of Javanese culture in Malay communities.

Duryodana Employs Drona to Have Bima Killed

Raffles Malay 21 is a clean manuscript. It is undated and unlocalized, but the paper is dated 1812 (Ricklefs and Voorhoeve 1977, p. 135) and its former owner took sail from Java in 1816. Circumstantial evidence suggests that it was inscribed in Batavia, like a number of other manuscripts in the Raffles collection,[7] between 1812 and 1816.

Errors of the scribal type show that Raffles Malay 21 is a copy. The exemplar is unknown. The fact that the manuscript was probably made in Batavia and that later versions of the text survive from the same city says little about the text's cultural provenance. Hooykaas's idea that this collection of stories was meant as "a guideline for the dalang" (1947, p. 129, my translation; a dalang is a *wayang* puppeteer) is too restricted, as later versions clearly belonged to lending libraries in Batavia, whose manuscripts tended to serve as reading matter in private and group reading sessions. Nonetheless the cultural domain indexed by the text was indeed *wayang*. The dramatis personae include the clown-servant Semar typical for Javanese-style *wayang* and, as Semar's son, a certain Belado or Beladu. The latter personage is rare.[8] I have encountered him only in *wayang* narratives from East Java and Madura. This suggests that the stories in Raffles Malay 21 were written with reference to an East Javanese *wayang* tradition.

Semar and Belado are said to be present at an audience (section 14 below[9]), but they play no active role in the episodes summarized here. They are there to evoke a certain image — that of a *wayang* scene in Javanese style. The text contains several other signs of Javaneseness as well. The story-world is labelled as socially Javanese through terms of address used in dialogues (such as *Man*, short for *Paman* "Uncle", and *Kakik* "young man") and the titles of protagonists (such as *Patih* "Chancellor", which is Old and Modern Javanese, and *Dangiang*, the standard title for Drona, which parallels Old Javanese *Ḍang Hyang* and Modern Javanese *Dhangyang*). Bima introduces himself with an epithetic phrase that is clearly Javanese (see section 10) and at a certain point in the corresponding manuscript Or. 3240 (though not in Raffles Malay 21) Bima's distressed mother exclaims "Oh my son, my life" in Javanese (*Aduh anakku nyawa sun*; in section 18). A place name, too, contains Javanese, as does a list of divine weapons (both in 10). This text, then, has a Javanese flavour. Whether it was actually composed in or by people from Java, in what sort of milieu, when, and for whom, is quite another matter. The language is too translocal and transcultural for it to be used as a criterion and Raffles Malay 21 does not go back to a known Javanese text. I will return to this issue below.

Meanwhile it is evident that Raffles Malay 21, the manuscript, was inscribed in a cultural milieu unfamiliar with the finer details of the mythology it reproduces and its onomastics.[10] This milieu cannot have been Javanese-speaking and was not in direct contact with a living *wayang* or textual tradition featuring the story of Bima's quest. It is reasonably certain that by the early nineteenth century the text was present in Batavia — where ethnic Javanese were not officially allowed to live until the 1810s (Abeyasekere 1989, pp. 13, 64)[11] — and it is indisputable that texts closely akin to it remained in use there, in Malay-reading circles, until the 1880s. But, whether the text was composed to satisfy British demand for texts and manuscripts as Pijnappel suggested for several Malay literary works (1870, pp. 145–46), or was already present in Malay-reading (and probably Malay-speaking) communities in Batavia before it was copied for Raffles there, or was collected elsewhere in the Malay lands and brought to Batavia for copying we do not know.

Echoing Van der Tuuk (1866, p. 101), Winstedt called Raffles Malay 21 "a collection of narratives with no plot to link them" (1991, p. 34). Although it is true, as comparison between manuscripts shows, that they were partly reconfigurable, the episodes summarized here — Bima's quest which leads into Drona's thrashing (Raffles Malay 21, pp. 153–66) and the three much shorter episodes that precede (pp. 148–52) — are represented as a series of events narrated in order of occurrence. They do belong together, building a climax that ends in the Pandawas' exodus from Astinapura and their founding a new settlement, Martawangsa. These episodes are neatly integrated into the overarching Mahabharata-derived mythology. In the long term they will find their resolution in the fratricidal war between Pandawas and Korawas (Malay *Perang Pandawa Jaya*).[12] Drona's betrayal of Bima, instigated by Duryodana, leads the Pandawas' advisers to conclude that the animosity between Pandawas and Korawas will not subside. In this text, then, the episode of Bima's quest is constructed as a crucial moment in *wayang* mythology.

At the court of Astinapura where they all live, the five youthful Pandawas and their 108 cousins the Korawas are no longer getting along well together.

1. Their grandfather Biasa arrives from his hermitage to warn the Korawas and Pandawas and Chancellor Sangkuni that, as he has been told by the seven sages and the gods, the cousins will come to blows over Astinapura and the Korawas will lose. He wants to prove this with a pair of scales brought down from heaven by Betara Guru (God Guru, i.e. Shiva). The heavier party will win. Sangkuni agrees, saying "let us see the Godhead's miraculous works" (*kita lihat kekayaan Dewata Mulia Raya*). The five

Pandawas indeed outweigh their 108 cousins. One by one the Pandawas descend but their side remains the heavier. Finally, when Bima places a hand on one scale with the Korawas on the other, the scales hang even. Biasa stresses that they must not fight.

2. Sangkuni reports in detail to King Destarata (the Korawas' father, who is blind). Destarata realizes that Bima will defeat his children and decides to kill him with his magical power (*kesaktian*) called "the oil of disintegration" (*minyak peleburan*). He summons Bima and tells him not to quarrel with the Korawas. If some of them do mischief (*berbuat jahat*), he should forgive their sins (*ampunilah dosanya olehmu*). He asks Bima to approach so that he can hug and kiss him. Bima finds this strange, as Destarata has never done this before. Bima stands near a statue. Thinking it is Bima, Destarata embraces it and it is shattered to pieces. Bima accuses Destarata of wanting to kill him. Were he not like a father to him (Bima's own father is deceased), Destarata would feel his fists. Bima returns to their uncle King Rama Widara (who supports the Pandawas). As the time for Bima to die has clearly not yet come, Destarata (like Biasa earlier) tells Chancellor Sangkuni to ensure that the Pandawas and Korawas do not fight. Sangkuni follows Bima to Rama Widara, who, again, says the same, with the Pandawas present. All return to Astinapura.
3. The Pandawas and Korawas make outings to seek amusement. One day, Sangkuni takes them to a grove with a tall jambu tree full of fruits. The Korawas climb it and shower the Pandawas with seeds. Bima shakes the tree and the Korawas fall to the ground. They run back to Astinapura shouting. Only now the Pandawas can eat the jambus. They return to Rama Widara, who says that they should not play with the Korawas anymore.

The years that follow are described in a few sentences. The Korawas and Pandawas become adults and the kingdom of Astinapura is divided in two, one half for each party. Duryodana is married. The next episode is again recounted in detail.

4. One day Duryodana asks Chancellor Sangkuni how they could kill Bima, the most evil one of them all. Sangkuni notes that because Bima is big now and endowed with sensibility and opinions (*tahukan budi bicara*), while even when he was still a child they were unable to deceive him (*tiada boleh kita perdayakan*), they should ask the Reverend Drona to kill him [by] deceiving him (*kita suruh membunuh pedayakan dia*).
5. They go to Drona's residence, Angsoka Panca, and tell him about the situation with the Pandawas. They should seek to be reconciled (*muafakat*), is Drona's advice. The Pandawas are like a fence and the Korawas like precious plants. If they are in harmony, all enemies will fear them. Duryodana counters that if the fence attacks the plants, they will be destroyed. Bima is that kind of person. But if he is killed, the other four will be subject to the Godhead's decree (*dalam hukum Dewatalah*).[13] Drona claims he could easily kill Bima, but he fears the blemish and misfortune this entails (*takut akan mala petakanya*). Duryodana is prepared to bear the consequences. If Drona wants, Duryodana will give him half of the country.
6. Drona tells them to fetch Bima, and Sangkuni goes to Rama Widara's residence to call him. When Bima has arrived, Drona says that he has given all his knowledge to the Korawas, but he wants to teach Bima as well. He has not done this so far, because his body is polluted (*karena tubuhnya itu lagi cemar*). There is this thing called the *kawitra* water (*air kawitra*). If Bima bathes in it, he will obtain magical powers (*beroleh kesaktian*). It is to be found in the pond (*telaga*[14]) Sagurangkah (later referred to as Sakurangga) at the foot of Mt. Mahameru. Bima should not tell his mother and brothers, lest they try to stop him. Drona does this out of love for Bima, in order that his body becomes pure (*suci*) like his brothers. Bima must quickly fetch the water so that Drona can bathe him in it. Bima leaves. Duryodana and his relatives rejoice when Drona predicts that Bima will die because there is a huge serpent (*naga*) in the pond.
7. Having travelled for some time, Bima arrives on a field where not even a single blade of grass grows. The serpent, angry whenever it

is unable to find food, has sprayed the forest that used to be there with its venom. Bima finds the pond, its water clear, and enters it. The serpent asks what he has come for; Bima wants water from the pond because Drona has said it will rid his body of pollution. According to the serpent, Drona intends to kill him (*sahaja engkau ini hendak dibunuhnya*). "You may be mighty, brave, and fierce, but you're not very clever" (*Sungguhpun engkau gagah berani dan perkasa, tetapi akalmu itu kurang*). Bima insists on getting the water nonetheless. This angers the serpent, who coils around him. Then Bima remembers a spell taught to him by God Bayu, "the formula of fierceness" (*aji perkasa*). He pronounces it and kills the serpent. With some of the water in a golden bowl, he goes to Angsoka Panca.

8. As he arrives there carrying the bowl, Drona, Duryodana, and the other Korawas are amazed. He explains how he killed the serpent and got the water. Drona empties the bowl before Bima's feet. Bima is furious: "No-one but me would have been able to get this water. Why did you spill all of it?" Drona says it was polluted by the serpent's blood. There is another place where the water that will rid his body of pollution can be found, namely in the middle of the sea (*di pusat tasik*). Bima sets off. Drona predicts Bima's imminent death.
9. Because he may disappear in that forbidding place (*tempat yang sukar*), Bima decides first to tell his relatives where he is going. He heads for King Rama Widara's residence, finding Lady Gunti (Rama Widara's sister, Bima's mother) and his brothers Darmawangsa, Rajuna, Sakula and Sadewa there. Bima recounts how he searched for the *kawitra* water to remove the pollution of his body, as Drona told him. Startled, Gunti realizes that Drona means to kill her son. Now, Bima says, he must go to the middle of the sea. Rama Widara warns him not to, as Drona means to kill him. Bima's heart is torn: he is at fault (*salah*) if he fails to do what his relatives say, he is also at fault if he does not follow Drona's instructions. He decides to go, but after everyone has gone to sleep. He says that Rama Widara is correct and promises not to go. All return to their quarters.

10. When night has fallen, Bima leaves through the back door and enters the forest. The next day, he reaches a field called Ing Tegal Amlagung.[15] It is inhabited by the ogre (*raksasa*) Inderabau who used to be a god (*dewa*) but was struck by a curse of blemish and misfortune (*kena sumpah mala petaka*) from Betara Guru. Betara Guru ordered him to go to earth, where he would be released from the curse. Inderabau has been eating all humans and animals passing by; the field is covered with bones and skulls. When he spots Bima, Inderabau roars and bares his fangs. Bima introduces himself as "Bimasena, the second of the Pandawas" (*sang Bimasena penggulu ing Pandawa*[16]). When Bima mentions that his *guru* has told him to get the *kawitra* water in the middle of the sea, Inderabau notes that Drona clearly intends to kill him. Bima and Inderabau fight "like hills clashing" (*seperti bukit bersabung*). As they stand holding each other by the waist, Inderabau claims he cannot be killed even if Bima stabs him with a variety of divine weapons,[17] but Bima says he will use his quintuple nails (*kuku pancanaka*). He does so and Inderabau dies. He changes back into God Indera, who is willing to serve Bima because he has annihilated his blemish and misfortune (*sudahlah ruat mala petakaku*). Bima tells him to return to his heaven; he will continue to search for the *kawitra* water. Indera warns him that the intention is not for him to get this water but to be killed. It is Duryodana who wants this. Bima does not care. Indera leaves.
11. Bima travels across forests, fields, and hills until he reaches the sea-shore. Wonderful corals are visible. He enters the sea and goes deeper and deeper until he has to swim. Battered by the waves, he continues towards the middle. He becomes exhausted, chokes, and dies. The current carries his body to the middle of the sea.

This is where Cod. Or. 3240 begins, and therefore a published Malay text and Dutch translation are available from this point onwards (Poerbatjaraka 1940, pp. 52–54, 36–37). The text is close to that in Raffles Malay 21, but a little more elaborate, especially as from time to time the descriptions that frame the dialogues are longer. I continue to follow Raffles Malay 21 and indicate significant differences in the notes.

12. When Betara Guru sees that Bima has died,[18] he descends, assuming the form of a pandit (*pendita*) named Begawan Tawaruji.[19] He creates an island in the middle of the sea with on it a golden pavilion (*maligai*) studded with jewels. When Bima's corpse has washed ashore, he brings him back to life. Bima goes towards the pavilion, noticing the pandit seated in it. He walks round in circles, but cannot find his way there and rather ends up farther away from it. Then Narawuji[20] approaches him and asks, "Bima, where are you going?" Bima is surprised that he knows his name. He is Begawan Narawuji, the master of this golden island. He claims to know not only Bima but also his ancestors, and also what Bima has come for. Drona, he says, does not really want Bima to find the *kawitra* water. Rather, his intention is to kill him, which is why he has directed him to this forbidding place. Bima realizes that Narawuji must be right, as Betara Indera said the same. This pandit must be a god. No human beings would reside on this island.

This is the ensuing stretch of dialogue in full:

> Bima said, "O Narawuji, where did you come from when you approached me?" His Holiness Narawuji said, "Dear Bima, I have lived here in the middle of the sea for all time." Bima said, "In that case, where is the *kawitra* water here in the middle of the sea?" His Holiness Tarawuji said, "O Bima, go home and take revenge for your death here in the centre of the sea. What would be the use of you taking the *kawitra* water here in the middle of the sea, as he did not order you to [really] take this water, but rather intended you to die.[21] Now you must quickly go home and take revenge on the Reverend Drona for your death, because he has been insincere to you." Bima said, "I fear the blemish and misfortune that thrashing [him] would bring; my blemish and misfortune would become even greater." His Holiness Tarawuji said, "You shall not suffer blemish and misfortune for it, because it is other teachers who [if maltreated] cause one to suffer blemish and misfortune. As to this teacher of yours, he has been exceedingly wicked, he wanted to kill you. Everything he said to you was insincere. Therefore you shall not suffer blemish and misfortune for it. But you must not kill

> him; do not go beyond a thrashing, so that he becomes aware of himself and does not want to do you harm again."[22]

Back to a summary. To enable Bima to return home, Narawuji teaches Bima his magical power (*kesaktian*) named "the formula Water Destruction" (*aji Jala Sengara*), which will allow him to walk on water. Bima takes his leave, goes to the sea-shore, pronounces the formula, and walks away. When he looks back, the golden island and Begawan Narawuji have vanished. Bima thinks (again) that this person cannot have been human but must have been a god. Now, if he returns to his relatives they will prevent him from beating Drona, so he heads straight for Angsoka Panca.

13. Drona gives audience to the Korawas. He thinks that Bima must be dead, as he has been away for a full day and night. Duryodana agrees. Then Bima arrives, looking angry. Drona notices and asks him with sugary words whether he has found the *kawitra* water. If not, he should not exert himself any further as Drona will go and get it himself. Bima claims that Drona did not want him to get the water but wanted him to be killed. If pupils were allowed to kill their teachers, Bima would kill him right now, but [instead] he must feel his fists.[23] Duryodana and his brothers tremble with fear. Bima pulls Drona face-down to the ground and slaps and beats him.

This is where Poerbatjaraka's text and translation end. The manuscript he used continues, however, as does Raffles Malay 21.

> The Korawas run away and hide in the grove. Only Sangkuni stays and begs forgiveness [for Drona]. When Sangkuni grabs Bima's hand, Bima pushes him aside and he rolls over the ground. Sangkuni warns him that he is committing a grave sin and incurring great blemish and misfortune (*besar dosanya dan mala petakanya*), as nothing causes more blemish and misfortune than a teacher thrashed; even saying bad things to a teacher is a grave sin (*berkata jahat lagi kepada guru itu besar dosanya*). Bima responds that that might be so if Bima had been at fault (*salah*), but if he has been upright (*benar*), this teacher deserves

to be thrashed. But, Sangkuni protests, Drona wanted Bima to get the *kawitra* water to rid his body of pollution. Bima tells Sangkuni to stop talking, or he will throw away both their heads. Sangkuni withdraws and quickly goes to Darmawangsa, for Bima will surely listen to him.

14. Darmawangsa and his brothers sit together with Semar and Belado in attendance. Sangkuni arrives in great haste and says that they should help Bima [*sic*], as he is thrashing Drona. They rush to Angsoka Panca.
15. As they arrive, Bima is holding Drona by the arm and beating him.[24] Darmawangsa clasps Bima's neck, the other brothers hold other parts of his body. Bima wants to throw them off but when he recognizes them, he stands motionless. Darmawangsa tells Bima to let the eminent teacher (*sang adiguru*) go, because he is their *guru*, but Bima will not do so before he has heard whether it was someone else who told Drona to kill Bima, or Drona himself. Drona says that he was ordered by Duryodana; he would have been crazy to send Bima away of his own accord. Bima asks why then did he not tell him. Drona was unaware that he was at fault (*salah*), as he did not intend to kill him.[25] Darmawangsa tells Bima (again) to let go because Drona was not at fault. Bima complies, Drona rises and sits down. Rajuna, Sakula, and Sadewa pay him obeisance but Bima, still angry, remains standing. He asks where that (*si*) Duryodana went, he wants to thrash him. Drona tells Sangkuni to go and find Duryodana.
16. Sangkuni looks for Duryodana and his brothers around the grove and eventually finds them crouching in the undergrowth, crying. Drona is calling for them. But Duryodana is afraid of Bima, who beats even his teacher. Sangkuni says there is no need to fear because Bima is not angry anymore, this having been forbidden by Darmawangsa. If Bima wants to kill him, Sangkuni will offer himself to him, rather than this ending in failure.[26] They come along with Sangkuni.
17. When they arrive there they feel fear. Drona accuses Duryodana of putting him up to it and Duryodana promises not to do such things again. Drona tells the Pandawas to listen to their relative

and forgive his sin.[27] Darmawangsa responds that he, too, wants to be reconciled (*muafakat*). Drona counsels Duryodana that whoever undertakes an action with evil ambitions will inevitably have to confront [the consequences of] his misdeeds.[28] Duryodana agrees. Drona says that they should (indeed) be reconciled and Darmawangsa, Rajuna, Sakula, and Sadewa agree. They go home, taking Bima along. Then Drona says emphatically (twice) to Duryodana that he will not take part in any further efforts to kill Bima and the Pandawas. Duryodana and his brothers return to Astinapura.

18. The Pandawas arrive at King Rama Widara's who is sitting with Lady Gunti, longing for Bima. Gunti asks Darmawangsa why Sangkuni called them away. He explains that Bima was thrashing Drona. Gunti wants to know why; Bima says that Drona committed a sin: he wants to kill him, at the orders of Duryodana. Bima recounts everything; Rama Widara and Gunti are distressed. Rama Widara realizes that the Pandawas and Korawas will be enemies. He suggests the Pandawas should distance themselves from the Korawas and build a new settlement, as inevitably they will be trying to deceive one of them (*niscaya mau juga anakku salah seorang diperdayakannya*). Darmawangsa agrees. With the five Pandawas and their followers, Rama Widara goes outside Astinapura. They arrive in a beautiful park called Martawangsa, where King Pandu (the Pandawas' late father) used to go to enjoy himself. Rama Widara suggests they settle here. They build a town complete with fortifications and a moat.

The text describes the beauty and prosperity of the new settlement, then moves to a new episode in the ongoing rivalry between the Pandawas and Korawas.

Two More Things that the Story Is Not

This is not the Old Javanese Nawaruci. That text is immensely more detailed. It is not a synopsis of it or of part of it either. There is a relationship, but it is not straightforward. Reduced to the barest essentials, part of the plot of this Malay episode parallels the beginning of Nawaruci. There are also remarkable similarities in the identity and names of certain story-specific characters that tend to vary from version to version. For instance, the ogre Inderabau (section 10) corresponds to Indrabāhu in the Nawaruci, while later Javanese versions have two ogres with totally different names (though they are manifestations of Gods Indra and Bayu). The Malay name Tawaruji, Narawuji, or Tarawuji corresponds to Nawaruci, while other versions (including the Old Javanese verse rendition of Poerbatjaraka 1940) tend to call this personage Dewa Ruci. Conversely, there are numerous differences of detail and, most importantly, the two versions diverge radically after Bima and Narawuji part ways. Prijohoetomo divided the Nawaruci into eight chapters (1934, pp. 3–4). The first three or four have a counterpart in sections 6–12, but Bima does not take revenge on his *guru* here. Rather, Nawaruci continues with an intricate plot in which Bima goes on to find the purifying water and then to perform austerities, becoming more powerful than the gods.

The Malay episode, on the other hand, has elements that are different or lacking in Nawaruci, but does correspond to other Old and Modern Javanese renditions in literary and *wayang* form. An example is the contents of the pond where Bima goes first to search for the purifying water (section 7). It is inhabited by one serpent not two as in Nawaruci (Prijohoetomo 1934, pp. 28, 89). This corresponds to early nineteenth-century *wayang* scenarios (which are from Central Java). A second example is the passage in which Narawuji claims to know Bima's ancestors (section 12). This has no equivalent in Nawaruci, though such a claim occurs in the Old Javanese poem (Poerbatjaraka 1940, pp. 20–21) and is standard in *wayang* scenarios, including the early nineteenth-century ones. Also, shared elements do not necessarily indicate that one is the source of the other. For instance, Poerbatjaraka (1940, p. 37) derives the name of the pond, Sakurangga, via a hypothetical Si Kurangga from the well (*sumur*) Si Dorangga found in Nawaruci, but it might also come from Sigrangga, the well's name in nineteenth-century *wayang*.

As shown above and unlike the Nawaruci, the present episode is solidly embedded in the overall narrative of the run-up to the Pandawa-Korawa war. Such mythological integration of individual episodes is a characteristic feature of the Modern Javanese *serat kandha* "books of stories" or *serat purwa* "books of antiquity". As signalled by the extended name of this genre — "books of stories of the *wayang* of antiquity" or *serat kandhaning ringgit purwa* — they recount the repertoire of *wayang*. They do this in chronological order. Also in the brevity and matter-of-fact style of its episodes, Raffles Malay 21 resembles a *serat kandha*.[29]

The episode of Bima's quest in Raffles Malay 21, then, may contain reminiscences of the Old Javanese Nawaruci, but other kinds of intertextual relationship are also possible. If Raffles Malay 21 has a literary counterpart in Javanese, it is likely to be a *serat kandha*, but it may equally well be an original composition in Malay in the manner of a *serat kandha*. Currently there exists a vast and dynamic multilingual and partly non-lingual web of tellings of and references to the story of Bima's quest in various media, some relatively durable and others ephemeral, including oral accounts and *wayang*. Although it was not as complex and involved fewer media, the story's multiform mode of existence was not substantially different in the eighteenth and nineteenth centuries. While literary renditions may on the whole have been endowed with greater authority than spoken narrations or dramatic performances — as tends to be the case today — the story was not exclusive to written texts. The Malay literary renditions were composed against the background of such a dynamic body of versions.

If the episode of Bima's quest is not in any straightforward sense "based on" the Nawaruci, exactly the same goes for the so-called adaptations of the Old Javanese poems Bhāratayuddha and Bhomāntaka, which were likewise told in *wayang* fashion. Judging by Braginsky's review, Parnickel has argued for the possibility that the Hikayat Sang Boma, based on the latter Old Javanese poem, was composed in the seventeenth century "in the bilingual milieu of one of the coastal towns of East Java", the same environment as the *serat kandha* (Braginsky 1976, p. 473). Coupled with my own findings on the Malay story of Bima's quest, including what can be concluded from its clown-servants, this points to the possibility that the Malay Hikayat Pandawa Jaya (Hussain 1992) came into being in similar circumstances. It has been thought to be based on a hypothetical Majapahit-era version of the Bhāratayuddha, timed around 1400 CE (Brakel 1980, pp. 155–57). Brakel surmises that such a version indeed existed by referring to a title, Pandawa Jaya, that was used in Majapahit times. However, there is no ground for assuming that this title belonged to an unattested text. It may have been an alternative name of the well-known Old Javanese poem or it may have referred to the story rather than a particular text narrating it.[30] When Van der Tuuk identified the Old Javanese Bhāratayuddha as the source of the Hikayat Pandawa Jaya, it was thought that knowledge of Old Javanese literature had largely been banished from Java with the establishment of Islam, and what remained had become corrupted. It is now known that this idea was mistaken.[31] Other Modern Javanese tellings of the Bhāratayuddha existed. In this case, too, the narrative was told in *wayang* style and some of the literary tellings were of the *serat kandha* variety.[32]

Before turning to an examination of the Malay story of Bima's quest, I must pause on one more thing that it is not: a paragon of virtuousness. A major difference between the Malay version and other tellings lies in its thematic emphases. The Malay text foregrounds matters like Drona's betrayal of his pupil and Bima's brutality towards his *guru*. There is a consensus, a shared assumption, among scholars of traditional Malay literature that this literature taught virtue. Overall this may be a valid generalization and, not unimportantly, exemplariness was an ideal actively promoted in Malay poetics and other metatextual commentary. But, in at least one realm of Malayophone writing and performance it was not straightforwardly the case. This is the realm from which the present episode springs. It represents idolatry, malevolence, and sin, and not all of it in a negative light.

Religiosity in the Story-World

Whereas the mystical and doctrinal domains of religiosity are notably absent from the episode of Bima's quest, it contains elements — beings, objects, practices, conditions, concepts — that were at odds with Islamic doctrine or normative practice, or in accordance with it. A number of such elements are conspicuously thematized by means of repeated and in some cases truly iterative reference, often using the same words and syntactic constructions, or by their place of occurrence in the structure of the narrative. This suggests that they were meant to be of interest to readers and listeners. These highlighted religious matters are deities (*dewa*, *betara*, *Dewata*), the possession and use of *aji* "magical formulas" and more generally *kesaktian* "magical powers", the use of a particular kind of water for removing pollutions and rendering one's body pure (*suci*), the moral concepts of *mempe(r)dayakan* "to deceive" and *salah* "to be at fault" versus *benar* "to be upright", the notion of *dosa* "sin", and, especially prominently, the fear of *mala petaka* "blemish and misfortune".

Several deities appear as dramatis personae and in sections 1 and 7 reference is made to "the gods" (*dewa2*) generally. They have superhuman abilities, such as God Guru's ability to bring down scales from heaven to weigh people's relative power (section 1), his ability to create an island with a structure on it (section 12), and his ability to revive Bima after he has drowned (ibid.). This is unsurprising, as a pantheon with certain extraordinary capabilities is part and parcel of the mythology represented in these texts. More interesting are two phrases which refer to Allah, but by the non-Arabic word *dewata* "godhead". In section 1 the idiom *kekayaan Allah* "God's miraculous works" is rendered as *kekayaan Dewata Mulia Raya* — literally, "the riches of the Great Exalted Godhead" — and *hukum Dewata* in section 5 is synonymous with *hukum Allah* "God's decree" (as to one's life or death). This is how *Dewata Mulia Raya* was used in Malay in the well-known Terengganu inscription of the early fourteenth century. It parallels the common use of designations like *Hyang Manon* "The Seeing Godhead" and *Hyang Widi* "The Supreme Godhead" instead of *Allah* in pre-nineteenth century Islamic texts in Javanese. Most remarkable, finally, in the divine realm as represented in the text is the figure of Narawuji. Initially he is said to be a pandit. As he is unique to this episode this could have easily been carried through, but rather it is stressed that he is divine not human (section 12, twice). A manifestation of Betara Guru, he is definitely not to be identified with Allah.

Two named magical formulas (*aji*) and a magical oil with similar function feature in these episodes (sections 2, 7, 12). Two of them are explicitly identified as *kesaktian* "magical powers". Bima is called "mighty and magically powerful" (*gagah dan sakti*) after showing his ability to counterweigh all 108 Korawas with one hand (section 1). *Kesaktian* is referred to in one other place, namely as something that Bima will acquire by bathing in the *kawitra* water (6). The story could have done without these references; human strength and force, with God's blessing, could have done the same narrative work. The fact that such magic is considered out of bounds for Muslims was insufficient reason to avoid them.

One thing that the *kawitra* water, the object of Bima's quest, will do is endow Bima with *kesaktian*. This places it in the same religious domain as the formulas and oil, but there is obviously more to it than that. It is never made clear what the *kawitra* water is exactly, but its salutary effects are mentioned over and over, and it is to be found "in the middle of the sea" (*di pusat tasik*) (section 6). The effects and location of this mysterious substance will have rung familiar to those readers and listeners who knew the Hikayat Sri Rama, the classic Malay rendition of the Ramayana narrative — a Muslim rendition, as Sweeney has stressed (1987, p. 26). Here the little monkey Hanuman, who is polluted with excrement, is told by Sri Rama (who in fact has sired Hanuman, albeit indirectly): "You must go to the middle of the sea to bathe and purify your entire body" (*pergilah engkau kepada pusat tasik mandi bersuci segala tubuhmu*). Hanuman leaves and returns in an instant, dripping with water and carrying various jewels and perfumes. He offers them to Sri Rama. Sri Rama acknowledges him as his son and later dispatches him to the island of Langkapuri to find Sri Rama's abducted wife Sita Dewi (Achadiati Ikram 1980, pp. 184–86). In the episode of Bima's quest the *kawitra* water is clearly depicted in the same light.[33] Besides endowing Bima with magical powers it will also clean off the pollution (*cemar, cemar-cemar*) of his body (sections 6, 7, 8, 9, 13) and make him pure (*suci*) (6, 9), so that Drona can teach him. The water can itself be polluted with blood (8). This is in line with Islam. Polluted and forbidden (Arabic *ḥarām*) could be considered the same category.[34] Blood defiles (Arabic *najis*). Water, on the other hand, cleanses.

As noted, scholars have paid little attention to the Malay episode on its own account. Braginsky is an exception when he characterizes it: "Another Javanese poem, Dewa Ruci, telling about Bima's mystical self-cognition, became, in the Malay paraphrase, a tale of perfidy and vengeance for perfidy [...]" (2004, p. 147). In the text itself, what Braginsky calls perfidy is referred to as *-pe(r)dayakan* "to deceive, trick" (sections 4 and 18). A kind of "moral of the story" is formulated by Drona in the reconciliatory meeting afterwards (17), in which he refers to Duryodana's scheme — disregarding, as the context shows, his own involvement — as "undertaking an action with evil ambitions". Besides these cover terms for what Duryodana and Drona do to Bima, mentioned before and after, the phenomenon is thematized more concretely in the regular observation, made by nearly everyone whom Bima meets, that his teacher does not really want Bima to find the *kawitra* water but intends to kill him. Even after Bima has recognized this as true (12), it is repeated.

More clearly relative and contextual than these religious personages, objects, and functions and immoral intentions is the contrast between being "at fault" (*salah*) and "upright, right" (*benar*) that is thematized several times. At one point Bima even notes that he is caught in a dilemma: he can do what his relatives want or what his *guru* has ordered; he will be at fault either way (section 9). But across the episode in its entirety, Bima is right and Drona at fault (13). A kindred but absolute concept is "sin" (*dosa*). Doing mischief (2), beating one's teacher[35] or even just saying bad things to them (13), putting someone up to mischief (17), and wanting to kill someone (18) are said to be sins. These types of sin are social; they can be grouped together as malice. Social pressure in general has an important moral function in this story. Even though Betara Guru in disguise has assured Bima that it is acceptable to beat Drona on account of his malicious intentions, and Bima is so infuriated that he actually follows this advice to commit malice to his teacher, Bima does still expect that his relatives will try to prevent him from going through with it.

A possible consequence of sinning is "blemish and misfortune" (*mala petaka*). The fear of bringing such calamity upon oneself is a motif that occurs throughout. Drona expresses this fear while Duryodana declares his willingness to bear it (5), Bima utters the same fear later (12), and Duryodana tries to get Bima to stop beating Drona with the warning that it will cause blemish and misfortune (13). In the story-world created here, not only the misfortune but also the blemish are to be taken literally, as actual disfigurement. Indera had become the horrible ogre Inderabau because he was struck by Betara Guru's curse (10). Blemish and misfortune should be avoided but if one does incur them, a solution is to have them annihilated and be delivered from them (both referred to as *ruat*, a Javanese loanword). This happened to Inderabau when he was killed by Bima. More mundane ways would be not to want to murder one's pupils and thrash one's teachers, but as this story testifies, the world would be quite a bit more boring for it.

While such malice disagrees with Islam, the notion of blemish and misfortune that are incurred by transgressing moral codes but can be annihilated has Hindu-Buddhist antecedents and "Javanese" connotations.[36] At the same time it is a Malay concern. This is clear, for instance, from its thematic prominence in the narrative poem that has been styled "the jewel of Malay Muslim culture", the Syair Bidasari (Millie 2004). Also, among the countless versions of the narrative of Bima's quest, blemish and misfortune feature most prominently in this particular rendition, the one in Malay.

These are signals that the kinds of religiosity thematized in the episode of Bima's quest — mostly from the realms of magic and morality — were of interest in Malay environments. Ideally, in order to investigate the cultural resonances of this text and others like it, one should have access to the themes that coloured the discursive ambience of the people who read and heard them. We have only educated guesses as to the place and time of writing of the text in Raffles Malay 21. It circulated among Malays in nineteenth-century Batavia, but next to nothing cultural is known about them, apart from the fact that they tended to be fervent Muslims.[37] It may also have been available in Malay-speaking circles elsewhere. We must therefore turn to more recent times and other parts of the Malay world for information.

Ethnographic studies of traditional communities in the Malay peninsula suggest that wickedness was a concern and, at least in private, a theme of discourse. In his ethnography of rural Negeri Sembilan, researched between 1978 and 1988, Peletz refers to "villagers' suspicions that fellow Malays are frequently motivated by greed, envy, and malice" (1996, p. 193). Such motivations were deemed unethical and these suspicions should not be aired in public (1996, p. 194). Under the heading of *ilmu*, the Arabic loanword which in the Malay context "is most commonly used to denote esoteric religious knowledge concerning the manipulation of spirits and the unseen forces of the natural world" (1996, p. 158), Peletz also noted that "[v]illagers assume — and fear — that many people in their social universe rely on *ilmu* to achieve what they are prevented by the formal rules of social interaction from accomplishing (or even setting out to accomplish)" (1996, p. 194). Owing in part to this assumption, practices involving *ilmu* persisted under the radar despite vehement orthodox Islamic opposition (1996, p. 194). According to this line of reasoning, *ilmu* is likely to be of long cultural standing, and indeed Peletz points out that this term approaches what in the past could also be called *sakti* and *kesaktian*, words still used by nineteenth-century observers (1996, pp. 57, 360 note 4). *Ilmu* today relates typically to magical formulas (Haron Daud 2001, p. 19), like *kesaktian* did in Raffles Malay 21. The Malay Concordance Project reveals that *ilmu* and *kesaktian* began to collocate in Malay texts around 1700.[38] Under flexible nomenclature, then, ill will and magic, taboo though they may be, are established cultural themes.

Malay *Javanaiserie*

They are thus among Malays, but Peletz notes that people of Javanese origin in particular are "believed to have dangerous forms of *ilmu*" (1996, p. 165). The prominence of this perception is confirmed by Miyazaki in his study of the image of Malays of Javanese ancestry in rural Johor, based on fieldwork in 1991. Although its variety and frequency have declined, "Malay magic is still very much a part of the daily life of the Malays" (2000, p. 90) and "many Malays [...] tend to believe that [Javanese-Malays] possess strong 'magical' powers and are skilled in sorcery" (2000, p. 83). This is a stereotype, of course, but it is influential: "The Javanese-Malays also often described themselves as magically powerful" (Miyazaki 2000, p. 84; see also p. 91). That this image extends to the language variety associated with the ethnic category follows from Sweeney's reference to a "widespread belief in the efficacy of written charms (*azimat, tangkal*) which are found (among

Malays) in Arabic, Thai, Javanese, and Malay" (1987, p. 110).[39] Most of those who employ these producers and tools of magic, whose efficacy is credited, in part at least, to their Javaneseness, are Malays. The history of rivalry and animosity between Java-based kingdoms and Malay kingdoms in Sumatra and later the Malay Peninsula that goes back to the first millennium CE (Leonard Andaya 2008) continues to resound, but it does not preclude Malays from making use of occult practices held to belong to and belong with Javanese.

Threatening otherness is not the only image of Javanese culture that has been of consequence among Malays. The idea that Javanese civilization was considered prestigious and paradigmatic, mentioned in the beginning of this chapter in connection with Overbeck and Robson's theories of cultural influence, finds support among most literary scholars and has been confirmed through historical research. Barbara Andaya, for instance, observes that the Malay sultanates of Palembang and Jambi in the seventeenth century engaged in "amusements such as Javanese wayang, dancing, and gamelan" and emulations of courtly "Javaneseness" in the form of tourneys, that the Javanese language was admired, and that at certain points Malays appearing at court were even required to don Javanese attire (1993, pp. 66–67). Vickers notes that, besides Panji narratives, "Javanese styles of shadow puppets, dance, and weaponry in the form of the *kris* with its various types of hilt [...] became firmly embedded in Malay culture" throughout insular and peninsular Southeast Asia (1987, p. 56).

These emblematically Javanese modes of discourse, genres of performance, and types of objects are public culture, civilized and positive. But, the Malay conception of Javaneseness was complex and knew darker shades as well. Its association with magic and sorcery is not recent. To mention a famous example, the iconic Hikayat Hang Tuah also connects Java with threatening magical objects and practices and individuals possessing them (Sulastin 1983, pp. 241–47).[40] What these two apparently conflicting images have in common is fascination. Rather than distinguishing objects of admiration and appropriation on the one hand and objects of discomfort and rejection on the other, it seems wise to recognize that a spectrum of select "Javanese" characteristics was part of the Malay cultural repertoire, while at the same time being alien, and remaining so. In other words, what is relevant was Javaneseness's difference, an alterity that was also one's own. The idea of "Javanese" — *Jawa*, the Malay adjective that refers to geography, ethnicity, culture, and language — functioned as a zone, both other *and* the same, onto which certain aspects of *Malay* culture could be projected, and in which certain issues that were problematic to *Malays* could be thematized.[41]

In either case this is a matter of representation, and therefore a term like *javanaiserie* would seem to be apt as a cover term for these practices.[42] In this connection the question of Javanese influence is beside the point. What counts is that these practices, public and concealed and in between, create a diegesis designed and felt to be "Javanese" and sometimes explicitly marked *Jawa*. Such a diegesis and style may be analyzed as *javanesque*. Alleged Javanese authorship of Malay texts, for instance, is an element of javanaiserie. Such a claim helps legitimize the work as extra-Malay at the same time that it *is* Malay. But javanaiserie could also involve actual translation or adaptation from Javanese, rather than first-hand Malay composition in javanesque style. Javanaiserie is a mode of diegesis, of worldmaking. Although the latter term may suggest artistic fantasy, these worlds can be narrative and indeed lived ones. Part of Malay magic, for instance, is javanesque and its practice is javanaiserie. As Bima's quest and revenge demonstrate, one thing that javanaiserie can do is to create a zone in Malay diegeses where, under javanesque cover, certain evils are justifiable and indeed alluring.

Javanaiserie has an artefactual component. This goes for texts and material culture, but the same applies to performances and magic. For this reason javanaiserie was not only able to circulate, but its cultural significance varied.[43] Javanesque narratives and performances, for instance, have been produced in Bali (Vickers 2005, pp. 266–67), in mainland Southeast Asia in Thai (Robson 1996)[44] and Khmer, in twentieth-century Europe and the United States of America (Cohen 2010; Spiller 2015) and in metropolitan Indonesia. Also for the self-conscious forms of Javaneseness promoted and practised in Java itself during high colonialism and the New Order period (Pemberton 1994) the label is not amiss. It should not come as a surprise that within the lingual tradition of Malay, heterogeneous and dynamic as it was, the cultural meanings of javanaiserie varied geographically and historically. Over the seventeenth to nineteenth centuries it certainly flourished in different ways in Batavia (where it was taken to new heights in the second half of the nineteenth century), Palembang and Jambi, and Kedah and Kelantan, but javanesque works and performance genres have been identified throughout the Malay World.

Over the centuries "Javanese stories" and "Javanese *hikayat*" have received a bad press in Malay cultural criticism. At least from Bukhari's damning judgement of the readers of *hikayat*, particularly a "Javanese" one, as infidels, stupid and witless, in 1603, javanesque narratives were typically branded "misguided" (*sesat*), "falsehood" (*dusta*), and "harmful" (*kecewa*) (as in Hussain 1992, p. 280; Hijjas 2010, p. 160; Gallop 2015; and other texts, discussed in Koster 1997, pp. 86–93; Braginsky 2002, pp. 46–48, and Chambert-Loir 2013, pp. 28–32). Nonetheless — only to mention major centres of Malay javanaiserie — up to the early twentieth century javanesque texts were composed and copied in Batavia (Chambert-Loir and Dewaki 2013) and Palembang (Overbeck 1932, p. 209; 1934, p. 104; 1935, p. 150) and *wayang Jawa* was staged in Kedah and Kelantan (Sweeney 1972, p. 24). There were ways of neutralizing the sin of immersing oneself in these narratives, ways not automatically to disqualify oneself for heaven. These methods are premised on the fact that diegeses are *ensphered* into each other.[45] A common strategy was to advertise these narratives, often in versified epilogues, as allegory (*ibarat*). The sphere of the dramatis personae's story-world could be interpreted as invoking a higher-order diegetic sphere that was more elementary (as not everything in the first-order narrative diegesis was represented here) and abstract. In the episode of Bima's quest and its brutal aftermath, this is the function of the "moral of the story" that Drona delivers to Duryodana (section 17). In the story-world, Drona comments upon and closes the diegetic sphere that, with hindsight, was constituted by Bima's dealings with Drona, Duryodana, and Sangkuni. At the same time Drona's counsel signals to overhearing readers and listeners, who have just enjoyed a sizable dose of un-Islamic religiosity and violence, that it can also be taken metaphorically in a higher and essentially moral diegetic sphere.

The second method, too, was applied as the narrative diegesis was dissolved and readers returned to the everyday sphere, their lifeworld, the one that would lead on to the hereafter. It was a ritual moment in Malay reading practice. Epilogues to sinful narratives tell the reader to repent (*bertobat*) or ask to be forgiven, as in this example from a Batavia-Malay javanesque *hikayat* finished in 1892: "And you are advised, after reading and hearing this, to ask much forgiveness and pray and beg for clemency from the Lord, the Honourable, the Forgiving, the Merciful."[46]

NOTES

I thank Adrian Vickers, Andrea Acri, Henri Chambert-Loir, Jan van der Putten, Leonard Andaya, Suryadi, Ulrich Kratz, and Willem van der Molen for their critical comments on earlier versions of this chapter and Suryadi, Henri, and Willem for their help in interpreting parts of the text in Raffles Malay 21. The Royal Asiatic Society of Great Britain and Ireland and the library of the School of Oriental and African Studies, both in London, have enabled me to study this manuscript.

1. It should be clear that I do not assume a stable and simple correlation between Malay language, ethnicity, culture, and territory. The same goes for Java(nese). I do examine some contexts where these categories are habitually superposed.
2. I use the term diegesis for a configuration of entities, processes, conditions, and moods constructed processually in the interplay between discourse, other symbolic productions, and situations (Arps 1996; 2006). A less pretentious synonym is worldmaking (Arps 2016), although this term is really too specific, suggesting that what is constructed is by default as comprehensive as a "world". In fact, diegesis may be highly selective and strongly focused on a particular stretch or aspect of reality. That reality may, moreover, be fictional.
3. For instance, the person whom Bima meets on an island in the ocean is a manifestation of Betara Guru, the king of gods. Bima has mysterious difficulties in physically reaching this person, whom he sees seated in a wonderful golden pavilion adorned with jewels in the middle of the island.
4. See Tanaya (1979) for texts of several of the Modern Javanese literary versions including the canonical one, and Arps (2000) for a Dutch translation of the latter. On the dating of that version — which, incidentally, represents an Islamization of the Old Javanese poem, casting Bima as a Sufi — see Arps (2000), p. 85. The first known dramatic rendition is examined in my article "The Benefits of Purity in Amarta and Surakarta: The Shadowplay of

Bima Suci, 1817–1818" (To appear in a volume on reflections of religious change in Javanese texts, edited by Toru Aoyama et al. (Tokyo: Institute of Languages and Cultures of Asia and Africa, Tokyo University of Foreign Studies)). More recent *wayang* representations of Bima's encounter with the deity are discussed in Arps (2016), pp. 559–72.

5. I have not had the opportunity to study this manuscript, only the other three.
6. This version is discussed in my monograph in progress on the ideology of the quest in modern Java and beyond.
7. The same paper dated 1812 as used for Raffles Malay 21 is found in other Malay manuscripts from the Raffles collection. One of them, Raffles Malay 15, "was written in Kampung Kĕrukut in A.D. 1815 (in Western numerals) or A.H. 1219 (in Western numerals) [A.H. 1219 was, however, A.D. 1804]" (Ricklefs and Voorhoeve 1977, p. 134). (The dating peculiarity according to the Islamic calendar does not affect my argument.) Kerukut or Krokot was (and is) a downtown neighbourhood in Batavia, founded as a Balinese settlement in 1687 (Oud Batavia 1922, p. 478) and inhabited, among others, by "educated Chinese Moslems" in the late eighteenth century (Salmon 1981, p. 16). Another such manuscript, Raffles Malay 78, "has many Batavia Malay words" (Ricklefs and Voorhoeve 1977, p. 143). Moreover Bijleveld, probably referring to Raffles Malay 21, mentions that a character's voice "is compared with that of a company lieutenant in Batavia" (Bijleveld [s.a.], p. 5). I have not been able to check this.
8. Or rather, this name is. The personage is commonly known as Bagong in Javanese *wayang* today.
9. I have divided Raffles Malay 21's episode of Bima's quest and the preceding episodes into numbered narrative sections for ease of reference. The criteria for division were heuristic and other segmentation is certainly possible. The numbering is ad hoc.
10. See the remark above about Bima's self-description. The name of the deity Bima encounters in the ocean, an important figure in all other renditions, is also corrupt. See the footnote to "Tawaruji" in section 12.
11. Although there were *kampung Jawa* in Batavia and ethnic Javanese did live there (Raben 2000, p. 97 *et passim*).
12. This is explicit in Or. 3240, where Drona's death is predicted. See the footnote to section 12.
13. I.e. as to whether they should live or die.
14. The lexical meaning of *telaga* in this text is "pond, lake" as in Javanese, not "well" as in Malay.
15. This reading of A NG-T-K-L A M-L-A K-W-NG is quite uncertain. It is a field (Javanese *tegal*, Malay *padang*). *Ing* is a Javanese locative particle. Van der Tuuk calls the place Melanggang (1879, p. 513), but the manuscript he used contains a rather different text. It is a forest there.

16. This is a version of a common epithet of Bima in Javanese.
17. The phrase in question reads *senjata dewa2 T-R cakra mungsala duduk angkusa*. The last four are weapons (*senjata*) and kindred metal instruments: *cakra* "discus", *musala* "mace", *du(k)duk* "thrusting spear", and *angkusa* "elephant goad". All are known in Old Javanese; most of the words derive from Sanskrit but *duduk* is Austronesian. What T-R stands for I do not know.
18. In Or. 3240, where it comes at the very beginning of the manuscript, this passage is more elaborate. Seeing that Bima has died, Betara Guru is angry with Drona who has listened to Duryodana. He ordains that Drona will die in the war with the five Pandawas (*perang Pandawa Lima*). Then he descends to earth.
19. Called Narawuji and Tarawuji later on in the text. These names go back to the Old Javanese name Nawaruci. See Van der Tuuk (1879), p. 21 on the names Tarujaya — no doubt born from a different reading of T-A R W J-Y — and Tawaruji, and (1881), p. 54 on Tawaruci. In his text and translation, Poerbatjaraka has silently emended the name that is actually used in Or. 3240, Tawaruji, to Nawaruci. The variation in names, exhibiting metathesis and variable readings of the Perso-Arabic script, suggest scriptural transmission of the text in an environment where the story was not familiar from other sources.
20. N-A R W J-Y, as his name usually is from here onwards, alongside a few cases of T-A R W J-Y.
21. It is implied that Drona is not going to teach Bima anything anyhow.
22. The manuscript reads as follows: Maka kata Bima, "Hai Narawuji, dari mana datangmu maka engkau mendapatkan aku ini?" Maka kata Begawan Narawuji, "Hai Kakik Bima, dari selamanya pun aku ada duduk pada pusat laut ini." Maka kata sang Bima, "Jika demikian, di mana tempatnya air kawitra itu di pusat laut ini?" Maka kata Bakawan Tarawuji, "Hai Bima, pulanglah engkau, balaskan kematianmu di tengah laut ini. Yang air kawitra itu di pusat laut ini apatah gunanya engkau ambil, karana engkau ini tiada disuruhnya mengambil air ini, sebenar2nya sahaja hendak disuruhnya mati. Sekarang sigeralah engkau pulang, balaskanlah kematianmu kepada Dangiang Drona itu, kerana ia tiada benar hatinya kepadamu." Maka kata sang Bima, "Aku takut akan mala petakanya memalu itu, bertambah2 mala petakaku." Maka kata Begawan Tarawuji, "Tiada engkau kena mala petakanya, karana lain gurunya yang memberi kena mala petaka itu. Akan gurumu ini terlalu jahat, hendak membunuh engkau. Barang katanya kepadamu itu tiada sungguh. Sebab itulah maka tiada kena mala petakanya. Tetapi jangan ia kaubunuh, sehingga engkau palu juga, supaya tahu ia akan dirinya, tiadalah mau ia berbuat jahat kepadamu lagi" (Raffles Malay 21, pp. 160–61; cf. Poerbatjaraka 1940, pp. 52–53).

23. "Jikalau murid harus membunuh guru sekaranglah engkau kubunuh, tetapi engkau rasai juga bekas tanganku ini" (Raffles Malay 21, p. 162). Poerbatjaraka's published text contains unnecessary emendations (1940, p. 54) and his translation errors (1940, p. 37).
24. In the version of Or. 3240 Bima's rage receives greater emphasis: Drona begs forgiveness but Bima thrashes him still more forcefully.
25. I am not certain of the interpretation. Rendered without added punctuation, Drona's response to Bima reads "Apatah lagi yang salah ayahanda itu mengapatah bicara anakku tiadalah ayahanda sadari lagi karana bukannya ayahanda hendak membunuh anakku."
26. Unusually, Sangkuni's offer to bear the brunt has no equivalent in Or. 3240.
27. The text is confused here. This is what it seems to come down to.
28. The text reads "barangsiapa memulai pekerjaan berjaga2 yang jahat itu niscaya menempuh juga kepada kejahatannya." *Berjaga2* does not make sense here. Or. 3240 reads *bercita2*, which does. Instead of the last clause, Or. 3240 reads "niscaya menempuh juga kepadanya kejahatan", i.e. "evil will inevitably confront him", which makes sense as well.
29. The present episodes are not in the published text (*Serat Kandhaning Ringgit Purwa* 1985–88). There is a huge narrative gap between vols. 4 and 5; if it was once part of this version of the *serat kandha*, the story of Bima's quest would have fallen here. Nor do these episodes have a counterpart in Leiden Cod. Or. 6381 and 6383 (the latter dated 1795 and from Gresik in East Java), although these *serat kandha* cover the same portion of the mythology as Raffles Malay 21 and likewise feature the clown-servants Semar and Bladho.
30. The reference to Pandawa Jaya from the Old Sundanese Bujangga Manik is probably about a particular text in Javanese that was studied by Bujangga Manik (late fifteenth to early sixteenth century) (Noorduyn 1982, p. 431), and that in the Sutasoma (late fourteenth century) to an episode in the narrative.
31. See Kuntara (1990) about manuscripts of Arjunawiwāha, another Old Javanese poem, provided with Modern Javanese glosses and paraphrases. See also Teeuw and Robson (2005), p. 64 about a Modern Javanese summary, from Madura, of Bhomāntaka.
32. See *Serat Gembring Baring* (1981), containing a *serat kandha*-type of work that incorporates fragments from the Old Javanese Bhāratayuddha (as well as, in fact, fragments of the Old Javanese poem of Bima's quest for purity). The antecedents of this work are unknown but the contents and style suggest both East Javanese and Yogyakarta-court connections. This work, too, features Bladho.
33. Later in the Hikayat Sri Rama there is mention of an abyss in the sea that leads to the nether parts of the earth, where it meets the water of life (*air ma'ulhayat*, Arabic *mā' al-ḥayāt*). Drinking and bathing in the water of life will render Sri Rama's followers mighty, brave, invincible, and immortal

(Achadiati Ikram 1980, pp. 210–11). In an Islamic context this water of life is known particularly from commentary on a passage in the Koran and from the narrative of Alexander the Great's quest for it (Drewes and Brakel 1986, pp. 156–57). Probably Hanuman in the earlier episode should be understood as having cleansed himself in the water of life and it is quite likely that those familiar with the notion also took *air kawitra* in the episode of Bima's quest as referring to it.

34. As suggested by a passage in the Laws of Malacca, a code in force in parts of the Malay peninsula, Sumatra, and Borneo up to the nineteenth century or even later. See Liaw (1976), p. 136.
35. Slapping (let alone thrashing) someone was a grave offense in both customary and Islamic law according to the Laws of Malacca. For instance, a free person who slapped an innocent slave should be fined. If the latter killed the former in retaliation, he was deemed not to have committed a crime according to customary law — though according to Islamic law he was a murderer and should be put to death (Liaw 1976, pp. 74–77).
36. In the Nawaruci, for example, Indrabāhu's disfigurement (Old Javanese and Sanskrit *mala* "impurity, defect") is caused by a sin (*doṣa*) that had to be annihilated (*lukat*, an Old Javanese synonym of *ruat*) (Prijohoetomo 1934, p. 32). It is likely that in Malay the ancient lexical meaning of *mala* faded over time as *mala pe(s)taka* (Old Javanese and Sanskrit *pātaka* "misfortune, punishment for sins") became a fixed collocation meaning "misfortune", though it retained the sense that the misfortune was incurred by a transgression. Hence my choice of "blemish" to render Malay *mala*.
37. As was noted, for instance, by the Central Javanese nobleman Sastradarma who, after visiting Batavia in 1865, wrote in his travelogue that he "used to believe that 'Javanese' and 'Muslim' were identical until he arrived in Batavia. There he learned that the Javanese, at least in the eyes of the original inhabitants of Batavia — themselves devout Muslims — are hardly more than heathens" (Van der Molen 2006, p. 113).
38. See <http://mcp.anu.edu.au/> (accessed 28 March 2014).
39. Magic is also associated with Thais and "forest-dwelling aborigines" (Peletz 1996, p. 162). This is relevant but I cannot go into it. The use of the Malay languages of Islam, Arabic and Malay itself, is self-explanatory.
40. It has been suggested that in Southeast Asia Java had a "reputation for possessing esoteric knowledge" as early as the ninth century CE (Wolters 1999, p. 35), but Wolters's suggestion hinges on the very specific interpretation of the word *siddhayātrā* in a Sanskrit inscription from Champa as "pilgrimage to a particularly sacred territory charged with magical power" (Coedès 1968, p. 316). In spite of much debate, the correctness of this interpretation has not been established. For Old Javanese, Zoetmulder simply glosses *siddhayātra* as "having a successful (auspicious) journey" (Zoetmulder and Robson 1982).

41. See Vickers (2004) for a discussion of the historical dynamics of Malayness in relation to Javaneseness.
42. This coinage is modelled after *chinoiserie* and *japonaiserie*, likewise historical styles of selective representation of other cultures that are also one's own. I use the term as a mass noun to denote the employment of "Javanese" characteristics. In French, of course, *chinoiseries* and *japonaiseries* are artefacts.
43. I can only identify the phenomenon and refer to a few individual studies. Comparative study is in order.
44. And in 1703 King Phetracha of Ayutthaya (r. 1688–1703) sought to buy female dancers and musical instruments from the ruler of Mataram in Central Java (Bhawan Ruangsilp 2007, pp. 171–72). He may not have succeeded in buying the dancers (2007, p. 251).
45. The notion of enspherement is inspired by Goffman's "frames" (1986), but conceived multi-dimensionally and allowing for fuzzy boundaries, so including "sphere" in the sense of "environment" or "ambience".
46. "Dan dipesankan habis membaca dan menengar harap biar banyak-banyak istifar dan salawat dan minta ampun pada Tuhan *Azizu l-Gafur l-Rahim*" (Nikmah Sunardjo 1989, p. 137).

REFERENCES

Manuscripts

Leiden University Library: Cod. Or. 3240. Described as Wayang Stories in Wieringa (2007), pp. 97–100.

Leiden University Library: Cod. Or. 3377. Described as Hikayat Tumpang (Carang) Kembang in Wieringa (2007), pp. 340–44.

Leiden University Library: Cod. Or. 6381. Described as Sĕrat Kaṇḍa niŋ Riŋgit Purwa in Pigeaud (1968), p. 364.

Leiden University Library: Cod. Or. 6383. Described as Sĕrat Kaṇḍa niŋ Riŋgit Purwa in Pigeaud (1968), p. 364.

Royal Asiatic Society, London: Raffles Malay 21. Described as Hikayat Pandawa Panca Kalima in Ricklefs and Voorhoeve (1977), p. 135.

Publications

Abeyasekere, Susan. *Jakarta: A History*. Singapore: Oxford University Press, 1989. Revised edition.

Achadiati Ikram, ed. *Hikayat Sri Rama: Suntingan naskah disertai telaah amanat dan struktur*. Jakarta: Penerbit Universitas Indonesia, 1980.

Andaya, Barbara Watson. *To Live as Brothers: Southeast Sumatra in the Seventeenth and Eighteenth Centuries.* Honolulu: University of Hawaii Press, 1993.

Andaya, Leonard Y. *Leaves of the Same Tree: Trade and Ethnicity in the Straits of Melaka.* Honolulu: University of Hawai'i Press, 2008.

Arps, Bernard. "The Song Guarding at Night: Grounds for Cogency in a Javanese Incantation". In *Towards an Anthropology of Prayer: Javanese Ethnolinguistic Studies*, edited by Stephen C. Headley. Aix-en-Provence: Publications de l'Université de Provence, 1996, pp. 47–113.

———. intr. and trans. "Déwa Rutji. Avontuur en wijsheid in een Javaans verhaal". In *Oosterse omzwervingen. Klassieke teksten over Indonesië uit Oost en West*, edited by Harry Poeze. Leiden: KITLV Uitgeverij, 2000, pp. 81–119, 215–16.

———. "Dance-Floor Politics in Easternmost Java". *IIAS Newsletter* 40 (2006): 11.

———. *Tall Tree, Nest of the Wind: The Javanese Shadow-Play* Dewa Ruci *Performed by Ki Anom Soeroto. A Study in Performance Philology*. Singapore: NUS Press, 2016.

Bhawan Ruangsilp. *Dutch East India Company Merchants at the Court of Ayutthaya: Dutch Perceptions of the Thai Kingdom c. 1604–1765*. Leiden and Boston: Brill, 2007. TANAP Monographs on the History of the Asian-European Interaction 8.

Bijleveld, B.J. "Malay Wayang Stories: The Primary Works". Unpublished paper, [s.a.].

Braginsky, Vladimir. [Review of B.B. Parnickel, Skazanie o Sang Bome (Hikayat Sang Boma), 1973.] *Bijdragen tot de Taal-, Land- en Volkenkunde* 132 (1976): 472–78.

———. "Malay Scribes on their Craft and Audience (with Special Reference to the Description of the Reading Assembly by Safirin bin Usman Fadli)". *Indonesia and the Malay World* 30, no. 86 (2002): 37–61.

———. *The Heritage of Traditional Malay Literature: A Historical Survey of Genres, Writings and Literary Views*. Leiden: KITLV Press, 2004. VKI 214.

Brakel, L.F. "Two Indian Epics in Malay". *Archipel* 20 (1980): 143–60.

Chambert-Loir, Henri. "Sebuah keluarga pengarang abad ke-19". In *Katalog naskah Pecenongan koleksi Perpustakaan Nasional: Sastra Betawi akhir abad ke-19*, edited by Henri Chambert-Loir and Dewaki Kramadibrata. Jakarta: Perpustakaan Nasional Republik Indonesia, 2013. Seri Katalog Naskah Nusantara 1, pp. 3–35.

Chambert-Loir, Henri and Dewaki Kramadibrata, eds. *Katalog naskah Pecenongan koleksi Perpustakaan Nasional. Sastra Betawi akhir abad ke-19.* Jakarta: Perpustakaan Nasional Republik Indonesia, 2013. Seri Katalog Naskah Nusantara 1.

Coedès, G. *The Indianized States of Southeast Asia*. Honolulu: The University Press of Hawaii, 1968.

Cohen, Matthew Isaac. *Performing Otherness: Java and Bali on International Stages, 1905–1952.* New York: Palgrave Macmillan, 2010.

Drewes, G.W.J. and L.F. Brakel, eds. and trans. *The Poems of Hamzah Fansuri. Edited with an Introduction, a Translation and Commentaries, Accompanied by the Javanese Translations of Two of his Prose Works*. Dordrecht and Cinnaminson: Foris, 1986. KITLV, Bibliotheca Indonesica 26.

Gallop, Annabel Teh. "Panji Stories in Malay". *Asian and African Studies Blog*, 29 June 2015. Available at <http://britishlibrary.typepad.co.uk/asian-and-african/2015/06/panji-stories-in-malay.html>.

Goffman, Erving. *Frame Analysis: An Essay on the Organization of Experience*. Boston: Northeastern University Press, 1986. First published in 1974.

Gonda, J. "Old Javanese Literature". In *Handbuch der Orientalistik. Dritte Abteilung: Indonesien, Malaysia und die Philippinen, unter Einschluss der Kap-Malaien in Südafrika. Dritter Band: Literaturen. Abschitt 1*, edited by H. Kähler. Leiden and Köln: Brill, 1976, pp. 187–245.

Haron Daud. *Mantera Melayu: Analisis pemikiran*. Pulau Pinang: Penerbit University Sains Malaysia, 2001.

Hijjas, Mulaika. "Not Just Fryers of Bananas and Sweet Potatoes: Literate and Literary Women in the Nineteenth-Century Malay World". *Journal of Southeast Asian Studies* 41 (2010): 153–72.

Hooykaas, C. *Over Maleise Literatuur*. Leiden: Brill, 1947.

Hussain, Khalid M., ed. *Hikayat Pandawa Lima*. Kuala Lumpur: Dewan Bahasa dan Pustaka, Kementerian Pendidikan Malaysia, 1992.

Juynboll, H.H. *Catalogus van de Maleische en Sundaneesche handschriften der Leidsche Universiteits-bibliotheek*. Leiden: Brill, 1899.

Koster, G.L. *Roaming through Seductive Gardens: Readings in Malay Narrative*. Leiden: KITLV Press, 1997. VKI 167.

Kuntara Wiryamartana, I. *Arjunawiwāha: Transformasi teks Jawa Kuna lewat tanggapan dan penciptaan di lingkungan sastra Jawa*. Yogyakarta: Duta Wacana University Press, 1990.

Liaw Yock Fang, ed. and trans. *Undang-undang Melaka: The Laws of Melaka*. The Hague: Nijhoff, 1976. KITLV, Bibliotheca Indonesica 13.

Millie, Julian, ed. and trans. *Bidasari: Jewel of Malay Muslim Culture*. Leiden: KITLV Press, 2004. KITLV, Bibliotheca Indonesica 31.

Miyazaki, Koji. "Javanese–Malay: Between Adaptation and Alienation". *Sojourn* 15 (2000): 76–99.

Molen, Willem van der. "A Land Overflowing with Milk and Honey: Sastradarma's *Description of Batavia*, 1867–1869". *Indonesia and the Malay World* 34, no. 98 (2006): 109–15.

Nikmah Sunardjo, ed. *Hikayat Maharaja Garebag Jagat: Suntingan naskah disertai Ttinjauan tema dan amanat cerita serta fungsi panakawan di dalamnya*. Jakarta: Balai Pustaka, 1989. BP 3058.

Noorduyn, J. "Bujangga Manik's Journeys through Java: Topographical Data from an Old Sundanese Source". *Bijdragen tot de Taal-, Land- en Volkenkunde* 138 (1982): 413–42.

Oud Batavia. *Gedenkboek uitgegeven door het Bataviaasch Genootschap van Kunsten en Wetenschappen naar aanleiding van het driehonderdjarig bestaan der stad in 1919.* Volume 1. Batavia: Kolff, 1922.

Overbeck, H. "Java in de Maleische literatuur (Hikajat Galoeh di-gantoeng)". *Djåwå* 12 (1932): 209–28.

———. "Bambang To' Sena: Een Palembangsch wajang-verhaal". *Djåwå* 14 (1934): 104–16.

———. "Bambang Gandawerdaja (een Palembangsch wajang-verhaal)". *Djåwå* 15 (1935): 150–61.

———. [Review of C. Hooykaas, Over Maleische literatuur, 1937.] *Tijdschrift voor Indische Taal-, Land- en Volkenkunde* 78 (1938): 292–333.

Peletz, Michael G. *Reason and Passion: Representations of Gender in a Malay Society*. Berkeley etc.: University of California Press, 1996.

Pemberton, John. *On the Subject of "Java"*. Ithaca and London: Cornell University Press, 1994.

Pigeaud, Theodore G. Th. *Literature of Java: Catalogue Raisonné of Javanese Manuscripts in the Library of the University of Leiden and Other Public Collections in the Netherlands. Vol. 2. Descriptive Lists of Javanese Manuscripts.* Leiden: Bibliotheca Universitatis Lugduni Batavorum, 1968. Bibliotheca Universitatis Leidensis, Codices Manuscripti 10.

Pijnappel Gz., J. "De Maleische handschriften der Leidsche bibliotheek". *Bijdragen tot de Taal- Land- en Volkenkunde van Nederlandsch Indië* 17 (1870): 142–48.

Poerbatjaraka. "Déwa-roetji". *Djåwå* 20 (1940): 5–55.

Prijohoetomo. *Nawaruci: Inleiding, Middel-Javaansche prozatekst, vertaling; vergeleken met de Bimasoetji in Oud-Javaansch metrum.* Groningen etc.: Wolters, 1934.

Raben, Remco. "Round about Batavia: Ethnicity and Authority in the Ommelanden, 1650–1800". In *Jakarta–Batavia: Socio-Cultural Essays*, edited by Kees Grijns and Peter J. M. Nas. Leiden: KITLV Press, 2000. VKI 187, pp. 93–113.

Ricklefs, M.C. and P. Voorhoeve. *Indonesian Manuscripts in Great Britain: A Catalogue of Manuscripts in Indonesian Languages in British Public Collections.* Oxford etc.: Oxford University Press, 1977. London Oriental Bibliographies 5.

Robson, Stuart O., ed. and trans. *Hikajat Andaken Penurat*. The Hague: Nijhoff, 1969. KITLV, Bibliotheca Indonesica 2.

———. "Java in Malay Literature: Overbeck's Ideas on Malayo–Javanese Literature". In *Looking in Odd Mirrors: The Java Sea*, edited by V.J.H. Houben, H.M.J. Maier, and W. van der Molen. Leiden: Vakgroep Talen en Culturen van Zuidoost-Azië en Oceanië, Rijksuniversiteit te Leiden, 1992. Semaian 5, pp. 27–42.

———. "Panji and Inao: Questions of Cultural and Textual History". *Journal of the Siam Society* 84.2 (1996): 39–53.

Salmon, Claudine. *Literature in Malay by the Chinese of Indonesia: A Provisional Annotated Bibliography*. Paris: Éditions de la Maison des Sciences de l'Homme, 1981. Études insulindiennes – Archipel 3.

Serat Gembring Baring. Jakarta: Proyek Penerbitan Buku Sastra Indonesia dan Daerah, Departemen Pendidikan dan Kebudayaan, 1981. Alih aksara Sri Sumarsih, Noharkesti, S. Ilmi Albiladiyah, Suratmin, K. Hadiwasita.

Serat Kandhaning Ringgit Purwa. Menurut Naskah Tangan LOr 6379. Jakarta: Djambatan, 1985–88. 9 vols.

Spiller, Henry. *Javaphilia: American Love Affairs with Javanese Music and Dance*. Honolulu: University of Hawai'i Press, 2015.

Sulastin Sutrisno. *Hikayat Hang Tuah: Analisa struktur dan fungsi*. Yogyakarta: Gadjah Mada University Press, 1983.

Sweeney, P.L. Amin. *The Ramayana and the Malay Shadow-Play*. Kuala Lumpur: Penerbit Universiti Kebangsaan Malaysia, 1972.

———. *A Full Hearing: Orality and Literacy in the Malay World*. Berkeley: University of California Press, 1987.

Tanaya, ed. *Bima Suci: Kaimpun sarta kataliti*. Jakarta: Balai Pustaka, 1979. BP 2795.

Teeuw, A. and S.O. Robson, eds. and trans. *Bhomāntaka: The Death of Bhoma*. Leiden: KITLV Press, 2005. KITLV, Bibliotheca Indonesica 32.

Tuuk, H.N. van der. "Short Account of the Malay Manuscripts Belonging to the Royal Asiatic Society". *Journal of the Royal Asiatic Society*, N.S. 2 (1866): 85–135.

———. "Eenige Maleische wajang verhalen toegelicht". *Tijdschrift voor Indische Taal-, Land- en Volkenkunde* 25 (1879): 489–537.

———. "Notes on the Kawi Language and Literature". *Journal of the Royal Asiatic Society*, N.S. 13 (1881): 42–58, 584.

Vickers, Adrian. "Hinduism and Islam in Indonesia: Bali and the Pasisir". *Indonesia* 44 (1987): 30–58.

———. "'Malay Identity': Modernity, Invented Tradition and Forms of Knowledge". In *Contesting Malayness: Malay Identity Across Boundaries*, edited by Timothy P. Barnard. Singapore: Singapore University Press, 2004, pp. 25–55.

———. *Journeys of Desire: A Study of the Balinese Text Malat*. Leiden: KITLV Press, 2005. VKI 217.

Wieringa, E.P. *Catalogue of Malay and Minangkabau Manuscripts in the Library of Leiden University and Other Collections in the Netherlands. Vol. 2. Comprising the H. N. van der Tuuk Bequest Acquired by the Leiden University Library in 1896*. Leiden: Leiden University Library, 2007. Bibliotheca Universitatis Leidensis, Codices Manuscripti 40.

Winstedt, Richard. *A History of Classical Malay Literature*. Kuala Lumpur: Council of the Malaysian Branch of the Royal Asiatic Society, 1991. Revised edition by Y.A. Talib.

Wolters, O.W. *History, Culture, and Region in Southeast Asian Perspectives*. Ithaca, NY: Southeast Asia Publications, Southeast Asia Program, Cornell University, 1999. Revised edition. Studies on Southeast Asia 26.

Zoetmulder, P.J. with S.O. Robson. *Old Javanese–English Dictionary*. 's-Gravenhage: Nijhoff, 1982.

5

RAMAYANA AND MAHABHARATA IN HIKAYAT MISA TAMAN JAYENG KUSUMA

Gijs L. Koster

This chapter examines the role of the great Indian epics in the process of signification in the Panji romance Hikayat Misa Taman Jayeng Kusuma (copied or written between 1860 and 1870), concentrating on five episodes in its narrative. It traces the intertextual presence of elements familiar from Mahabharata and Ramayana, and suggests that the hikayat's *most probable sources are New Javanese* (wayang kulit purwa) *and Malay* (hikayat's) *adaptations of episodes of these epics, the creation of which was more or less contemporary with the* hikayat's *probable date of composition, and not Old-Javanese ones in the form of* kakawin. *The unknown author of the* hikayat *freely combines disparate elements from these adaptations to create what may be called mirror-texts commenting on the* hikayat's *narrative and thus adds new layers of meaning to it. The chapter closes with some considerations about how and why the* hikayat *foregrounds its own fictionality, relating this to what Malay poetics calls creative amplification* (memanjangkan), *a key characteristic of all narrative in the genre of the Panji romance.*

Keywords: Literary criticism, intertextuality, traditional Malay literature, Old-Javanese poetry, *wayang kulit purwa.*

Introduction

> First the story is told that the gods were sitting together in the Hall of the Lotus of Illusion, discussing a plan to send Betara Indera Naya and his wife down to incarnate in the Illusionary Abode. Since the Pandawa kings had long ago gone back to the heavens, the Illusionary Abode had become a deserted place and their land was about to become forest again. The gods therefore liked the idea and all agreed with Betara Kala's proposal.[1]

With these words opens the narrative of a bulky Malay Panji romance, entitled Hikayat Misa Taman Jayeng Kusuma (henceforth called HMTJK), that according to its editor, Abdul Rahman Kaeh (1976), was possibly copied or written between 1860 and 1870.[2] On Betara Kala's proposal, so the *hikayat* subsequently tells us, Betara Indera Naya and his wife Dewi Mandurati descend to earth and incarnate as the king and queen of Koripan, whose sons then become the kings of the Javanese kingdoms of Koripan, Daha, Gagelang and Singasari, and whose daughter marries the king of Manjapahit.

The above council-scene invites us to see a connection between the story told by the *hikayat* — centrally concerned with the love between Crown Prince Raden Inu Kertapati of Koripan (often referred to as Panji) and Princess Candera Kirana of Daha — and the Indian epic Mahabharata, and thus puts us on the track of intertexts that may perhaps be suitable for the interpretation of the *hikayat.* The passage also reflects the traditional Javanese belief that ancient history began with the Pandawa kings, and was then continued by the line of Javanese kings descended from the first king and queen of Koripan (Ras 1976*a*, p. 61; Robson 1992, pp. 28–29).

In order to gain a somewhat clearer picture of the role played in the process of signification in Panji romances in general by the great Indian epics Mahabharata and Ramayana I will in this chapter, as a case study, examine a number of relevant episodes in HMTJK in which intertextual relations with these two works can be traced. I must here forego the presentation of a more complete intertextual analysis of the *hikayat*, since that would require too much time and space.

I will close my chapter with a brief consideration of how and why HMTJK foregrounds its own fictionality, relating it to the principle of creative amplification (*memanjangkan*) that dominates in romance and, among others, operates by intertextually adding layers of meaning.

Summary of HMTJK

After HMTJK has introduced the major kingdoms of Java and the leading position occupied among these by Koripan, its narrative may be summarized as follows: Because they are still childless, the king of Koripan and the other rulers of Java (the grandchildren of Betara Indera Naya and Dewi Mandurati) vow to perform sacrifices to the gods if these grant them children. Each of the kings then duly begets sons and daughters. Descending from heaven, two gods, who are man and wife, incarnate on earth as Raden Inu Kertapati (henceforth RIK), the crown prince of Koripan, and Raden Galuh Candra Kirana (henceforth RGCK), the oldest daughter of the king of Daha (Kediri). Each of the new-born princes and princesses is betrothed with a prince or princess of one of the other kingdoms, and thus RIK is betrothed with RGCK.

In the celebrations the kings forget to redeem their vows, thus angering the gods. When RIK, on having become an adult, has his servant Semar paint a portrait of his fiancée RGCK, Betara Durga makes her invisible and takes her place, in the shape of an ugly old hag. On seeing the portrait Semar has made RIK refuses to marry RGCK and takes a princess of another kingdom as wife. When on a visit in Daha he beholds the beauty like that of a heavenly nymph of the real RGCK, whose hand has meanwhile been promised to another prince, he falls madly in love and swears he will make her his.

However, in order to make RIK aware that he has mistreated his beloved, to give him an opportunity to show his love and loyalty to her, to punish the Javanese kings for not redeeming their vows, and to prevent RGCK's marriage with a prince who is not destined for her by *karma*, Betara Kala abducts RGCK from Daha and puts her down with her maid-servants in the forest of Segara Gunung. There they all change names to hide their origin, RGCK now calling herself Ken Segerba Ningrat. When the king of Segara Gunung finds her and her maids, they claim to be mere humble folk from the forest-covered South, but he is so impressed by her that he adopts her as his own daughter.

The disappearance of RGCK triggers the departure of a series of search-parties, beginning with that of RIK, who leaves Koripan to look for his abducted fiancée. His search-party is followed by those of other princes, who, conforming to the particular need for motivation at that moment in the narrative, set out either in search of one of the main protagonists, their own betrothed, or a brother or sister who has disappeared. In the course of their circumambulations, which take them all over Java and even to the land of the Malays, RIK and the other royal searchers, RGCK also included, often disguise themselves as fierce warriors, subject many kingdoms and conquer many princesses, making them their wives.

In scenes fraught with dramatic irony RIK and RGCK as well as the other royal searchers and searched during their quests occasionally meet, sometimes suspecting each other's real identity but often also quite unaware of it, because they all constantly adopt new aliases and all sorts of disguises as low-class people: humble folk from the forest-covered south, hermits, nuns, knights-errant, champions of war, puppeteers of the shadow-play, *gambuh*-dancers.[3] Nevertheless the royal qualities of the princes and princesses shine through the veil of their disguises and lead to their gaining an ever higher substitute status in the course of the narrative. Their circumambulations are also attended by constant interventions by the gods. Occasionally also appearing in the guise of a giant (*raksasa*) or an ogre (*buta*), these either help or obstruct the efforts of the searchers to meet the object of their quest.

The narrative of HMTJK culminates in a confrontation of all the searchers and the searched from the different kingdoms in a big battle. This battle — which among others teaches the lesson that man and woman must not fight with each other — is fought between the troops led by Misa Edan Sira Panji Jayeng Kusuma — as RIK at this stage in the narrative calls himself — and those led by Prabu Anom — as

RGCK now calls "himself". RGCK, now the ruler of the kingdom of Tambak Kencana miraculously conjured up with the help of a magic ring, and her deputy Pangeran Tambak Kencana (RIK's sister Raden Ratna Wilis in disguise) detain at their court the fiancées of two of RIK's allies. Because Betara Kala is aware that the *lelakon* of Kelana Merta Jiwa — RGCK's identity before she became Prabu Anom — will soon end, he intervenes in the battle: descending from heaven he engineers the defeat and capture of the knight-errant (*kelana*) Misa Edan Sira Panji Jayeng Kusuma (RIK) and of his numerous allies.

All the Javanese kings now gather in Tambak Kencana and at their request RIK and his men are released. Betara Kala lifts the spell that has been cast upon the searchers and searched so that each prince and princess regains his or her identity as a princess or prince. Initially RGCK is still unwilling to forgive RIK, but when Betara Kala orders her to love him again they make up. In token of their gratitude to the gods the kings and all their relatives now go to the Southern Ocean to redeem their vows. Amidst all kinds of festivities RIK and RGCK, followed by the other betrothed couples, are married and installed as rulers. The abdicated kings go to Mount Indera Kila to practise austerities.

HMTJK as a Panji Romance

All romance arises from an intertwining of two components: love and adventure.[4] Depending on the emphasis given to the one or the other component we may, therefore, distinguish between more "lyrical" and more "epic" Panji romances. The Panji romance Syair Ken Tambuhan may be called "lyrical" in the sense that it dwells on the experiences, emotions and thoughts of the lovers at the expense of the element of action and adventure (Koster 1997, pp. 193–94). The nucleus of plot underlying all Panji stories is a circular movement which leads the hero from identity through alienation back to identity again. It requires that after the idyllic day-world of known identity in the initial situation has been disturbed, the hero disguises for others his real status and identity, sometimes even forgetting it. If I speak of the main protagonist as a "hero" or "he", I do so only for convenience, because the hero may be female as Syair Ken Tambuhan shows.

In disguise the hero is sent on a quest through adventures in a night-world which involves separation, loneliness, tyranny, humiliation, and other ills, and moves through the narrative as a "signifier-errant" (the name of *Ken Tambuhan*, RGCK in disguise, means "Lady-in-Waiting Unknown") which is correctly interpreted by the good characters and misread by the evil, unworthy or ignorant ones. The return movement is set into motion by the hero's adoption or gaining of some other substitute identity. The hero very much brings about the return to his/her real identity by constantly representing and reminding the other characters of his royal status in every act, word and gesture (Koster 1997, pp. 173–74). In HMTJK identity is ultimately only completely recovered because the gods lift the curse which they have placed on the lovers as punishment for the failure of the kings to redeem their vows.

If Syair Ken Tambuhan may be characterized as a "lyrical" Panji romance, then HMTJK is perhaps best characterized as an "epic" one. Although it still gives ample scope to the love component, it also gives just as much, if not more, space to the adventure component. Different from other Panji romances, such as Syair Ken Tambuhan, it does not send just one — or, as in other romances, two — protagonists through the plot-pattern of the quest, but, as we have seen in the summary above, many more. And instead of limiting its action to the peregrinations between the palace and royal garden of Koripan by RIK and RGCK, as happens in Syair Ken Tambuhan (Braginsky 2004, p. 173), it makes its many teams of searchers and searched roam through all the kingdoms of Java, and even beyond, as they go through a bewildering variety of adventures (Koster 1997, pp. 193–94).

Betara Naya Indera's Descent to Earth

Having seen something of HMTJK as a sample of the genre of the Panji romance, let us turn to the intertextual echoes of Mahabharata in this *hikayat*. When Betara Naya Indera has accepted the decision of the gods that he and his wife must incarnate on earth in Koripan we are told: "Thereupon Betara Guru gave him his war-club, to become a rainbow, a storm-wind and sunset-clouds when he confronted an enemy; Betara Kala gave him his sash, to become a blue banner with the white sign of his supreme authority (?). And Betara Indera gave him an arrow called Pasupati and Betara Wishnu gave his *keris* Kalamisani to Betara Naya Indera."[5]

It is possible that this passage was inspired by similar passages in other Panji stories, such as the one in Hikayat Panji Kuda Semirang, where we are told that, on seeing that Arjuna, obeying the decision of the gods, has incarnated on earth together with his wife Subadra, Betara Guru orders Betara Kala to give him among others a blue banner (*tunggul wulung*). Betara Kala also gives him a *keris*, called Kalamisani, which he has created by extracting one of his own tusks (Poerbatjaraka 1940, pp. 2–3).[6] There is, however, in this passage one weapon, the arrow Pasupati, the mention of which undeniably is an echo of an episode from Mahabharata, albeit in one of its Javanese adaptations.

This adaptation may be the *kakawin* (Old-Javanese heroic epic in an Indian metre), entitled Arjunawiwaha ("The marriage of Arjuna"), that was composed about AD 1030 by King Erlangga's court-poet Mpu Kanwa (Zoetmulder 1974, pp. 234–49). In this *kakawin* we are told that a powerful demon king is preparing to attack Indra's heaven. Indra decides to seek assistance from a human being with extraordinary qualities and chooses Arjuna, one of the five Pandawa brothers, who at that time is doing penance on Mount Indrakila (also the place to which the abdicated Javanese kings withdraw at the close of HMTJK). Indra first puts Arjuna's steadfastness in yoga to the test by sending seven celestial nymphs down to seduce him, but in vain. Next, he visits Arjuna disguised as an old sage. He has a long discussion with him on the true meaning of power and pleasure. When Indra is satisfied he reveals his identity and returns to heaven.

Shiwa then descends, disguised as a hunter, and has a dispute with Arjuna on the question of who defeated a boar that ravages the forests. Finally Shiwa reveals his identity and, when Arjuna worships him, grants him the magic arrow Pasupati. Later, when Arjuna considers returning to his brothers, the other Pandawas, he is summoned by Indra and requested to assist the gods in their scheme to destroy Niwatakawaca, who can only be killed by a human being. With the help of the nymph Suprabha, the secret of Niwatakawaca's invulnerability is discovered, and, when that demon king marches against the gods, he is finally killed by Arjuna with his magic arrow Pasupati. As a reward Arjuna may stay in heaven for seven (heavenly) days and contract a sevenfold marriage with seven celestial nymphs, the first two of who are Suprabha and Tillotama. After having consummated these marriages one by one, Arjuna finally returns to his brothers on earth (Zoetmulder 1974, pp. 234–35; Ras 1976*a*, pp. 62–63).

The Birth of HMTJK's Two Main Protagonists

Having established the divine authority and Arjuna-like *kesaktian* of the first king of Koripan and his descendants by telling how the gods provided Betara Indra Naya with the necessary weapons before his descent to earth, the *hikayat* then tells of the births of the children of the Javanese kings after they have made their vows to the gods. When RIK is born, so we are told, there is a lunar eclipse and thunder rumbles, as if ordering Betara Kerma Jaya to incarnate. As his name for use by intimates (*nama timang-timangan*) he is given that of Raden Asmara Jaya ("Prince Victorious Love") whereas his full formal name is Raden Inu Kertapati Anakan Asmara Ningrat ("Crown Prince Kertapati, the Duplicate of the God of Love in the World"). His father predicts that he will subject all of Java and that all princesses will fight among themselves to become his. As his playmates (*teman bermain*) he is given the sons of low-ranking courtiers: Jerude, Punta, Persanta, Semar and Jemuris (Abdul Rahman Kaeh 1976, pp. 7–9).

About the birth of RGCK we are told that, after practising austerities and worshiping the gods, the king of Daha beseeches Sangyang Sukma to grant him children. Thereupon, Betara Kala persuades Dewi Segerba, who dwells in the heavenly garden Tamansari and is longing for her absent husband Betara Kerma Jaya, to incarnate on earth and to join her husband there. While Dewi Segerba descends to earth, Dewa (sic)[7] Durga unsuccessfully makes a pass at her, upon which the shocked goddess transforms herself into a golden lotus flower (*bunga tunjung kencana*) that falls down in the royal palace in Daha. When the king and queen eat the flower, Dewi Segerba incarnates into the daughter that is born to them, Crown Princess Candera Kirana, whose full formal name is Raden Galuh Kusuma Ningrat Lasmi Puri ("Crown Princess Flower in the World, Beauty of the Palace"). Her father predicts she will be fought over by all the rulers of Java. As her attendants (*kedayan*) she is given the daughters of low-ranking courtiers: Bayan, Sanggit, Pasungan and Pasiran (Abdul Rahman Kaeh 1976, pp. 11–14).

Here the quest of the two main protagonists of HMTJK — RIK and RGCK — to be reunited with each other is suggested to have in a way already started before the crown princess of Daha is abducted by Betara Kala: in their previous existence as gods — as the God of Love, Kama, and the Goddess Suprabha (the Javanese form of her Malayized name *Segerba*) — they were in fact already a married couple. From the start they are therefore bound to each other by the law of *karma*. In my study of Syair Ken Tambuhan in Koster (1997, pp. 183–90, 192), I have demonstrated that a similar suggestion — one that may well be found in *all* Panji romances — is made by systematic and quite consistent intertextual allusions to myths about divine married couples that are told about in Old Javanese *kakawin*, Middle-Javanese *kidung* and, more recently, *wayang kulit* plays.

By allusions to these myths the marriage of RIK and RGCK at the close of Syair Ken Tambuhan is represented as a repetition and commemoration of the exemplary divine marriages of the days of yore, and the entire poem is turned into an allegory — *pasemon* would be the Javanese term for this — of the power of love between man and woman. Lovers, marriage partners of matching status and perhaps even twin-souls from another existence: what marriage could surpass in quality this thrice-blessed and guaranteed union? However, if we examine the particular pair of divine lovers of which RIK and RGCK are suggested to be earthly incarnations in HMTJK we run up against a major problem: no matter how appropriate this combination of the God of Love with the heavenly nymph Dewi Segerba may seem to an outsider, they do not form a pair in accepted Hindu-Javanese mythology.

Most probably we have here a conflation of two divine pairs known in Old Javanese *kakawin* as well as subsequent literary tradition. One of these married couples is that formed by Arjuna and Suprabha (Malay *Segerba*). As for Tillotama (Malay *Nila Utama*), the second of the seven nymphs he acquires, she is also mentioned in HMTJK, but only in descriptions of other princesses than RGCK. As we learn from Zoetmulder (1974, pp. 237–43), whereas much of Kakawin Arjunawiwaha's story is also found in Wanaparwa, the third book of Mahabharata that deals with the twelve years of exile of the Pandawas in the forest, Suprabha and the celebration of Arjuna's wedding with the seven nymphs do not occur in the Indian epic.

Although it is not impossible that, together with the arrow Pasupati, Dewi Segerba (Suprabha) and Nila Utama (Tillotama) have entered HMTJK via Mpu Kanwa's Old-Javanese Kakawin Arjunawiwaha, they are more likely to have done so through a much later adaptation of this poem, such as the New-Javanese Arjunawiwaha epic created in the eighteenth century by Yasadipura I, the court poet of the Surakarta kings Paku Buwana the III^{d} and IVth (Ras 1976*a*, p. 67), or through adaptions of the *kakawin* in the *wayang kulit purwa* plays variously called Mintaraga, Ciptaning Mintaraga, Arjuna Mintaraga or Arjunawiwaha (Ras 1976*b*, p. 60; Irvine 2005, pp. 184–85).

The other divine married couple with which the previously mentioned one seems to have been conflated, consists of the God of Love, Kama, and the Goddess of Love, Ratih, also known as Yangyang Kusuma. In Old-Javanese literature we meet them in the late twelfth century Kakawin Smaradahana ("The Burning of Kama") by Mpu Dharmaja. It tells that to Ratih's immense sadness her husband has to leave her to carry out the order from Indra and the other gods to bring Shiwa, who is doing severe penance on Mount Meru, out of his meditation and to make him desire his spouse, Uma, who is still a virgin. Kama's efforts to disturb Shiwa by attacking him with his flower-weapons succeed, and in a dream Shiwa sees Uma sitting on his lap. Awakening an instant later and noticing Kama's presence, he assumes his terrifying shape and scorches Kama to ashes with his fire.

Besought by Indra to revive Kama, Shiwa consents to let him live again, but only in an immaterial form. When news of Kama's death reaches Ratih, she is overcome with grief. The sage Wrhaspati acquaints her with Shiwa's decision that she and her husband shall both continue their existence in invisible form, she in women, and he in men. When she expresses her profound repugnance for such a formless life, which can hardly be called a life at all, and pleads that they be granted a rebirth, the sage assures her that this will definitely happen in the future.

Ratih now accepts her fate and decides to follow her husband in death. She goes to the place where he was burnt and throws herself into the flames, which Shiwa causes to flare up again. Kama and Ratih now meet, but, as they are bodiless, they cannot unite. Therefore, Kama enters the heart of Shiwa and Ratih that of Shiwa's spouse, Uma. From the moment Shiwa is struck by Kama's arrow, the passion of love takes possession of his heart. Now he unites with Uma.

Later, on a pleasure trip, Uma sees the ashes of the god and goddess of love. Moved by compassion and gratitude she obtains from Shiwa the promise that they shall be reborn. After several other rebirths Kama finally descends to earth as king of Java. Ratih is reborn in Janggala (Kahuripan) where she is known as Kiranaratu. Thus, by the grace of Shiwa, His Majesty Kameswara now reigns in Dahana (Daha) with Dewi Kirana as queen (Zoetmulder 1974, pp. 291–95).

In fact, HMTJK's story of the birth of RIK and RGCK, besides some remarkable differences, also shows considerable similarity to the story told in Hikayat Panji Kuda Semirang (copy finished 1832) about the births of its main protagonists (Poerbatjaraka 1940, pp. 1–5, 35; Abdul Rahman Kaeh 1989, pp. 92–93) — also married couples in their previous existence. Here HMTJK's story may therefore well have been constructed on the basis of that romance. That the attendants given to RIK and RGCK after their birth in both romances bear the same names need perhaps not surprise us, since these names are quite usual in Malay and Middle-Javanese Panji romances (Braginsky 2004, p. 160; Zoetmulder 1974, p. 429).

What *is* striking here is not only the generally similar way in which this story is structured, but also that here, too, the queens of both Koripan and Daha become pregnant after eating a lotus flower. Dewi Segerba and Banjaransari in combination may also well have entered

HMTJK from another Panji romance, such as Syair Ken Tambuhan, an edition of which was published by Teeuw (1966) on the basis of several manuscripts of which the oldest is dated 1791. There, too, that nymph, occasionally also called Nila Utama, is described as residing in the heavenly garden Banjaransari, where she is the guardian of the Flower Wijaya Mala by which the dead can be revived. In the *syair* we are told this flower grows from the milk of her breasts and is then used by Betara Kala to bring RIK and Ken Tambuhan (RGCK) to life again on the orders of Betara Guru, "so that the puppeteer may spin out his story" and "so that the shadow-play may thereafter long continue" (Teeuw 1966, pp. IX, 20*d*–63*a*).[8]

A *Wayang Kulit Purwa* Performance in Lasem[9]

But, let us leave the question of HMTJK's relation to other Panji romances and go to another episode in the *hikayat* that puts us on the track of what seem echoes from Mahabharata. In that episode RIK's half-brother Raden Asmara Agung and RGCK's half-brother Raden Gunung Sari, after already having gone through several identity changes in earlier adventures during their search for her, on arriving from Melayu in Lasem, disguise themselves as travelling *dalang* (puppeteers of the *wayang kulit*) — Dalang Mangku Jaya and Dalang Sungging Anom — who are accompanied by two assistants (*panjak*). At that time the ruler of Temasik happens to be in Lasem for the marriage of his son, Raden Kembar Dahang, with the princess of Lasem, Raden Puspa Danta.

When, at the orders of the king of Lasem, his Chief Minister looks for a *dalang* and his troupe and meets the two disguised princes, he is dumb-struck by their appearance, thinking to himself: "It is not proper they are puppeteers, they should be waited upon in the great hall of the palace, maybe they are gods in disguise."[10] Invited to perform in the palace, the two *dalangs* are, in spite of their seemingly humble status, received with great courtesy. The only exception is Raden Kembar Dahang, who fails to see the real signifieds behind these two signifiers-errant and treats them with condescension, even telling them: "Don't be afraid of me, just play",[11] words which only earn him the ridicule of the other courtiers. The two *dalangs,* quite in keeping with their real identity, only react to his lack of good manners with a diplomatic smile.

Before the two *dalangs,* who are the main attraction, take the stage, one of their assistants, Kuda Kerta Negara, opens the performance of a *wayang kulit* play entitled "The Shadow-Play about King Boma and Lord Samba"[12] by singing *kidung* and *kakawin* (Abdul Rahman Kaeh 1976, p. 160).[13] When Dalang Sungging Anom, after having taken over from Kuda Kerta Negara, has gotten well into the play, he sets eyes on Raden Puspa Danta, Raden Kembar Dahang's fiancée, whose appearance is like that of a newly-tinted golden puppet and who looks all the more ravishing for not having formally dressed for the occasion (*memakai*). As his desire for her is rising while he sings *kidungs*, completely forgetting himself, he reaches the episode in which Maharaja Boma wants to make Dewi Januwati his wife.

The *dalang* now tells the story how, although Boma has already several times tried to coax her with sweet words (*bujuk*), Dewi Januwati nevertheless keeps crying because she does not like having Boma as her husband. Not only does she refuse to stop crying, he cannot even approach her because she threatens to kill herself if he does. At his wit's end, Boma finally calls Samba and asks him if he does perhaps have a medicine for women who do not like their husband, something Samba denies with a smile. When Boma then requests Samba to coax Dewi Januwati for him, so that her heart will soften towards him, Samba answers with a smile: "How should I know how to coax her, sir; after all, she is your wife, so that you should coax her",[14] an answer that elicits a roar of laughter from the audience. Dalang Mangku Jaya then takes over from Dalang Sungging Anom and continues the play with the episode about how Samba elopes to the forest with Dewi Januwati, after which Kuda Kerta Negara finishes the performance (Abdul Rahman Kaeh 1976, pp. 156–63).

The *hikayat* then tells us that, because Raden Puspa Danta keeps refusing to enter the bedroom to consummate their marriage, Raden Kembar Dahang unwisely decides to hire Dalang Sungging Anom to coax her for him. Predictably the *dalang* performs his job only too well and ends up making love to her. When Raden Kembar Dahang finds out what has happened, a fight breaks out in the palace, in which the king of Temasik is killed. Raden Kembar Dahang is defeated by Dalang Sungging Anom and flees to the forest, where he practises austerities hoping to conquer back his wife, something which, so a god appearing before him tells him, is impossible, because the Princess of Lasem is not destined by *karma* to be his (Abdul Rahman Kaeh 1976, pp. 163–76).

The *lelakon* about King Boma and Lord Samba enacted in HMTJK has probably been derived from Hikayat Sang Boma ("The Story of Lord Boma"), which was itself written in the fifteenth or sixteenth century on the basis of now-lost archaic *wayang purwa* plays (Braginsky 2004, pp. 154–56) and not from the Old-Javanese Kakawin Bhomantaka ("Bhoma's Death"), which was composed by an unknown author in the twelfth century.[15] In Hikayat Sang Boma[16] we are told that Brama (Sanskrit: *Brahma*) and Bisnu (*Vishnu*) decide to resolve a dispute over who is the older of the two by playing hide and seek. While hiding in the earth, Bisnu seduces the earth-goddess Pertiwi (*Parthivī*), and she gives birth to the monstrous giant Boma (*Bhauma*), who is invulnerable and holds the flower of immortality. Boma's exploits then begin with his defeating Maharaja Daniswara in a duel and settling in his residence, Trajutrisna.

Now Brama and Bisnu create a young man, Derma Dewa, and a girl, Derma Dewi from two flowers of the *nagasari*-tree. The couple marries and settles on Mount Tenunan. After some time, Derma Dewa abandons his wife at the wish of Bisnu, who incarnates on earth as Kresna (Krishna), and Derma Dewa himself incarnates as Kresna's son, Samba. Throwing herself into Derma Dewa's funeral pyre, Derma Dewi thereupon incarnates as the beautiful Januwati (*Yajñavatī*), the daughter of Maharaja Jantaka.

When Boma's request for Januwati's hand is rejected, he kills her father in anger and carries her off to Trajutrisna, trying to persuade her to marry him. At her request Boma attacks heaven and forces the God Indra to give him two heavenly nymphs, Nila Utama (*Tilottama*) and Sukarba (*Segerba*, Sanskrit: *Suprabha*) to become Januwati's maids. Also at her request he begins to devastate the abode of the hermits, although his father Bisnu had explicitly advised him when he was young not to cause them trouble.

At the behest of the hermits, Samba arranges an expedition against Boma and defeats his commanders. On the way, in an enchanted garden, he meets three heavenly nymphs, who are hiding there from the approaches of the God Kama, and he marries one of them, Tunjung Sari. On reaching Mount Tenunan he remembers his former wife Derma Dewi and meets Januwati with Nila Utama's help. When Samba tries to free Januwati, the ogress who guards her abducts her and hides her deep in Boma's palace.

When Boma's ogres have captured the two lovers and are ready to burn them alive, Hanuman, the commander of the monkey-army in Ramayana, intervenes and kills Boma. In the ensuing battle, in which, besides Samba's father and other relatives of his, the Pandawas, too, take part, Samba and Arjuna also are killed. The supreme deity, Betara Guru, now brings the dead back to life, but initially refuses to revive Samba. As Tunjung Sari and Januwati are preparing to ascend Samba's funeral pyre, his servant Semar meanwhile defeats all the gods in heaven, including Betara Guru, and thus wins his master's being revived from death. Samba and Januwati celebrate their wedding, and Samba becomes ruler of Kresna's kingdom, Darawati Purwa (Braginsky 2004, pp. 152–53).

By creating in their play their own allusive adaptation (*pasemon*) of the story of the conflict between Boma and Samba over who shall win Januwati, in HMTJK the two *dalangs* teach the unfortunate Raden Kembar Dahang of Temasik a lesson in what is and what is not truly princely and manly behaviour. They do so by casting him allegorically in the role of the enamored but terrifying ogre — a creature far beyond the pale of refined courtly society.

The desires of this ogre — who is ridiculed as a naïve sucker — are frustrated by a handsome young prince, who steals his wife from him. Raden Kembar Dahang's role is therefore perhaps somewhat comparable to that of the *senex amator* ("old man in love"), who is the favourite butt of much Western comedy. By telling the story of Samba's elopement to the forest with Januwati Dalang Sungging Anom not only casts himself in the role of that handsome young prince, but also predicts what will happen next in the narrative of HMTJK, namely his seduction of, and making love to, Raden Puspa Danta.

As Braginsky has pointed out, Hikayat Sang Boma has much in common with its Old-Javanese predecessor, Kakawin Bhomantaka, so that one could in principle also imagine the possibility that the *kakawin*, and not the *hikayat*, has here served as inspiration for HMTJK's narrative. What these two works share, is that they both combine a Puranic Krishna legend telling of the struggle of the Yadawa with Bhoma — a conflict mentioned several times in Mahabharata — with a romance about king Samba and his wife Jajñawati — a story that in Sanskrit literature is only known from a poem by Dandin (AD sixth–seventh century).

However, as Braginsky has indicated, there are also considerable differences between their narratives. In my opinion, these differences make clear that HMTJK here has not relied on Bhomantaka but on Hikayat Sang Boma as an intertext. Whereas Krishna is the hero in the *kakawin*, in the *hikayat* he is Samba. Bhoma, who in the *kakawin* is the guardian of princess Jajñawati, is turned into an enamored ogre and claimant to her hand, while the focus of the action shifts, from Krishna's heroic struggle with evil and destruction represented by Bhoma, to the romantic relations in the love-triangle Samba–Januwati–Boma (Braginsky 2004, p. 154).

A *Gambuh*-Performance in Gagelang

Hikayat Sang Boma surprisingly also functions as an intertext in another episode in HMTJK, in which a performance of *gambuh* — a genre of dance-drama enacting episodes from Panji tales[17] — is given in the palace of the king of Gagelang. Among the spectators are the two knights-errant to whom the king has just submitted when they arrived, namely RIK, who is now called Sira Panji, short for Misa Edan Sira Panji Jayeng Kusuma, and his half-brother Raden Carang Tinangluh, who is now called Kelana Anom Perwira, short for Misa Kelana Jaya Wira Sukma. At this moment in the narrative we come to the last of three temporary and unaware reunions of the two lovers, RIK and RGCK, before they will be brought together for good.

To understand the *pasemon* of the dance-drama that is performed, an overview of the vicissitudes gone through by RIK and RGCK until then is helpful. The first unaware reunion of the two lovers occurs when RIK, who has begun his quest disguised as the Hermit Master over His Body (*Ajar Raga Pati*), changes his name to that of a warrior, Misa Jayeng Kusuma Sira Panji Jayeng Seteru. Bringing with him his newly acquired wife, Raden Ratna Langoe a princess of the defeated kingdom of Wengker, RIK then enters the kingdom of Segara Gunung, the ruler of which submits to him and gives him his three children, including RGCK, who had been adopted by the king when he found her in the forest, disguised as Ken Segerba Ningrat.

On the advice of his retainer, Kebu Sendubama — really Semar in disguise —, RIK consoles himself by sleeping with the Princess of Segara Gunung because she reminds him of RGCK. She gives herself to him, greatly impressed as she is by his handsome appearance like that of the god Kerma Jaya, but even when Betara Kala tells her who he really is, she still persists in telling him that she is of obscure descent. Leaving Segara Gunung, Sira Panji, taking Ken Segerba Ningrat (RGCK) and a very jealous Raden Ratna Langoe with him, arrives in Wiradesa, a dependency of Kembang Kuning, which is being attacked by the king of Surabaya over its refusal to give him the hand of one of its princesses. The king of Wiradesa decides to submit to Sira Panji, who then stays there with his two wives, while always longing for RGCK.

In Wiradesa the jealous Raden Ratna Langoe frames Ken Segerba Ningrat (RGCK), so that Sira Panji (RIK) accuses her of infidelity and even beats her. She does this by having one of her maid-servants, Ken Pangejangan, place the *keris* and clothes of the son of the king of Kembang Kuning in her rival's bedchamber. While Sira Panji is searching for the culprit and Ken Segerba Ningrat only wants one thing — to run away from that horrible man — Betara Kala arrives and transports her through the air to Mount Wilis, saying that all this has happened because her parents have still not fulfilled their vow. To ensure that she and her maid-servants will remain unrecognized Betara Kala now disguises them as nuns (*endang*) on Mount Wilis, and changes their names. Ken Segerba Ningrat's name now becomes Endang Kusuma Jiwa.

Betara Kala tells Sira Panji, who has remained behind in Wiradesa, that Ken Segerba Ningrat was in reality none other than his fiancée and that he was tricked by Ratna Langoe into quarrelling with RGCK. The lady-in-waiting who has helped her mistress slander Ken Segerba Ningrat is killed by Kebu Sendubama (Semar) and Sira Panji now falls ill with love-sickness (*sakit edan*). Leaving the prince of Wengker behind to guard over Sira Panji's wife Ratna Langoe, Kelana Anom Perwira (Raden Carang Tinangluh of Koripan) takes the distraught Sira Panji to Mount Wilis to ask the recluse living there, Sang Pelinggih,[18] for a medicine to cure his illness.

On the advice of the recluse, Sira Panji invokes the help of Endang Kusuma Jiwa (RGCK) which leads to their second unaware reunion, at which her appearance strikes him as somehow familiar. Strongly attracted to her he even humbles himself by performing the most menial work for her, such as working in the garden. Feeling Sira Panji may get too close with her, Endang Kusuma Jiwa departs with her companions, leaving behind for him a letter and her sash. When he spots the women, Betara Kala puts her and her companions under a spell and changes them into men, because he deems the time for the final reunion of the two lovers not yet to have come. Endang Kusuma Jiwa now takes the name of Misa Jejuluk Sira Panji Maring Daha.

Finding only the nun's sash and letter, Sira Panji (RIK) leaves Mount Wilis. While roaming all over Java he defeats the kingdom of Banjaransari. When he and his men reach Gagelang they change their names before entering the kingdom. Previously called Misa Jayeng Kusuma Sira Panji Jayeng Seteru he now calls himself Misa Edan Sira Panji Jayeng Kusuma, and his half-brother, Kelana Anom Perwira, now calls himself Misa Kelana Jaya Wira Sukma. The king of Gagelang submits to the two knights-errant, and on their entrance into the palace he is strongly reminded of RIK and his half-brother Raden Carang Tinangluh.

RIK and RGCK's third unaware reunion occurs when Misa Jejuluk (RGCK) also arrives in Gagelang, disguised and with the alias of Kelana Merta Jiwa Sira Panji Maring Daha. On meeting each other the commanders of both armies have a strong mutual feeling of recognition. During an audience with the king of Gagelang, who is happy to learn that the two newcomers have no hostile intentions, Sira Panji (RIK) does not recognize RGCK, who is disguised as Kelana Merta Jiwa and claims to be the child of humble folk from the forest-covered South, but he nevertheless keeps feeling strongly attracted to "him" and always accompanies "him".

HMTJK's story of the performance of the *gambuh* dance-drama is as follows. At the request of the queen of Gagelang the assembled knights-errant one evening decide to enact a *gambuh* dance-drama, beautifully dressed as female dancers. On the proposal of the warrior Kuda Kerta Negara, RGCK's maid-servant Ken Bayan in disguise, they choose as *lakon* to be danced one which they call "The Love-Sickness of Betara Kangsa Dewa"[19] and then divide the roles among themselves. Kelana Merta Jiwa (RGCK) takes the role of Betara Kangsa Dewa. "His" companion, Kelana Panji Kayangan, who really is RIK's half-sister Raden Ratna Wilis in disguise, is given that of Betara Kangsa Dewa's wife. Kuda Kerta Negara, RGCK's maid-servant Ken Bayan, acts the part of the Princess of Wengker, RIK's wife Raden Ratna Langoe. Kuda Warsa Pati, in fact Ken Bayan, a maid-servant of Raden Ratna Wilis, plays Kangsa Dewa (not: Betara Kangsa Dewa) and Kuda Jaya Perang plays the minor role of Kuda Warsa Danta.

Kelana Kusuma Agung, RGCK's brother Raden Asmara Agung of Daha, then invites the other warriors present to play the gamelan. Sira Panji (RIK), while himself choosing to play the *selukat*, instructs Kelana Kusuma Agung to play the *gender*, and someone else to play the *saron*; Misa Merga Asmara, actually Raden Wira Pati of Manjapahit, is to play the *gambang*; Misa Kusuma Yuda, really Raden Jayeng Kusuma of Singasari in disguise, is to play the *rebab*; Kelana Prabu Desa, actually Raden Gunung Sari of Daha, to whom Raden Ratna Wilis of Koripan — now disguised as Kelana Panji Kayangan — is betrothed, is to play the *kecapi*; Raden Wijaya Kusuma, a son of the king of Melayu, is to play the *keromong*, and Raden Teruna Jaya, son of the king of Kembang Kuning, is to play the *suling*. The other warriors are instructed to act as their assistants (*panjak*).

After the *gamelan* has played an introductory piece, bringing the audience in the right mood for the play, Kelana Merta Jiwa gets up and slowly circles the stage, leading Kelana Panji Kayangan by the hand. The sight of the two dancers gently swaying their buttocks drives Sira Panji

(RIK) and Kelana Prabu Desa (Ratna Wilis's fiancé) almost crazy with love-sickness, rendering them unable to take their eyes off them; RIK is even so distracted that he plays false notes on his *selukat*, and is coyly criticized for this by Kelana Merta Jiwa. Then Kelana Merta Jiwa gets up again, and flipping "his" sash over his breast like a shoulder-cloth, starts to dance, swaying gently with the buttocks, like the leaves of the *Pandanus*-tree when they are blown by the wind. Then, after having danced for a while, "he" flips the sash back and, covering his mouth with its tip, softly sings a *kidung*, instilling feelings of love in all those who hear it. After that "he" sings a *kakawin* telling the story of (Betara) Kangsa Dewa and then pauses after one episode.

From behind the screen (*kelir*) Misa Kelana Wira Sukma, in fact Raden Carang Tinangluh, RIK's half-brother, now appears, acting as the brother (?) of Betara Kangsa Dewa. Having danced for a while, he stands still in front of Betara Kangsa Dewa, who then gives instructions for his attendants to prepare, because the next day he wishes to go on a hunt in the forest. After Kuda Kerta Negara, really RGCK's maid-servant Ken Bayan, in the role of the Princess of Wengker, has told Betara Dewa Kangsa, she approves of his intention to go hunting, Kelana Panji Kayangan gets up and starts to dance, softly singing a *kidung* called Dewi Derma Dewi. Enters the palace Betara Kangsa Dewa who, after having sat down beside Dewi Derma Dewi, tells her he will leave for the hunt the next day. She orders her two maid-servants to prepare everything for her husband's departure and they disappear behind the screen.

Betara Kangsa Dewa, played by Kelana Merta Jiwa (RGCK), thereupon leads his wife Dewi Derma Dewi to their bedroom, and the two dancers slowly circle the stage while singing coaxing *kidungs* (*kidungan pembujuk*). Remembering "his" fate back in the days when "he" was still in Segara Gunung, Kelana Merta Jiwa is unable to hold back "his" tears as "he" and Kelana Panji Kayangan then sit down again. Now Kuda Kerta Nagara, who plays the role of the Princess of Wengker, Ratna Langoe, appears from behind the *kelir* in female dress. "He" and Kuda Mangku Jaya, who plays her maid-servant Ken Pangejangan, dance while singing a *kidung* about how the Princess of Wengker calls Ken Pangejangan; they then stand still and a dialogue follows in which the Princess of Wengker orders Ken Pangejangan "Steal me the girdle, ceremonial garment and creese of Kangsa Dewa, and place them on Dewi Derma Dewi's cushion, because I am very jealous that she is so much loved by her husband, Betara Kangsa Dewa."[20]

When evening falls and all Gagelang is crazy with love-sickness, the dance-drama reaches the episode in which Ken Pangejangan has planted the false evidence of Dewi Derma Dewi's unfaithfulness on her cushion. Now Kelana Merta Jiwa stands up and leads Kelana Panji Kayangan by the hand, dancing and singing *kidung* and *kakawin* about when Betara Kangsa Dewa came back from the hunt and took his wife on his lap in his bedroom, coaxing her with sweet words. Both the singing Kelana Merta Jiwa and the watching Sira Panji are in tears. Kelana Merta Jiwa dances on until Betara Kangsa Dewa finds the planted objects on Dewi Derma Dewi's cushion. Accusing her without due examination of the facts, he angrily hits her with his horse-whip until she faints and then he runs out of the bedroom with his creese drawn, looking for the culprit, that is, for Kangsa Dewa, who has meanwhile been hidden by the palace-servant Kuda Warsa Danta, a role played by the second maid-servant of Raden Wilis.

With everyone in the audience now in tears, the play then reaches the episode in which Ken Pangejangan is killed by Kuda Warsa Danta. Then it tells how Dewi Derma Dewi enters the forest to practise austerities and how Betara Kangsa Dewa goes mad for love-sickness and is carried up a mountain by his brother. The *gambuh* performance ends when it is fully daylight: having sung a *kidung* about Dewi Derma Dewi's stay in the forest, Kelana Merta Jiwa finally sits down again and bows to the ruler, upon which the audience disperses. But then, so HMTJK tells us, just when Sira Panji suspects that Kelana Merta Jiwa must really be the beloved whom he has been searching for so hard all this time, Kelana Panji Kayangan to his utter despair tells him that "he" has actually found the corpses of some women in the forest, one of which looked exactly like that of Ken Segerba Ningrat. Thus, once again, the lovers fail to be united.

Who is the *gambuh* performance's Betara Kangsa Dewa and to what intertextual background does the name of this character refer us? And why does he appear on stage with Dewi Derma Dewi, a figure who comes from Hikayat Sang Boma? In Mahabharata there is no mention of a Betara Kangsa Dewa, but in Indian Hindu mythology he can be found under the name Kangsa in the Devi Bhagavatam Purana ("Old Books of the Goddess"), which have been dated between the sixth and the fourteenth century of the Christian era. Scholars have suggested that these late *purana*, that have been ascribed to the same author as the one to whom the composition of Mahabharata is traditionally attributed, namely Vyasa, were probably written in Bengal.[21]

In the text of those Purana, Part I, Fourth Book, Chapter XIX, entitled "On Chanting Hymns to the Devi", we find a passage which goes: "O Mother! Kamsa, Bhauma, [...] and other vicious kings respectively are dwelling on earth. Dost Thou better kill them and relieve the burden of the Earth."[22] As we learn from Zoetmulder, there is in fact also a number of *kakawin* about Krishna's great deeds in his youth, in which we find mention of an evil demon, called *Kangsa*. Thus Mpu Panuluh's Kakawin Hariwangsa (middle of the twelfth century) opens by telling that Wishnu has incarnated himself in Krishna for the protection of the world and the extirpation of the evil demonic beings (Bhoma, Kangsa, Kalayawana), who harass the gods and can be killed only by a human adversary (Zoetmulder 1974, pp. 250, 273).

The Puranic legend, Krishnawijaya ("Krishna's Victory") or Kalayawanantaka ("The Death of Kalayawana") first narrates the same story of Krishna's fight with the demon Kalayawana, which also forms the introduction to Kakawin Krishnayana, and then continues with the story of Subhadra's elopement with Arjuna. It begins: Wishnu descends to earth as Krishna and the god Basuki as his brother Baladewa, in order to annihilate the demons. Kangsa and Kalakanja have already been killed. The demon Kalayawana, infuriated by the death of Kangsa, conceives of a plan to destroy Dwarawati and kill Krishna and Baladewa. Ultimately the demon is killed by Krishna (Zoetmulder 1974, pp. 387–88).

Kakawin Krishnandaka ("The Death of Krishna"), which is also called Kakawin Kangsa and also treats of Krishna's youth, tells the story of the slaying of the demon Kangsa by Krishna. About this *kakawin,* Zoetmulder remarks that the similarity of its narrative to the stories of Krishna's youth in the *puranas* is unmistakable, but that there are too many deviations to enable us to assume a direct relation with them. With regard to the time of its origin he reports that he was told by one informant in Bali that it was considered very late, going no further back than the nineteenth century, but was unable to verify this statement. Its narrative may be summarized as follows: In the country of Madhura, King Basudewa reigns over the Yadus, Wrsnis and Andhakas. His brother Kangsa is of partly demonic origin through his mother Pragmini, a descendant of the demon king Lawana. Kangsa terrorizes the Yadus and Krishna puts an end to him by killing him by his disc (Zoetmulder 1974, pp. 392–94).

However, a likelier source than the Old- or Not-so-Old Javanese *kakawin* from which the author of HMTJK may have derived the figure of Betara Kangsa Dewa is in my opinion the *wayang*. According to Hardjowirogo (1982, pp. 153–55) and Irvine (2005, pp. 230–31) in the *wayang* there is a character called Raden Kangsa who is the bastard son of the ogre king Gorawangsa, born as the fruit of Gorawangsa's seduction of Dewi Maerah, wife of king Basudewa of Mandura. As a young man he returned to seek the throne of Mandura. He sacked the kingdom seeking for the three children of Basudewa (Kakrasena, later called Baladewa; Narayana, later Krishna; Dewi Rara Ireng) who found refuge from him with Antagopa and his wife Sagupi in their thatched hut.

Helped by Bima and Arjuna, Kakrasena and Narayana finally defeat the ogre in a great battle, in which he is killed by Krishna's deadly disk and Baladewa's ploughshare. A different story of Kangsa's death — although obviously not unrelated with the one reported by Hardjowirogo — is found in a redaction of Hikayat Pandawa Lima contained by Ms. Raffles Malay 2 in the Royal Asiatic Society, London. There we are told how Krishna successfully persuades his young son Prajamena not to fear facing Sangkuni in battle. He does so by telling him how, when hiding from Kangsa as a young child together with Baladewa, he had by accident killed the demon with a stone pestle. To prevent Krishna and Baladewa from risking their lives and being lured out by Kangsa to join in the fighting matches for children he had organized in the marketplace, their adoptive parents had tied a heavy stone pestle to the feet of both (Van der Tuuk 1875, pp. 67–68). Plays about Kangsa can actually be found to have been performed in *wayang* until the present day and they all seem to be concerned with Kangsa's fight to the death with Krishna. Looking for plays about Kangsa I found two handbooks for the performance of Javanese *wayang kulit purwa*, respectively published in 1980 and 1981, mentioning a play called Kangsa Lena ("The Death of Kangsa"). In a publication of 1943 concerning *wayang wong* (*wayang* performed by human actors) a title of a *lakon* is mentioned as Kangsa Menyabung Jago ("Kangsa's Cockfight"), which has a counterpart in a Sundanese *wayang golek* performance (*wayang* performed with wooden puppets) filmed in 1999, and a comic strip book, both referring to the title Kangsa Adu Jago.[23]

The question now arises: is the combination of the two Hindu-Javanese mythical traditions — that about Kangsa and that about Boma — in the *gambuh* play's *pasemon* about Sira Panji's mistreatment of Ken Segerba Ningrat and his subsequent going mad with love-sickness a mere accidental conflation or is there another explanation for it? In my opinion we must see it as intentionally created. By representing Ken Segerba Ningrat (RGCK) as Dewi Derma Dewi and RIK as Betara Kangsa Dewa they are respectively described as the ideal wife, who always loyally follows her husband everywhere, even unto death, and as the ogre of a husband, who is utterly unappreciative of all these qualities of his wife, and who so completely forgets all the rules of civilized, courtly behaviour that he can even physically abuse her.

A *Gambuh*-Performance in Tambak Kencana

Finally, there is one more episode — once again one telling of a theatrical performance — that merits to be discussed for its intertextuality. In that episode we are told how two knights-errant, who have also joined the swelling forces of Sira Panji (RIK) and his allies in Gagelang, namely Misa Kusuma Yuda (Raden Jayeng Kusuma of Singasari) and Misa Merga Asmara (Raden Wira Pati of Manjapahit), disguised in female dress as *gambuh*-dancers, go on a spying mission to the kingdom of Tambak Kencana.

That kingdom has been conjured-up by a giant (*raksasa*), who in reality is RIK's older brother Raden Kerta Buwana, who was put under a curse by the king of Koripan when against his father's wish he left the *negeri* to search for his sister, Raden Ratna Wilis. The giant has created the kingdom in order to be able to guard over the two princesses he has obtained during his perambulations. One of them is RGCK's sister, Raden Nawang Kusuma of Daha, Raden Carang Tinangluh of Koripan's fiancée, whom the *raksasa* has abducted on Betara Kala's instruction, so that Raden Kembar Dahang of Temasik will not marry her, because it is not his *karma* to do so.

The other is Raden Puspa Juwita of Manjapahit, who is the fiancée of Raden Jayeng Kusuma of Singasari. When RGCK, disguised as the fierce warrior Misa Jejuluk Sira Panji Maring Daha, conquers Tambak Kencana, she kills the giant and, as Betara Kala has predicted to Raden Kerta Buwana of Koripan when giving him the ring, by being killed by RGCK he returns to his human shape. The new rulers of Tambak Kencana, Prabu Anom (RGCK) and Pangeran Tambak Kencana (Raden Ratna Wilis of Koripan), thus not only are reunited with a relative/brother, but also acquire the two princesses the giant has abducted, and even make them their wives.

In the episode about the *gambuh*-performance in Tambak Kencana we are told that the two spies sent by Sira Panji (RIK), namely Misa Kusuma Yuda (Raden Jayeng Kusuma of Singasari, whose betrothed is Raden Puspa Juwita), and Misa Merga Asmara (Raden Wira Pati of Manjapahit), on arrival in Tambak Kencana change their names into respectively Ken Lara Danta and Ken Lara Gading. Everyone who beholds the pair in their pretty dresses is struck by their beauty which equals that of their own ruler, Prabu Anom. When invited to perform there, they arrive at the royal palace, the dancers themselves have quite different feelings on beholding Prabu Anom and Pangeran Tambak Kencana with their wives, the two abducted princesses, and think "What a pity that you (that is, the two princesses) have such destitute people as husbands. What can one do about it; it is the will of the highest deity."[24]

The drama the two disguised princes perform is then described in HMTJK as follows. After an introductory piece by the *gamelan* has been played by their assistants (*panjak*) the two dancers stand up, flip their sashes over their shoulders, and dance, while singing a *kidung* called Lara Tangis. Prabu Anom and Pangeran Tambak Kencana are deeply moved hearing their voices that somehow sound familiar. The two dancers then dance the story of how Carang Kembar Kusuma has lost his sister,[25] and the audience watches in tears as it sees Carang Kembar Kusuma, danced by Lara Danta, weep all the way through the forest, as he is searching for his sister.

Then follows the story of how Carang Kembar Kusuma enters the kingdom of Ceribon in disguise and how, when he presents himself in audience before its king, he sees that his sister has already become the First Queen of Ceribon.[26] When Gambuh Lara Danta sits down and makes a deep bow to Prabu Anom, Lara Gading takes over from "her". "She" flips "her" sash over the shoulder and sings the Kidung Smaradana. Continuing the dance, Lara Gading then, as HMTJK tells us, comes to "the episode in which Cara Kembar Kusuma asks Lord King Brahma for help, who then calls together all the recluses, ordering them to come down the mountain to go help Carang Kembar Kusuma."

The *hikayat* then continues: "And all the retainers of the two princes (that is, of the two *gambuh*-dancers, GK), then stood up, dressed in the manner of mountain-folk. Looking as if they were real recluses, they accompanied Carang Kembar Kusuma, who wanted to go to war with the king of Ceribon."[27] Thereupon, so HMTJK tells, both *gambuh*-dancers danced, accompanied by their retainers, who were all dressed as recluses. As Prabu Anom, Pangeran Tambak Kencana and the rest of the audience watched the dance, they roared with laughter, and the *gamelan* started to play louder and louder. Finally the dancers reached the episode in which Carang Kembar Kusuma arrived with his troops in Cirebon and then, when evening fell, the performance came to an end.[28]

Obviously, we have here another case of *pasemon*. But how can one solve the riddle it poses to its audience? One clue for its solution is provided by the name of the play's protagonist, who has lost his sister and goes in quest of her, namely Carang Kembar Kusuma. This name has been made up from two names that must be quite familiar to Prabu Anom (RGCK) and his court. One is that of Raden Carang Tinangluh of Koripan, whose fiancée, Raden Nawang Kusuma of Daha, has by Prabu Anom been made "his" wife. The other is that of Raden

Kembar Dahang of Temasik, who previously, before losing her in his turn to the *raksasa* (the cursed Raden Kerta Negara of Koripan), had abducted Raden Nawang Kusuma from Daha to take revenge for the humiliation inflicted on him by Dalang Sungging Anom (Raden Gunung Sari of Daha) who had seduced and stolen his wife, Raden Puspa Danta of Lasem.

A clue is thus given to the audience that the dance-drama's story — which is about a brother who searches for his sister, in disguise spies out the situation at the court of Ceribon, finds her there having been made the wife of that kingdom's ruler, and then, together with his allies, the recluses, goes to war with that king — has something to do with Prabu Anom's wife, Raden Nawang Kusuma. However, the problem then remains that Raden Carang Tinangluh is not her brother but her *fiancé*: the brother who searches for her is Raden Gunung Sari. Now it is not unusual for a riddle on the one hand to drop a helpful clue, yet on the other to put some obstacle in the way of its solution. It seems that the story speaks of the search by a brother for his sister in order to create just such an obstacle. Nevertheless, what is unmistakably suggested is: Prabu Anom (RGCK) threatens to get away with committing a highly improper act, namely that of making the *fiancée* of Raden Carang Tinangluh of Koripan "his" wife.

That, in fact, the reference to a brother who is searching for his sister can be seen as simultaneously posing an obstacle and giving a valid clue for solution, becomes clear if we look at the real identities of the two *gambuh*-dancers. One (Lara Danta) is in reality Raden Jayeng Kusuma of Singasari who is engaged to Raden Puspa Juwita of Manjapahit, who has been made "his" wife by Pangeran Tambak Kencana (Raden Ratna Wilis of Koripan). The other (Lara Gading) is Raden Puspa Juwita's brother, Raden Wira Pati of Manjapahit. What we then have is a story about rescuing one's sister/fiancée from an improper marriage with a ruler of a kingdom called Ceribon. Why that ruler is called king of Ceribon and not of some other kingdom remains unclear, but what is now obvious is that the lakon's *pasemon* criticizes Prabu Anom and Pangeran Tambak Kencana for improperly making the fiancée/sister of certain princes allied with Sira Panji their wives.

We can only understand this criticism's full implications once we perceive with which intertext HMTJK in fact invites us to connect the story of Raden Carang Kembar Kusuma enacted by the two dancers. The clue that leads us to this intertext has been smuggled in quite surreptitiously, at the beginning of the episode about the spying mission. It consists of the mention of the epic Ramayana in the description of the female dress which the two warriors put on to disguise themselves on arrival in Tambak Kencana as *gambuh*-dancers. In this reference — the one and only explicit mention made of Ramayana in the entire *hikayat* — we are told that they both "wore a long skirt of *geringsing*-cloth on which a story from Ramayana had been depicted in gold".[29]

Unfortunately we are not told which episode of that long epic has been depicted on their dresses, but a useful hint seems to be given by HMTJK where it tells how the *panjak* of the *gambuh*-troupe all dress up as the recluses who at the request of Carang Kembar Kusuma have been ordered by Lord Berma Raja (*Sang Berma Raja*) to help him in his war waged against the king of Ceribon in order to free the unnamed princess from her marriage with him. Representing a scene that is similar to a *budhalan* (army-on-the-march scene) in the *wayang kulit purwa* (Brandon 1993, p. 22), these *panjak* perform a quaint dance of recluses-turned-warriors, which is accompanied by ever louder and faster *gamelan* music, and by the roaring laughter of the public which their antics provoke.

Perhaps the intertextual foil against which the story of Carang Kembar Kusuma is meant to be understood is the famous episode towards the close of Valmiki's Ramayana — which is also found with fairly close similarity in Hikayat Seri Rama[30] as well as in the *wayang kulit purwa* plays at the close of the Rama-cycle (Braginsky 2004, p. 67; Irvine 2005, pp. 45–47) — about the abduction of Rama's wife Sita Dewi by Rawana.[31] In that episode we are told how Rawana spirits Sita Dewi away to the island of Langka, where he installs her in his palace and assiduously courts her, hoping she will surrender to him body and soul. Rama enlists the support of the Monkey King, Sugriwa, and of his lieutenant, the white monkey Hanuman, who on a spying mission locates Sita Dewi's whereabouts. Sugriwa's monkey-army then builds a causeway across the waters to Langka and after a long battle Rama finally kills Rawana and regains his wife.

If we read the episode about the dance-drama in Tambak Kencana against the foil of the story of the abduction of Sita, we can regard the play that is performed as a not very precise allegory, since only one of the two *gambuh*-dancers is there to regain his bride. It seems that HMTJK, in order to somewhat disguise its intertextual relation with Ramayana, has replaced the army of monkey-helpers by a hilarious army of recluses-turned-warriors. But even then a problem still remains: the Berma Raja mentioned in Hikayat Seri Rama — the most likely source used for this episode in HMTJK — is Rawana's grandfather and can therefore not figure as his enemy. Assuming we may indeed read the story of the dance-drama in Tambak Kencana against Hikayat Seri Rama's episode about the abduction of Sita, we may conclude that by enacting their *lakon* the *gambuh*-dancers are condemning the behaviour of Prabu Anom, and by implication also that of Pangeran Tambak Kencana, as that of an evil demon.[32]

Fictionality and Creative Amplification

Above I have indicated the intertextual presence of elements from Mahabharata and Ramayana in HMTJK, suggesting that their most probable sources are New Javanese and Malay adaptations of episodes of these epics, the creation of which was more or less contemporary with the *hikayat's* probable date of composition, rather than the Old-Javanese adaptations in the form of *kakawin*. We have also seen how the episodes examined in HMTJK quite creatively — one might also say, eclectically — combine elements taken from unrelated intertexts and how they thus create additional layers of meaning within the *hikayat*.

In the episode of the *gambuh*-performance in Tambak Kencana this eclectic use of sources can also be seen by the fact that not all its intertextual connections are concerned with Hikayat Seri Rama. In fact, as is the case in the story of the dance-drama about Betara Kangsa Dewa and Dewi Januwati, so here, too, are we reminded of the prominent role played by Hikayat Sang Boma as an intertext in the composition of HMTJK. As Hikayat Sang Boma tells us about the three heavenly nymphs Samba meets in the enchanted garden, one of whom, Tunjung Sari, will later become his wife, "the oldest one was called, Tunjung Maya, the middle one Tunjung Biru and the youngest Tunjung Sari."[33]

Surprisingly, in HMTJK's episode about the *gambuh*-performance in Tambak Kencana the name Tunjung Sari is used as that of a hall where heavenly nymphs reside (Abdul Rahman Kaeh 1976, p. 385). Even more curious is the mention at the very start of HMTJK's narrative of the name of another of these nymphs, Tunjung Maya, as that of a hall where the gods are meeting. The mention of this name here, as well as that of Tunjung Sari later, seem to function as a marker warning the reader or listener that he or she is dealing with a work of fiction.

Another way in which HMTJK emphatically foregrounds its own fictionality is by creating "mirror-texts". This device is not just found in modernist literature — e.g. in André Gide's novel *The Counterfeiters of 1925*, in which a character is engaged in writing a novel similar to the novel in which he appears — but also in older literatures, and is used because it opens up possibilities for reflexivity and self-reference. We have a case of a mirror-text when the primary story and the embedded one can be paraphrased in such a manner that both paraphrases have one or more elements in common, so that the subtext functions as a sign of the primary text (Hawthorn 1992, pp. 149–50). The plays we have seen performed in the three episodes discussed above by some of the protagonists of HMTJK are examples of such mirror-texts.[34]

As Braginsky has pointed out, "motifs of a theatrical show and, to a lesser degree, of performance in general play an extremely important role in Panji romances." Not only do "the heroes often appear before the reader as puppeteers or directors and performers of dance dramas or narrators of classical poems (*kakawin* and *kidung*)", but also, so Braginsky observes, "[...] the world is presented as a *sui generis* theatre in these romances, with deities — primarily Batara Kala — as directors. Joys and misfortunes that befall its heroes are motivated constantly by Batara Kala's being anxious about 'the continuation of the play' or 'avoidance of an interruption in the *dalang's* performance" (Braginsky 2004, p. 161).

In HMTJK, too, Betara Kala expresses this anxiety when he decides to abduct RGCK from Daha to the forest of Segara Gunung, among others thinking to himself: "Let me separate all of them (i.e. RIK, RGCK, and the other couples of engaged princes and princesses) so that the performance may long continue."[35] And indeed, throughout HMTJK we see Betara Kala as well as some other gods intervene in the events, in order to direct the efforts of the protagonists. No doubt, this strong streak of the theatrical in the Panji romance has much to do with the close proximity of the *wayang*. This proximity also manifests itself in the fact that the narrator of Panji romances by convention must in his prologues and comments appear in the role of a *dalang*.

Another effect of these divine interventions is to draw attention to the story's fictionality. Instead of an unchanged repetition of traditional myth and sacred truth the narrative in the Panji romance is thus shown to be merely an uncontrolled and unauthorized creation by a self-willed, playful author who lurks behind the mask of the intervening gods and directs the fate of the characters in his story.

Muhammad Bakir, owner of a manuscript lending library in Batavia at the end of the nineteenth century and author of many *wayang* stories, in his parody on romance, Syair Buah-Buahan, jocularly expresses this notion of the fictionalizing writer, when he indicates that the unlikely events in his story happen "because the writer wants to spin out his story" and "by the will of the person who writes it".[36] In HMTJK the writer avails himself of the gods and makes them interfere in his story all the time in order to spin it out as much as he can.

As HMTJK demonstrates, it is the art of creative, imaginative amplification — called *memanjangkan* in Malay poetics (Koster 1997, pp. 84–85) — that produces a Panji romance. As we have seen, the intertextual appeal made by HMTJK to adaptations of Mahabharata, and Ramayana, while it creates *pasemon* commenting on episodes, events and characters in its own narrative,[37] forms an important part of its amplification.

An outspoken statement of the principle of *memanjangkan* is found in the prologue of the Panji romance Hikayat Cekel Wanengpati ("The Story of Valiant Knight Bachelor"), which goes: "Verily this is a story about people in the days of yore, rendered from Javanese into Malay (?), which is told by a puppeteer and sage, who is an expert in composing poetry in the land of Java. It was rendered into Malay and, in order to become a soother of the feelings of yearning, it was made into a play. But how can sadness disappear? Feelings of yearning, too, cannot be spoken. Yet this the puppeteer speaks about in order to extinguish his feelings of passionate love. And the puppeteer spins out this play in order that the *tembang*, *kidung* and *kakawin* of all those who are wise and discreet will be continued by making known the passion in his heart."[38]

In HMTJK the work's fictionality is perhaps most poignantly expressed when the two *gambuh*-dancers, asked on arrival in Tambak Kencana from where they have come, answer: "We have come from the village of stories."[39] But why, so we may ask, is it for HMTJK so important to foreground its own fictionality? As Robson has made clear, we should not underestimate the enormous authority the Panji romance as a great myth of kingship and an embodiment of superior Javanese courtly culture enjoyed, not only on Java, but also among the Malays. Thus in the chronicle Hikayat Banjar the title Panji and the place names of Daha and Koripan are used as a way to establish a claim to the throne. And the chronicle Sejarah Melayu (Raffles MS. 18) tells us how Sultan Mansur Syah of Malacca went on a state-visit to Majapahit with Hang Tuah and other retainers, to ask for the hand of the Batara's daughter, Raden Galuh Candra Kirana (Robson 1992, p. 38).

For many Malays, however, every genre of literature in which the Hindu-Javanese gods played an important role — the *wayang kulit purwa*, the Panji romance and other types of romance — also posed considerable problems. Thus Nuruddin al-Raniri's Serat al-Mustakim ("Straight Bridge to Heaven", composed 1644), a book on religious law (*fikh*) and the observance of religious obligations (*ibadat*), condemns Hikayat Indraputra and Hikayat Seri Rama as "filth" (*najis*) and a swerving away from Origin, like the Torah and the Gospels.

By the more strict Muslims to attend a *wayang* performance — and also to read romance — was considered to be reciting from the wrong book, namely the Book of the Devil (*mengaji dari Kitab Syaitan*);

TABLE 5.1
The Identity Changes of HMTJK's Two Main Protagonists

RIK	RGCK
(Dewa Kama)	(Dewi Segerba)
Raden Inu Kertapati	Raden Galuh Candra Kirana
Ajar Ragapati	Ken Segerba Ningrat
Misa Jayeng Kusuma Sira Panji Jayeng Seteru	Endang Kusuma Jiwa
Misa Edan Sira Panji Jayeng Kusuma	Misa Jejuluk Sira Panji Maring Daha
	Kelana Merta Jiwa Sira Panji Maring Daha
Raden Inu Kertapati	Raden Galuh Candra Kirana Daha

to them it meant to surrender oneself to a world of mere semblance and sinful seduction, a turning to a pseudo-origin, to a cosmic order that had been toppled by the revelations of the Prophet (Koster 1997, pp. 8–9, 235–39). It seems that the HMTJK's foregrounding of its own fictionality,[40] like its opening with the invocation "In the name of God, the Merciful and the Compassionate", was among others intended to help its Muslim readers not to stray too far from the right path and to protect the *hikayat*'s writer against possible criticism for indulging in heathen pleasures.

NOTES

1. "Sebermula, maka tersebutlah perkataan segala dewa-dewa duduk di Balai Tunjung Maya, berbicara hendak menyuruhkan Betara Naya Indera laki isteri turun menjelma ke mayapada. Selama-lama raja Pandawa kembali ke kayangan, maka sunyilah mayapada ini. Akan negeri Pandawa itu pun hampir akan jadi hutanlah. Maka segala dewa-dewa itu pun sukalah. Semuanya membenarkan bicara Betara Kala itu" (Abdul Rahman Kaeh 1976, p. 1).

2. I use the edition by Abdul Rahman Kaeh (1976) of manuscript MS 35 in the collection of Perpustakaan Negara Malaysia. According to him MS 35 was probably composed or copied between 1860 and 1870 (Abdul Rahman Kaeh 1976, pp. ix–x). According to Abdul Rahman Kaeh (1977, pp. 23–24) the owners, copyists, and main connoisseurs of Panji romances were often noble ladies from the palace-milieu or came directly from the sultan's family. There is evidence in HMTJK linking the *hikayat* to Indonesia: the king of Koripan has a letter type-written by a clerk, who is referred to as a *barit ketik* (Abdul Rahman Kaeh 1976, p. 25). *Barit* means "messenger, office-clerk". *Ketik* is a loan-word derived from the Dutch verb *tikken* ("to typewrite"). The typewriter was invented in the 1860s and began to be commercially produced on a still modest scale by the mid-1870s. Available at <http://en.wikipedia.org/wiki/Typewriter> (accessed 23 December 2013).
3. In the words used for this in HMTJK respectively: *Wong kidul alasan, ajar, endang, kelana, misa, dalang, gambuh.*
4. About the close resemblance between the Panji tale as a variety of the love-and-adventure genre and the romances of Greek antiquity see Braginsky (2004), pp. 162–63.
5. "Maka Betara Guru pun memberikan gadanya iaitu akan jadi seperti kuwung, ribut dan teja tetekala ketemu musuh. Dan Betara Kala pun memberikan sabuknya akan jadi tunggul wulung ciri wenangraya putih. Dan Betara Indera pun memberikan sebilah panah bernama Pasupati dan Betara Visnu pun memberikan kerisnya Kalamisani kepada Betara Naya Indera" (Abdul Rahman Kaeh 1976, pp. 1–2).
6. About *tunggul wulung* also see Poerbatjaraka (1940), pp. 339–40. See Poerbatjaraka (1940, pp. 165, 211) for the words *Tunggul Wulung* used as the name of a brother of Panji (RIK).
7. That this is really in the manuscript's text also appears from other passages in HMTJK, where Durga, who in the *wayang kulit* normally figures as Bathari Durga, the vicious and evil wife of Betara Kala (Hardjowirogo 1982, p. 43; Irvine 2005, pp. 208–9), is clearly regarded as a male god.
8. '"Kalaukan panjang perkataan dalang'" (Teeuw 1966, pp. 6.151c–d); '"supaya panjang lelakon kemudian'" (Teeuw 1966, p. 9.3d). For more details about the spread in Panji romances of the motif of being born through incarnation into a flower or an areca-nut, which upon being eaten leads to pregnancy, see Harun Mat Piah (1980), pp. 62–64.
9. Only after presenting this chapter in Singapore I learned that Stuart Robson had already published a finely-wrought essay about this episode (Robson 2006), the findings of which seem quite compatible with my analysis.
10. "Tiada patut dalang, layak diadap di peseban agung, mungkin ia ini dewa-dewa yang menyamar" (Abdul Rahman Kaeh 1976, p. 157).

11. "Janganlah takut akan beta, bermainlah!" (Abdul Rahman Kaeh 1976, p. 160).
12. "[L]elakon Maharaja Boma dengan Sang Sambu [sic]" (Abdul Rahman Kaeh 1976, p. 160).
13. The word apparently used for describing the singing is *tembang*. About the practice of the sung performance of works of Javanese literature, see Arps [s.a.]. About *kidung*, see Zoetmulder (1974), pp. 121 –25, 143–51, 407–38.
14. "Di mana pula yayi tahu membujuk tuanku, pun bini tuanku, tuankulah yang membujuknya" (Abdul Rahman Kaeh 1976, p. 162).
15. For Kakawin Bhomantaka and a discussion of its relationship to Indian literature, see Zoetmulder (1974), pp. 313–24. See also the introduction in Teeuw and Robson (2005).
16. For an edition of Hikayat Sang Boma, see Sang Boma (1953).
17. For detailed information about *gambuh* performances, see Vickers (2005).
18. Sang Pelinggih must probably be read as Sang Pelangi Lord Rainbow. In Hikayat Panji Kuda Semirang a recluse of that name, who dwells on Mount Sela Warna and helps RIK to be reunited with RGCK, see Lukman Ali and M.S. Hutagalung (1996), pp. 120–22, 277.
19. "'Lelakon Betara Kangsa Edan'" (Abdul Rahman Kaeh 1976, p. 315).
20. "Curikan aku sabuk dan kampuh dan keris Kangsa Dewa itu, taruhkan di atas bantal Dewi Derma Dewi itu kerana sangat sakit hatiku akan ia sangat dikasihi oleh lakinya Betara Kangsa Dewa itu" (Abdul Rahman Kaeh 1976, p. 317).
21. See <http://en.wikipedia.org/wiki/Devi-Bhagavata_Purana> (accessed 30 January 2014).
22. See <http://www.sacred-texts.com/hin/db/bk04ch19.htm>, which quotes from Shrimad Devi Bhagavatam. Transl. Swami Vijnanananda (Hari Prasanna Chatterji), 1921, Part I, p. 319, line 16 (accessed 30 January 2014).
23. See the titles listed for the search term "kangsa" in the catalogue of the Leiden University Library, on the site <www.library.universiteitleiden.nl> (accessed 30 March 2017).
24. "Sayangnya tuan bersuamikan orang papa! Sudahlah dengan kehendak Sanghyang Sukma" (Abdul Rahman Kaeh 1976, p. 386).
25. "[L]elakon Carang Kembar Kusuma kehilangan saudaranya" (Abdul Rahman Kaeh 1976, p. 387).
26. "[C]eritanya Carang Kembar Kusuma masuk ke negeri Ceribon menyamar mengadap ratu Ceribon. Maka dilihatnya saudaranya sudah jadi permaisuri Ratu Ceribon" (Abdul Rahman Kaeh 1976, p. 387).
27. "Lelakon Carang Kembar Kusuma Minta tolong kepada Sang Berma Raja. Maka Sang Berma Raja pun mengerahkan segala ajar-ajar turun dari gunung pergi membantu Carang Kembar Kusuma. Maka segala kedayan itu pun berdirilah masing-masing memakai cara wong gunung, seperti ajar-ajar sungguh, pergi mengiringkan Carang Kembar Kusuma hendak perang dengan Ratu Ceribon itu" (Abdul Rahman Kaeh 1976, p. 388).

28. "Lelakon Carang Kembar Kusuma sampai di negeri Ceribon" (Abdul Rahman Kaeh 1976, p. 388).
29. "[M]emakai tapih geringsing lelakon Ramayana semburna kencana" (Abdul Rahman Kaeh 1976, p. 381).
30. For an edition of Hikayat Seri Rama, see Ikram (1980).
31. There is also the early tenth century Kakawin Ramayana, the oldest great work of poetry preserved in Javanese literature. For a summary and discussion of its date and authorship, see Zoetmulder (1974), pp. 217–33.
32. As one of the reviewers of this chapter has rightly pointed out, in the *lakon* enacted at Tambak Kencana other connections with Ramayana may also be seen, such as the prince and princess wandering through the forest, or RGCK like Sita remaining loyal to her husband in all her manifestations.
33. "[Y]ang tua namanya Tunjung Maya, yang tengah Tunjung Biru dan yang bungsunya namanya Tunjung Sari" (Sang Boma 1953, p. 84).
34. About the function fulfilled by theatrical interludes in Panji romances, also see Braginsky (2004), pp. 161–62.
35. "Biarlah aku pisahkan mereka semua supaya berpanjangan lelakon ini selanjutnya" (Abdul Rahman Kaeh 1976, pp. 78–82).
36. "Sebab pengarang mau panjangkan; Dengan takdir orang yang mengarang" (Koster 1997, pp. 10, 248–49).
37. It must be noted that the *pasemon* I have discussed in this chapter are created by characters in the *hikayat's* narrative, who are themselves of course manipulated by the writer and that they comment only on events or persons in the narrative. Since we have almost no information about the concrete historical context(s) in which HMTJK has been performed and functioned there is no saying whether the *hikayat* also contains *pasemon* to extra-textual realities.
38. "Bahawa ini cerita orang dahulu kala daripada bahasa Melayu dan Jawa (?), diceriterakan oleh dalang dan bujangga yang paramakawi di tanah Jawa. Dipindahkan dengan bahasa Melayu, maka akan menjadi penghibur rasa yang dendam dilelakonkan. Dalam itu pun masygul dimana kan hilang? Dendam pun tiada terbilang. Akan perinya juga pun dalang katakan akan pemadam hati yang birahi. Maka dalang panjangkan lelakon ini supaya menjadi lanjut tembang dan kidung dan kekawin segala yang arif bijaksana daripada menyatakan asyikin dalam kalbu" (Winstedt 1977, p. 55). The above prologue is spoken by what may be called a "paper-*dalang*" and not by a real one of flesh and blood. For a fascinating description of how a real *dalang* — in this case a Malay puppeteer performing a *lakon* of the *Wayang Siam* — does his *memanjangkan*, see the chapter "Tree Hours from Three Minutes" in Sweeney (1980), pp. 41–53.
39. "Beta sekalian datang dari dusun cerita" (Abdul Rahman Kaeh 1976, p. 383).
40. For the problematic place of fiction and fictionality in traditional Malay literature, see Koster (1997), pp. 4–5, 9–10, 55, 63–64, 86–93, 243–51.

REFERENCES

Abdul Rahman Kaeh. *Hikayat Misa Taman Jayeng Kusuma: Sebuah cerita Panji Melayu*. Kualu Lumpur: Dewan Bahasa dan Pustaka, 1976.

———. *Hikayat Misa Taman Jayeng Kusuma: Sebuah kajian kritis*. Kualu Lumpur: Utusan Publications, 1977.

———. *Panji Narawangsa*. Kuala Lumpur: Dewan Bahasa dan Pustaka, 1989.

Arps, Bernard. "Tembang in Two Traditions: Performance and Interpretation of Javanese Literature". [S.l.: s.n.] Ph.D. thesis. Leiden, [s.a.].

Braginsky, V.I. *The Heritage of Traditional Malay Literature: A Historical Survey of Genres, Writings and Literary Views*. Leiden: KITLV Press, 2004. VKI 214.

Brandon, James R. *On Thrones of Gold: Three Javanese Shadow Plays*. Honolulu, Hawaii: University of Hawaii Press, 1993. Reprint.

Hardjowirogo. *Sejarah wayang purwa*. Jakarta: Balai Pustaka, 1982. Sixth edition. BP 1698.

Harun Mat Piah. *Cerita-cerita Panji Melayu*. Kuala Lumpur: Dewan Bahasa dan Pustaka, 1980.

Hawthorn, Jeremy. *A Glossary of Contemporary Literary Theory*. London: Edward Arnold, 1992.

Ikram, Achadiati. *Hikayat Seri Rama: Suntingan naskah disertai telaah amanat dan struktur*. Jakarta: Penerbit Universitas Indonesia, 1980.

Irvine, David. *Leather Gods & Wooden Heroes: Java's Classical Wayang*. Singapore: Marshall Cavendish Times Editions, 2005.

Koster, G.L. *Roaming through Seductive Gardens: Readings in Malay Narrative*. Leiden: KITLV Press, 1997. VKI 167.

Lukman Ali and M.S. Hutagalung, eds. *Hikayat Panji Kuda Semirang*. Jakarta: Pusat Pembinaan dan Pengembangan Bahasa Departemen Pendidikan dan Kebudayaan, 1966.

Poerbatjaraka. *Pandji-verhalen onderling vergeleken*. Bandung: A.C. Nix & Co., 1940.

Ras, J.J. "The Historical Development of the Javanese Shadow Theatre". *Review of Indonesian and Malaysian Affairs* 10.2 (1976*a*): 50–76.

———. *De schending van Soebadra: Javaans schimmenspel*. Amsterdam: Meulenhoff, 1976*b*. Oosterse Bibliotheek.

Robson, S.O. "Java in Malay Literature: Overbeck's Ideas on Malayo-Javanese Literature". In *Looking in Odd Mirrors: The Java Sea*, edited by V.J.H. Houben, H.M.J. Maier and W. van der Molen. Leiden: Vakgroep Talen en Culturen van Zuidoost-Azie en Oceanië. Semaian 5, 1992, pp. 27–42.

———. "The Play's the Thing". In *Milde regen: Liber amicorum voor Hans Teeuw*, edited by Willem van der Molen. Nijmegen: Wolf Legal Publishers, 2006, pp. 209–17.

Sang Boma. *Hikayat Sang Boma*. Djakarta: Balai Pustaka, 1953. Second edition. BP 279.

Sweeney, Amin. *Authors and Audiences in Traditional Malay Literature.* Berkeley: University of California Center for South and Southeast Asian Studies, 1980.

Teeuw, A. *Shair Ken Tambuhan.* Kuala Lumpur: Oxford University Press/University of Malaya Press, 1966.

Teeuw, A. and S.O Robson, eds. *Bhomāntaka: The Death of Bhoma.* Leiden: KITLV Press, 2005. Bibliotheca Indonesica 32.

Tuuk, H.N. van der. "Geschiedenis der Pandawa's naar een Maleisch handschrift der Royal Asiatic Society No. 2 in Fol". *Tijdschrift voor Indische Taal-, Land-, en Volkenkunde* 21 (1875): 1–90.

Vickers, Adrian. *Journeys of Desire: A Study of the Balinese Text Malat*. Leiden: KITLV Press, 2005. VKI 217.

Winstedt, R.O. *A History of Classical Malay Literature*. Kuala Lumpur: Oxford University Press, 1977. 2nd impression.

Zoetmulder, P.J. *Kalangwan: A Survey of Old Javanese Literature.* 's-Gravenhage: Nijhoff, 1974. KITLV Translation Series 16.

6

THE DEATH OF ŚALYA
Balinese Textual and Iconographic Representations of the Kakawin Bhāratayuddha

Helen Creese

IN MEMORIAM
Supomo Suryohudoyo (12-8-1931 – 8-7-2016)

The twelfth-century Kakawin Bhāratayuddha ("The War of the Bhāratas") is unique in Old Javanese kakawin literature because it was the work of two authors, Mpu Sĕḍah and Mpu Panuluh. Mpu Panuluh began his contribution to the poem from Canto 32, at the point in the narrative when Śalya becomes commander-in-chief of the Kaurawa forces. To this part of the text — a poem in its own right within the larger work — the poet gave the name Śalyawadha, "The Death of Śalya". Mpu Panuluh's section of the kakawin is marked by a number of major diversions from the Sanskrit narrative of the Mahābhārata, including the animosity between Śalya and Aśwatthāmā and the introduction of the figure of Śalya's wife, Satyawatī, who later performs sati, taking her life on the battlefield in order to follow her beloved husband in death. It is precisely these episodes that dominate later

Balinese reworkings of the Bhāratayuddha narrative in poetry and art. This chapter examines the narrative continuities between Mpu Panuluh's contribution to the twelfth-century Javanese kakawin and later textual and visual representations produced in Bali.

Keywords: Old Javanese literature, Balinese literature, *kakawin*, Balinese art, Bhāratayuddha, Mahābhārata, Śalya, Mpu Panuluh.

Introduction

On 6 September 1157 CE, Mpu Sĕḍah, a poet at the court of King Jayabhaya of Kaḍiri, began to compose the Old Javanese *kakawin*, the Bhāratayuddha, "The War of the Bhāratas". This long narrative poem of 731 stanzas retells the story of the war between the Pāṇḍawas and the Kaurawas described in the "battle" books of the great Sanskrit epic, the Mahābhārata, that is, from the preparations for battle in the Udyogaparvan (Book 5) to the annihilation of the Kaurawa forces and the slaughter of the five sons of the Pāṇḍawa heroes on the night after the battle from the Sauptikaparvan (Book 10). In the introductory tribute to his patron in Canto 1, Mpu Sĕḍah, who composed the first section of the poem, reveals that his retelling of the story of the great war between the Pāṇḍawas and the Kaurawas is presented in homage to another mighty hero, his patron, King Dharmeśwara, or Jayabhaya, who has vanquished all his enemies (Supomo 1993, pp. 7–8). This *kakawin* therefore serves also as an allegorical panegyric to the world-conquering East Javanese monarch who ruled from c. 1135 to 1157 CE.

The Javanese textual antecedents of the central narrative of the Bhāratayuddha can be traced back to the tenth-century Old Javanese *parwa* (Sanskrit *parvan*), the earliest Old Javanese prose renderings of the Mahābhārata. The Bhāratayuddha recounts the Mahābhārata battle narrative in its entirety, although only nine of the Sanskrit epic's total of eighteen books are extant in Old Javanese versions, and only two of the six battle books — Book 5, the Udyogaparwa and Book 6, the Bhīṣmaparwa. The question of whether these "missing" battle books, Books 7–10 — the Droṇaparvan, Karṇaparvan, Śalyaparvan and Sauptikaparvan — were also rendered into Old Javanese prose and served the Bhāratayuddha poets as sources for their composition has never been satisfactorily resolved (Supomo 1972; 1993; Zoetmulder 1974, p. 98). Nevertheless, it seems probable that earlier Old Javanese versions of these sections of the epic must once have existed. The events in the battle depicted in the Bhāratayuddha follow the Sanskrit epic narrative in broad outline and in each episode direct links to the Sanskrit text have been established (Supomo 1993, pp. 14–29). Moreover, the poem's twin poets also show themselves to be familiar with the broader narrative world of the epic tradition and clearly assume the same knowledge on the part of their audience.

The Bhāratayuddha holds a special place in Old Javanese literature, both as an object of Western intellectual inquiry and as a primary source of later artistic inspiration in the literary, performing and visual arts of Java and Bali, a position perhaps rivalled only by the other great Indian epic, the Rāmāyaṇa. Because of its importance in the *kakawin* tradition as the earliest and most wide-ranging Javanese poetic expression of the Mahābhārata, the Bhāratayuddha has attracted considerable scholarly interest ever since it was first brought to the attention of the West in 1817 when Thomas Stamford Raffles published an extract of 138 stanzas from the poem in *The History of Java* (Raffles 1817). The *kakawin* later became the focus of major studies throughout the twentieth century, with the first critical edition of the text appearing in 1903 (Gunning 1903), followed by a Dutch translation in 1934 (Poerbatjaraka and Hooykaas 1934), my own undergraduate thesis (Griffith 1976), and, most recently, Supomo's complete edition and English translation (Supomo 1993). Zoetmulder (1974) also paid close attention to the Bhāratayuddha in his survey of Old Javanese literature.

The number of complete and partial manuscript copies of the Bhāratayuddha belonging to both the Balinese and Javanese manuscript traditions is testament to its popularity down through the centuries (Pigeaud 1967, pp. 178–80; Supomo 1993, pp. 37–46). In addition to the preservation of the *kakawin* as a literary work in its own right, the core Bhāratayuddha narrative lived on in popular culture through the *wayang* shadow puppet theatre. Then, in the eighteenth and nineteenth centuries, it found new life in Java when it was reworked in Javanese *macapat* and *kawi miring* verse forms (Cohen Stuart 1860; Kats 1984;

McDonald 1983; 1986; Supomo 1993, p. 260; 1997). In Bali, where Old Javanese literature and Hindu religious traditions have continued in an unbroken line until the present, the Bhāratayuddha and its legendary epic heroes and their exploits retained a firm grip on the local imagination. It remains one of the most well known and best loved works and for generations has been a rich source of inspiration for myriad forms of Balinese artistic endeavour.

In addition to its narrative impact and intrinsic poetic qualities, the authorship of the Bhāratayuddha is also of singular interest. For reasons forever shrouded in mystery, Mpu Sĕḍah was unable to finish his commission and the task of completing the *kakawin* instead fell to another court poet attached to Jayabhaya's court, named Mpu Panuluh. In the final stanza of the poem, Mpu Panuluh records that he took over from Mpu Sĕḍah at the point in the story where Śalya is elected commander-in-chief of the Kaurawa army (Bhāratayuddha [BY] 52.13; Supomo 1993, p. 256):

> However, I was not alone in composing this story, for there was a pupil of His Majesty, famed throughout the world, the most eminent *mpu* Sĕḍah, who wrote the first part; it is faultless in its poetic qualities. It was from the episode of Śalya becoming commander-in-chief that the task was entrusted to me, this clumsy man who is so lacking in poetic feeling. How regrettable that the sweetness of the court poet's poem should have a bitter coating.

Later Javanese tradition has created a romantic legend around the change in authorship, claiming that King Jayabhaya's queen had served Mpu Sĕḍah as a model for Śalya's devoted wife, Satyawatī, thus arousing his patron's suspicions. However, since Satyawatī appears only in the section of the poem created by Mpu Panuluh, who also speaks in glowing terms of his fellow poet in the epilogue to the *kakawin*, it seems unlikely that Mpu Sĕḍah had somehow fallen from grace, but rather that illness, infirmity or death prevented him from finishing the work. This dual authorship, and specifically Mpu Panuluh's contribution to the *kakawin*, provides the starting point for this chapter in which we turn our attention to the later history of the centuries-long Bhāratayuddha tradition in Bali, through an exploration of the enduring influence of

Mpu Panuluh's particular creative genius on Balinese literature and painting.

Mpu Panuluh — Royal Poet and Teller of Tales

Kakawin literature is largely an anonymous tradition, leaving us with little more than a handful of names of authors of some of the most significant classic works that have survived the journey down through the centuries. Even then, most names are pseudonyms, descriptive epithets rather than personal names. Panuluh, for example, from the root word *suluh* "torch", "light" means "illumination". Nevertheless, we perhaps know more about Mpu Panuluh than any other poet, not only from the Bhāratayuddha but also from what he reveals about himself in his earlier composition, the Hariwangśa, "Hari's Lineage". In these works, Mpu Panuluh reveals something of his journey along the path towards the status of master poet (*mpu*) and of his relationship with his patron, King Jayabhaya. He depicts his patron as the embodiment of the three major elements of power in ancient Java: the divine — as the deity "Wiṣṇu himself", the political — as a victorious ruler, and the aesthetic — as a peerless poet in his own right and a source of poetic inspiration. In the epilogue of the Hariwangśa, Mpu Panuluh recalls how, as an inexperienced young man, he had gone wandering on hill and shore in search of poetic inspiration with rather unhappy consequences (Hariwangśa 54.1–2; Zoetmulder 1974, pp. 163–64):

> Back from my wanderings, I had the boldness to appear in the presence of His Majesty King "Sprouting-beauty" to offer him the story I had composed. A foolish thing to do, for it was devoid of all poetic feeling and had an irregular metre. It immediately aroused his anger, because of his disappointment that his coaching in verse-writing had achieved no results. While his temper expended itself in a vehement dressing down, I was so frightened that I tried to ward it off with my writing board.
>
> And now, in spite of all of this, I come forth with my work, nothing daunted. If I become an object of ridicule, what can I do? If they censure me for brazenness, let them. At least my work may help promote the invincibility of the king and the prosperity of the world. It is my hope that those who will deign in their condescension to occupy themselves with it, either by reciting or listening to it, may find it of some profit.

Mpu Panuluh concludes the poem (Hariwangśa 54.3) by expressing the hope that his poem telling of Krĕṣṇa's heroic deeds will enhance the splendour of the temple of his poet-king "who is praised for erecting book-monuments". He appears to have succeeded. By the time Jayabhaya sought a poet to continue Mpu Sĕḍah's Bhāratayuddha, Mpu Panuluh had clearly grown sufficiently in stature and confidence to be deemed worthy of this important commission by the king.

Although Old Javanese poets drew strongly on Sanskrit mythology, heroes and poetics in their poems, these cultural and intertextual links did not preclude them from innovative reworking and re-inscription of the epic narrative. The Bhāratayuddha is no exception. Clear though its genealogical ties to the Mahābhārata are, there are also some striking differences, particularly in Mpu Panuluh's rendering of the tale. Indeed, when he took over from Mpu Sĕḍah, Mpu Panuluh did not merely continue the narrative that his fellow poet had begun. With the change of authorship came a change in style and thematic treatment and, perhaps more importantly, an attempt to compose an original and creative work — in fact a separate poem. As Zoetmulder (1974, p. 282) remarks: "Cantos 32 to 45 are as it were a poem in themselves, worked out independently from the epic, for which the name Śalyawadha ('The death of Śalya') would be highly appropriate." This is, in fact, precisely the task that Mpu Panuluh's patron, King Jayabhaya, had commissioned (BY 52.10; Supomo 1993, p. 256):

> But now as if putting me through an ordeal that threw me into utter confusion, he summoned me, and insisted that I should be in charge of composing a tale of yore, narrating his victory in battle, at the time when he was Krĕṣṇa and was renowned as the protector of the five Pāṇḍawas during the war. These glorious deeds of days gone by are celebrated as "The Death of Śalya" in "The War of the Bhāratas".

The transition between the two poets takes place at a natural division of the narrative about two-thirds of the way through the poem: Mpu Sĕḍah composed Cantos 1–31 (485 stanzas, covering the first four battle books of the Mahābhārata, namely the Udyogyaparvan, Bhīṣmaparvan, Droṇaparvan and Karṇaparvan. Mpu Panuluh then dealt with the remaining two books, the Śalyaparvan and Sauptikaparvan in Cantos 32–52 (246 stanzas).

In his Śalyawadha section of the Bhāratayuddha, Mpu Panuluh makes four major narrative interventions. The first centres around Śalya's ambiguous position as both Kaurawa ally and a member of the extended Pāṇḍawa family. The perception of potentially divided loyalties results in a major confrontation between Śalya and Droṇa's son, Aśwatthāmā, when the latter accuses Śalya of duplicity. The second is Nakula's mission to visit Śalya in order to seek a last minute peaceful resolution to the conflict soon after his uncle has been appointed as commander-in-chief of the Kaurawas. The third and most enduring intervention is the exposition of the loving relationship between Śalya and his wife Satyawatī, his poignant leave-taking as he goes to meet his fate and her heartrending act of self-immolation (*sati*) on the battlefield as she joins him in death. The fourth and final intervention is the means of Śalya's death when he is slain, not by the spear of Sanskrit tradition, but by Yudhiṣṭhira's Kalimahoṣadha book-weapon. These narrative variations appear to have no counterpart in the Sanskrit epic, but in the Indonesian archipelago they must nevertheless have resonated with Javanese worldviews and have rapidly become entrenched in local understandings, for they also inspired a rich Balinese tradition of later textual and visual representations of Śalya's central role in the Bhāratayuddha narrative. Below, I trace the enduring impact of each of these creative interventions in the epic story through their adaptation into new *kakawin* compositions and into new literary forms written in Balinese language, as well as in their depiction in classical and modern Balinese painting.

Sālya in Bali — Reframing the Bhāratayuddha

A significant number of the Bhāratayuddha manuscripts from Bali have interlinear Balinese glosses that guided generations of literary experts through the interpretation and meaning of the Old Javanese text. These glosses may have served primarily for the vocalization and interpretation of texts in ritual and other contexts. Glossed manuscripts provide evidence of the textual strategies that ensured the preservation of both the form and content of *kakawin* down through the centuries. They are also witnesses to individual Balinese interpretations of the Bhāratayuddha in whole or in part, representing a bridge between the language of the ancient Old Javanese *kakawin* text and its later reworkings in Balinese language. There are also a number of prose summaries (*parikan*), which may have served a similar function. The earliest known copy of the Parikan Bharatayuddha (K 826) comes from the Kirtya collection established only in the late 1920s (*Mededeelingen* 1931). There are also several copies of the — or a — Parikan Bharatayuddha in the Hookyaas-Ketut Sangka Collection (HKS 3287, 4300, 6005, 6291, 6229). It has not yet been possible to ascertain if these are copies of a single work or independent summaries of the Bhāratayuddha.

Although the entire poem remained a source of poetic and artistic inspiration in Bali, Mpu Panuluh's section of the Bhāratayuddha and, in particular, his four major narrative interventions — the quarrel between Śalya and Aśwatthāmā, Nakula's visit to his uncle, the Śalya and Satyawatī episode and Śalya's death — are precisely the scenes that appear to have captured the imaginations of nineteenth-century Balinese poets and artists as well as modern Balinese painters. Supomo (1993, pp. 38–40) indicates at least eleven independent manuscripts of the Bhāratayuddha belonging to the Balinese tradition that reproduce only Mpu Panuluh's contribution to the poem. When sections of the larger work were selected for copying and study, the resulting text could become an independent poem with its own title. There are, for example, two copies of a *kakawin* entitled Kakawin Senapati Śalya found in the HKS Collection (Hinzler 1993; Creese 2004*b*), HKS 3176 and 5303. This work, which dates from the turn of the twentieth century and, as its title suggests, relates the events from the time of Śalya's appointment as commander-in-chief until his death at Yudhiṣṭhira's hand, in fact simply comprises Cantos 32–42 of the Bhāratayuddha, a total of 77 stanzas with Balinese gloss.

A parallel interest in both the entire Bhāratayuddha narrative and in Mpu Panuluh's personal contribution to it is found in the later Balinese tradition. There are three major *macapat* verse-form reworkings of the Bhāratayuddha in Balinese language and metres. Two of them, the Kidung Bratayuda and the Gaguritan Bharatayuddha, include the complete narrative, while the third, the Gaguritan Śalya, details only Śalya's exploits. None of these Balinese works can be dated with certainty but each of them has direct intertextual links with the original twelfth-century *kakawin*, attesting to its ongoing significance in Bali.

The Kidung Bratayuda is the oldest known Balinese version of the Bhāratayuddha, written in *macapat* metres. There are three copies dating from the late nineteenth century in the Van der Tuuk Collection (1896) of Leiden University Library. The first of these, LOr 3924 (2), comprises seventeen cantos. It narrates the story from the time of Krĕṣṇa's initial mission on behalf of the Pāṇḍawas to seek peace with the Kaurawas in Canto 1 until the death of Ghaṭotkaca in Canto 31 (Brandes 1901, pp. 172–73; Juynboll 1912, p. 97). The manuscript includes an unverified colophon date noting that the text was copied in the year 1600 *śaka* (1678 CE), suggesting it may be quite an early Balinese rewriting. The second manuscript (LOr 3814) is a palm-leaf, *lontar* manuscript which contains two episodes that are also found in Van der Tuuk's manuscript: Krĕṣṇa as envoy (Cantos 2–4) and Abhimanyu's death (Cantos 13–14), plus a third episode drawn from Mpu Panuluh's section of the poem that is not included in LOr 3924 (2) and describes Śalya's leave-taking from Satyawatī. There is also a second copy of LOr 3814 in the Van der Tuuk Collection, a transcription on paper written in Balinese characters, LOr 4129. A connection between Van der Tuuk's interest in this Balinese *gaguritan* version of the Bhāratayuddha and the series of paintings he commissioned that are described below cannot be ruled out.

The Gaguritan Bharatayuddha, a *macapat* version of the entire Bhāratayuddha written in Balinese, closely parallels the narrative structure of the *kakawin*, even incorporating a paraphrase of Mpu Sĕḍah's introductory homage to Jayabhaya. It comprises 12 cantos. There is one copy in the Kirtya Collection, K 5128 (Soreyana 1987, pp. 86–88), and four copies in the HKS Collection (HKS 2253, 2480 4505, 5438), all from the collection of Puri Kaba-Kaba in Tabanan. It appears to be of relatively recent date.

The Gaguritan Senapati Śalya is a *gaguritan* in Balinese language and *macapat* metres, comprising 139 stanzas in three cantos. The opening stanza specifically cites the Bhāratayuddha as its source. The poem details the events beginning in Canto 36 when Śalya's appointment as commander of the Kaurawa forces is confirmed. The Balinese poet apologizes for "cutting into" the story at this point. He incorporates Mpu Panuluh's section of the *kakawin* in its entirety, but transposes the episode describing Satyawatī's death and the final stages of the war drawn from the Sauptikaparvan, in which Duryodhana's flight and Dropadī's lament at the deaths of her five sons are related (BY Cantos 50.1–51.32). The poem thus ends when Śalya and Satyawatī are reunited in heaven (BY 45.12). The Gaguritan Senapati Śalya was first recorded as K 590/6 in the initial catalogue listing of Balinese manuscripts published by the Kirtya Liefrinck-Van der Tuuk, established in Singaraja in North Bali in 1928 (*Mededeelingen* 1931) and therefore must have been written no later than the early twentieth century. There are also four copies of this poem in the HKS collection (HKS 7/9, 1125, 2946, 5411).

It is striking that later Balinese poets and copyists appear to have had little inclination to make alterations to the narrative or to compose the many branch or satellite poems that are evident in the Rāmāyaṇa tradition (Creese 2011). The same continuity with the original *kakawin* tradition is also evident in Balinese paintings and, in the sections that follow, I will trace the intertextual links between Mpu Panuluh's twelfth-century narrative interventions in the *kakawin* and a number of Balinese paintings dating from the mid-nineteenth to the late twentieth century.

Iconographic Representations of the Śalyawadha

Two major collections provide material for considering the poetic and visual intertextuality of the Bhāratayuddha. The first major source is the Van der Tuuk Collection of paintings (LOr 3390), acquired by the Leiden University Library in 1896, comprising 482 illustrations on European paper in 307 folios. The paintings arrived in Leiden in 1896 and 1897 as part of Van der Tuuk's legacy in considerable disorder. Three more drawings (LOr 17.994), apparently sent by Van der Tuuk to contacts in England, were added to the collection in 1982 (Hinzler 1986, p. 3). A comprehensive description of the collection is found in Hinzler's two-volume catalogue (1986, 1987), which includes a reproduction and details of the iconography and narrative setting of each of the paintings. The catalogue has recently been made accessible online in the Digital Repository of the Univerity of Leiden library.

It seems probable that Van der Tuuk commissioned these paintings directly and provided the paper and paints to the artists. As Hinzler (1986, p. 13) notes, he may have planned to use the illustrations as explanatory plates in his posthumously published Kawi–Balinese–Dutch dictionary (Van der Tuuk 1897–1912), in the same way that he had done for his Batak–Dutch dictionary (Van der Tuuk 1861). Except where he makes reference to the terms written on the paintings as lemmata in his dictionary, however, no reference by Van der Tuuk to these paintings has thus far come to light in any of his voluminous letters or papers.

The images represented in the Van der Tuuk Collections are drawn from nineteen different literary works. The Bhāratayuddha paintings in this collection belong to the category of "mythological" paintings that illustrate stories from the Ādiparwa, Māhabhārata and Rāmāyaṇa epic cycles. Scenes from the Rāmāyaṇa–Uttarakāṇḍa cycle make up over half the paintings, but the Bhāratayuddha is also well-represented with thirty-five paintings depicting scenes and figures from the narrative (Hinzler 1986, pp. 35–37).

All the Van der Tuuk Bhāratayuddha paintings are painted in traditional *wayang* or classical style; most have inscriptions in Balinese or Old Javanese language in Balinese script identifying the figures who are depicted in them (Hinzler 1986, pp. 7–11). The style is characterized by key iconographic features relating to facial characteristics that indicate the refined or coarse character of the figures, as well as to headdress, hairstyle and costume which are indicators of rank and status. Many scenes include one or more of the four *parekan* clown figures familiar from the *wayang* shadow theatre — Twalen and Merdah who are the companions of the Pāṇḍawas, and Delem and Sangut from the Kaurawa faction. The inclusion of these companions provides a visual representation of their role in the performing arts as mediators between the high language of the noble figures, on the one hand, and the everyday and comic on the other (Forge 1978, pp. 13–17; Vickers 2012, p. 30).

Hinzler (1986, pp. 4–5) has identified the work of fourteen individual artists in the Van der Tuuk Collection on the basis of their stylistic characteristics, colour palette and other technical details. Thirty paintings depict narrative scenes from the Bhāratayuddha. The eight paintings relating to Śalya's role in the war discussed in detail here make up the largest narrative subset of these Bhāratayuddha depictions. There are also a number of paintings of paired epic characters on a plain background familiar from the Bhāratayuddha, including one showing Śalya and Bhīṣma (LOr 3390, p. 154), in the set of eighteen paintings by Artist No 7 (Hinzler 1986, pp. 24–25; LOr 3390, pp. 151–68) but these portrait images will not be considered further here. All but two of the Bhāratayuddha narrative paintings were painted by two artists: Artist No 4, who has been identified by Hinzler (1986, p. 21) as I Ketut Gede of Singaraja and the unidentified artist, Artist No 5, from Badung. This concentration of effort suggests that Van der Tuuk commissioned two of his most prolific artists to work specifically on the Bhāratayuddha narrative.

I Ketut Gede painted twelve of the Bhāratayuddha narrative paintings. His first group of seven works (Hinzler 1986, pp. 77–87; LOr 3390, pp. 29–35) centres on the heroic deeds of Bīma's son, Ghaṭotkaca, who meets his death at the hands of Karṇa. This evidently popular narrative episode, is based on Mpu Sĕḍah's section of the *kakawin* (BY Cantos 17–19). Two further paintings (Hinzler 1986, pp. 475–79; LOr 3390, pp. 305, 306) are of Bhīma's slaying of Śakuni (BY Canto 43), which immediately follows the account of Śalya's death. I Ketut Gede's remaining three paintings are discussed below and deal with Nakula's embassy to Śalya (Hinzler 1986, pp. 472–75; LOr 3390, pp. 303, 304; see Figures 6.6, 6.7) and the latter's death in battle (Hinzler 1986, pp. 479–80; LOr 3390, p. 307; see Figure 6.13).

Working in Badung, South Bali, the unidentified Artist No 5 depicts sixteen scenes spanning the entire Bhāratayuddha narrative, including Krĕṣṇa's mission as envoy to the Kaurawas and adviser to the Pāṇḍawas (Hinzler 1986, pp. 232–35; LOr 3390, pp. 150, 171, 176–77); Arjuna paying homage to Bhīṣma lying on his bed of arrows (Hinzler 1986, pp. 226–27; LOr 3390, p. 145); and the exploits of three key heroes in battle — Bhīma (Hinzler 1986, pp. 227–28, 230–31, 261–63; LOr 3390, pp. 146, 148, 175), Abhimanyu (Hinzler 1986, pp. 229–30, 266–67;

LOr 3390, pp. 147, 178; see Figure 6.14) and Ghaṭotkaca (Hinzler 1986, pp. 267–68, 483–84; LOr 3390, p. 179; LOr 17.994, p. 3). Four of his paintings are concerned with the Śalya episode (Hinzler 1986, pp. 255–56, 258, 260–61; LOr 3390, pp. 170, 172, 174; see Figures 6.1, 6.2 and 6.10). The remaining two Bhāratayuddha narrative paintings both depict Śalya and Satyawatī and were painted by the only two artists to sign their works, Ida Made Tlaga of Sanur (Artist No 10) and Ida Putu Hema of Badung (Artist No 6) (Hinzler 1986, pp. 163–65, 231–32; LOr 3390, pp. 104, 149; see Figures 6.11 and 6.12).

Because of Van der Tuuk's pivotal role in acquiring the paintings, a degree of caution is necessary in presenting them as representative of indigenous Balinese interest in literary narratives. We do not know whether Van der Tuuk selected specific scenes from the *kakawin,* or allowed the painters free rein. Nevertheless, all thirty narrative paintings of the Bhāratayuddha portray key moments in the *kakawin* narrative. Moreover, the interdependence of text and image is highlighted by striking parallels between the scenes that are depicted in these paintings and the narrative choices made by the authors of the Balinese *gaguritan* works described above in the transformation of the Old Javanese *kakawin* into Balinese linguistic and metrical forms. For example, I Ketut Gede's paintings reflect the Kidung Bratayuda's interest in Krĕṣṇa's role as envoy and in the deaths of Abhimanyu and Ghaṭotkaca and, as we have seen, both painters take up the Śalya story that is the focus of both the second Kidung Bratayuda manuscript and the Gaguritan Senapati Śalya. Such parallels suggest that certain episodes and figures from the *kakawin* tradition did resonate widely with both Balinese poets and artists in the late nineteenth century. On balance, it seems reasonable to conclude that even if Van der Tuuk commissioned the paintings the resulting artworks exemplify enduring local concerns and input.

The second major source of illustrations on which I have drawn is the Virtual Museum of Balinese Painting (Vickers et al. 2011). Thanks to this significant new resource, it is possible to access and view online a vast and eclectic collection of Balinese paintings dating from the nineteenth to the late twentieth century belonging to a wide range of private and public international collections. The search facility and narrative links on the website reveal the central importance of literary works as the inspiration for Balinese painters. Twenty-seven different narratives are incorporated into this collection, including all the major Old Javanese *kakawin*. Paintings depicting scenes from the Bhāratayuddha form an important narrative subset of this collection, indicating that not only Van der Tuuk and his network of painters were drawn to the text.

A detailed analysis of the entire Bhāratayuddha painting corpus is beyond the scope of the current study. Instead, the focus here now returns to Mpu Panuluh's section of the poem and specifically to his narrative interventions in the Death of Śalya episode as depicted in seven of the Van der Tuuk paintings and a selection of other Balinese works in classical and modern styles from the Visual Museum Collection. In the discussion that follows each of these interventions will be treated in narrative sequence in order to highlight the intertextual links between poem and painting.

Intervention 1. The Confrontation between Śalya and Aśwatthāmā

The figure of Śalya dominates Mpu Panuluh's section of the Bhāratayuddha. Nevertheless, prior to assuming command of the Kaurawa forces, Śalya has already played a role in the course of events, as retold in Mpu Sĕḍah's contribution to the *kakawin*. Śalya makes his first appearance early in the poem (Canto 3.2) as a member of Duryodhana's trusted coterie of close advisers who determine the Kaurawa battle strategy. In Canto 10.19, he plays a more prominent role in the direction of the narrative when he slays Uttara, crown prince of Wirāṭa, unleashing the grief and anger in the Pāṇḍawa camp that inflames their warrior-like zeal and leads to the downfall of Bhīṣma, the Kaurawa commander and highly respected teacher of both sides in the conflict. As the slaughter continues and Droṇa, appointed to succeed Bhīṣma, is in turn slain by Dhrĕṣṭadyumna, Karṇa assumes command of the Kaurawas. Śalya then enters the core battle narrative when Karṇa requests him as his charioteer in order to provide a worthy match for Arjuna and Krĕṣṇa in the forthcoming battle (Canto 21).

The mighty Śalya is initially humiliated to be asked to take the role of charioteer but agrees on the condition that he may say whatever he likes to Karṇa in the course of battle. As the battlelines are drawn up, Karṇa boasts that he will defeat his opponents effortlessly. Śalya responds with jeers and insults to which Karṇa cannot respond because of his earlier promise to allow Śalya to speak his mind freely. In the final confrontation between Arjuna and Karṇa, Śalya seemingly aids the enemy when, at a sign from Śalya, Krĕṣṇa, who is acting as Arjuna's charioteer, presses down the wheel of the chariot. As a result, Adrawalīka, the formidable snake arrow that Karṇa has just launched, misses its target, allowing Arjuna to gain the victory. In this way, Śalya is directly implicated in the death of Karṇa.

An understanding of the fraught relationship between Śalya and Karṇa — as well as of the animosity that later flares up between Śalya and Aśwatthāmā — assumes an underlying knowledge on the part of poet and audience of the broader Mahābhārata narrative. The seeds of discord have been sown in earlier sections of the Udyogaparwa that are not included in the *kakawin,* which begins only with Krĕṣṇa's final attempt to sue for peace (corresponding to *adhyāya* 5.80 of the Sanskrit text). Śalya's sister, Madrī, is Pāṇḍu's second wife and the mother of the twins, Nakula and Sahadewa. As the Pāṇḍawa's maternal uncle, Śalya therefore faces considerable conflict in loyalty when he is duped into allying himself with the Kaurawas in spite of his initial intention to join forces with the Pāṇḍawas.

As preparations for the battle advance, Śalya departs with a fully equipped army to answer Yudhiṣṭhira's call to arms. On the way he stops at a sumptuous rest-house where Duryodhana regales him with every honour and comfort in an attempt to win him over to the Kaurawa cause. Believing it is Yudhiṣṭhira who has offered this hospitality and having accepted it, Śalya has no choice but to acquiesce when Duryodhana unexpectedly comes forward and claims his allegiance in return. Nevertheless, Śalya proceeds first to the Pāṇḍawa camp to tell Yudhiṣṭhira what he has done. Yudhiṣṭhira enjoins Śalya to become Karṇa's charioteer, as fate will surely dictate, and to protect Arjuna when he is threatened in battle by undermining Karṇa's prowess. The course of war is thus pre-determined. Karṇa faces Arjuna fully aware of Śalya's duplicitous position as "a foe even when he pretends to be an ally", in the words of the parallel Sanskrit text (Karṇaparvan 27.95; Meiland 2005, p. 19). And so it turns out. In Mpu Panuluh's Bhāratayuddha, however, it is Aśwatthāmā rather that Karṇa who emerges as Śalya's principal enemy.

With Karṇa slain, Duryodhana must seek a new champion. In the Sanskrit epic, he asks Aśwatthāmā to choose a new general to lead his forces. Aśwatthāmā, who is one of Śalya's most loyal supporters and comes to his assistance on more than one occasion in the battle that follows, immediately champions Śalya (Śalyaparvan 9.6.17–20; Meiland 2005, pp. 88–91):

> "Tell us therefore who should be the general of my army and who can lead us in unity to defeat the Pándavas in battle." The son of Drona replied: "Let Shalya be the leader of our army. Lineage, appearance, vigor, reputation, majesty — he possesses every virtue. Abandoning his own nephews, he has remembered his debts and come over to our side. With his great army and mighty arms he is like a second Skanda! We shall be able to achieve victory if we make this king our general, best of monarchs, just as the gods were victorious when they made Skanda their general."

In the epic, Śalya accepts his role readily. In the Bhāratayuddha on the other hand, rather than Aśwatthāmā, it is Śakuni who proclaims Śalya's virtues, although still sounding a cautionary note about Śalya's potentially divided loyalties (BY 34.2–3; Supomo 1993, p. 226):

> [He] is worthy to be your protector, for he is most reliable in battle. He is a valiant and mighty king, who is concerned with the welfare of others; he is famed for his meritorious deeds throughout the three worlds. Could an enemy survive if he dared to oppose him on the battlefield? However, the limits of his affection are difficult to ascertain.
>
> His attachment is certainly unwavering. Here is some proof. Everyone knows that he is Nakula's uncle, and therefore he is an enemy to you. Yet he has not turned against you, nor does he wish to leave you. The only problem is that he has surrendered his life to the Pāṇḍawas.

In the *kakawin*, Śalya is reluctant to accept the command at first and only agrees to lead the Kaurawa forces after first urging Duryodhana to seek a reconciliation with the Pāṇḍawas. Only if they refuse will the Kaurawas have a moral justification for the carnage that will surely follow and Śalya will then slay them all. As Śalya prevaricates, Aśwatthāmā swiftly launches his attack on him for once more seeking to aid the enemy. In his vehement denunciation, he addresses Duryodhana directly (BY 35.5–12; Supomo 1993, p. 227):

> Hah! King Śalya is showing his partiality. He is persistently in sympathy with our malicious enemies, the evil Pāṇḍawas.
>
> Remember that Arjuna should have been killed by Karṇa, for his arrow had been aimed straight at him. But Śalya, Karṇa's charioteer, hindered him and disturbed him, whilst Arjuna seeing a signal [from Śalya], ducked and avoided being struck by the arrow.
>
> The conclusion is that he has not wavered in his affection for your enemy. He is, in fact, Nakula's uncle! Indeed it would be better if he went over to the Pāṇḍawas, because he is in truth an enemy, even if he professed to be an ally.

Śalya rebuts the accusation and challenges Aśwatthāmā:

> Fie upon you, base son of a brahmin. How dare you be so arrogant? It is clear to me now that you will die at my hands.
>
> How could I, Śalya, be insincere in my affection for the king of Hāstina? I shall have no trouble in gaining victory for him. But since my only wish is for the well-being of the king and his relatives, would it be wise if I kept silent about such a matter?
>
> You have harshly and loudly criticised my truthful words, and you are boasting as if you are really a brave man. So excuse me, come forward and meet my weapon, or if you are afraid to die, throw yourself at my feet.

Aśwatthāmā responds in kind:

> Bah, Śalya! Come on, attack me! Do not be faint hearted. I shall be delighted to see your dexterity. Now your life is at an end, and you will have to suffer retribution. I will ensure that your soul be disgraced in the abode of Yama.
>
> If the king of Hāstina pays any attention to you at all, then I will leave rather than be forced to see you there on the battlefield. I would be

loath to witness the death of the worthless weakling. There is no doubt that it is I who will bring victory to my king.

These dramatic narrative moments are depicted in two paintings from the Van der Tuuk collection, both painted by Artist No 5. Figure 6.1 shows Karṇa with Śalya as his charioteer mortally wounded by Arjuna's arrow; the ghosts and demon figures (top right) and the snake arrow, Ardawalīka (top, centre), have also been shot (Hinzler 1986, pp. 259–60). Figure 6.2 then illustrates the first stage of the confrontation between Śalya and Aśwatthāmā. The iconography of the composition clearly conveys the threatening stance of the two protagonists (Hinzler 1986, pp. 255–56): Śalya (left) addresses Duryodhana (centre). On his right is Aśwatthāmā pointing menacingly at Śalya. Their rivalry is mirrored in the drawn *kris* of their respective companion figures, Sangut and I Delem.

As the Bhāratayuddha reveals, their confrontation escalates and the two heroes assume their demonic *triwikrama* (Balinese *pamurtian*) forms and threaten the annihilation of the world (BY 35.13–14; Supomo 1993, p. 228):

They quarrelled vehemently, for both were as brave and as famous as the embodiment of Rudra. In an instant they both assumed the form of Rudra, as if desiring to burn and destroy the three worlds.

And so the whole audience was in commotion, people screaming in uproar, and throwing their arms around the legs of the two adversaries. Duryodhana made every effort to restrain them. Both finally calmed down, then the son of Droṇa left.

This moment of crisis is depicted on several Balinese *tabing* (square cloths placed as a backdrop behind the offerings in homes and temples). These images of the Śalya-Aśwatthāmā confrontation, in which the protagonists assume their demonic (*pamurtian*) forms, also include the companion figures of the heroes. Similar *tabing* illustrating this scene are found in the collections of the National Museum of Ethnology, Leiden (B 90-06) and the Australian National Gallery (Maxwell et al. 2014, pp. 117–19). Two Kamasan *pamurtian* paintings, depicted in Figures 6.3 and 6.4, are linked artistically and genealogically. The earliest portrayal, Figure 6.3, dating from 1840–50, is by Modara (I Wayan Gereha), the most famous Kamasan artist working in the mid-nineteenth century. The later work, Figure 6.4, is by Nyoman Laya

FIGURE 6.1

Karṇa, with Śalya as his charioteer, is mortally wounded. Artist No 5 (LOr 3390, p. 173).

FIGURE 6.2

Aśwatthāmā confronts Śalya. Artist No 5 (LOr 3390, p. 170).

FIGURE 6.3

Śalya and Aśwatthāmā in demonic form. Modara (1840–50) (Nyoman Gunarsa Museum).

FIGURE 6.4

Śalya and Aśwatthāmā in demonic form. I Nyoman Laya, early twentieth century (Vickers et al. 2011).

(died 1933), who was a nephew of Modara and active in the early twentieth century (Vickers 2012, pp. 74–76). Figure 6.5 illustrates the firm grip of this traditional iconography on a well-known modern painter, Mangku Mura (1920–99) (Forge 1978, p. 8; Vickers 2012, pp. 87–88). This painting was one of several works commissioned by Anthony Forge in 1972 and is now in the collection of the Australian Museum.

FIGURE 6.5

Śalya and Aśwatthāmā in demonic form. Mangku Mura, 1972 (Australian Museum, E074176).

When their anger has abated and the two warriors resume their human forms, Aśwatthāmā leaves and takes no further part in the war. Vowing only to fight after Śalya has been slain, he re-enters the story following

Duryodhana's final defeat at the hands of Bhīma in the Sauptikaparvan (BY Cantos 50–51), when he returns by night to wreak havoc in the Pāṇḍawa camp and, after attacking "like the God of Death descending to the world" (BY 50.13), kills the five young Pāṇḍawa princes, the five sons of Dropadī.

Intervention 2. Nakula's Embassy to Śalya

A second major change inserted into the epic narrative by Mpu Panuluh immediately follows the installation of Śalya as commander of the Kaurawa forces. As the war moves into its final phase, at Krĕṣṇa's suggestion, the Pāṇḍawas send Śalya's beloved nephew, Nakula, as an envoy to discover how he might be defeated. This episode demonstrates clearly the interdependence of the *kakawin* text and later Balinese iconography. Nakula, a relatively minor figure, plays no role of this kind in the Sanskrit epic, although in one episode before the outbreak of hostilities in the Sabhāparwa, he does journey to his uncle's kingdom of Madra where he is well received and handsomely treated. Here in the Bhāratayuddha, on the other hand, his embassy functions as a crucial narrative device to contextualize the preordained fate that awaits Śalya on the plain of Kuru when he finally comes face to face with Yudhiṣṭhira.

Nakula's mission is depicted in two paintings by the Singaraja artist, I Ketut Gede. In Figure 6.6, Nakula and Twalen pay homage to Yudhiṣṭhira, while Krĕṣṇa and Mredah look on (Hinzler 1986, pp. 479–80). Even before Nakula arrives, the burden of his divided loyalty is preying on Śalya's mind (BY 36.4; Supomo 1993, p. 228):

> He was deeply upset that he now had to fight against the Pāṇḍawas, for Nakula was indeed his own nephew. This affection for his near kinsman was the source of his distress.

Nevertheless, Śalya is startled when his nephew unexpectedly appears and prostrates himself at his uncle's feet, declaring it would be better to die at his uncle's hand now than to be forced to face him in battle (BY 36.12; Supomo 1993, p. 229):

FIGURE 6.6

Yudhiṣṭhira orders Nakula to visit Śalya, Kṛĕṣṇa is in attendance. I Ketut Gede (LOr 3390, p. 307).

> If I dare encounter you on the battlefield, I would be committing a most perfidious sin and be branded as one who is disrespectful toward one's teacher. Therefore thrust your kris into my throat.

Śalya explains to Nakula how he has been entrapped by Duryodhana to fight on the side of the Kaurawas since, once a vow has been uttered, it becomes a truth and must be fulfilled, no matter what else may happen. But he then gifts to Nakula the means of his defeat (BY 36.15–17; Supomo 1993, p. 230):

> As far as my life is concerned, I leave it in your hands. My only request is that my opponent shall be the son of Dharma [Yudhiṣṭhira],

> for by using the book as his weapon, he will be the cause of my death.
>
> The reason for this is that I am invincible in battle. Rudra has given me a great favour, an inconceivable gift, so that the most powerful of weapons that are capable of slaying *yakṣas* and *asuras*, will be rendered ineffectual when they strike my breast and will make no impression upon me.
>
> However Paśupati has ordained that I shall be slain by a man who practises the Law, well-versed in scriptures, devoted to fasting and reciting mantras, and who steadfastly uses the book as his sword to destroy the six inner enemies. This is the means by which I will be released to return to the abode of Rudra.

Nakula returns to the Pāṇḍawa camp in tears. In Figure 6.7 (Hinzler 1986, pp. 472–74), the artist, I Ketut Gede, combines two episodes which occur sequentially in the Bhāratayuddha: on the right, Nakula pays homage while, on the left, Śalya restrains Satyawatī, who has drawn her *kris* and is threatening to end her life. And, as the narrative segues from battle tactics to the personal, Mpu Panuluh now introduces his most important addition to the Sanskrit narrative, the figure of Śalya's wife, Satyawatī.

Intervention 3. Śalya and Satyawatī

The moment that Nakula has taken his leave, a dejected Śalya takes refuge in the inner court seeking out his beloved wife, Satyawatī. He finds her in despair, her *kris* drawn, preparing to take her life then and there, not because she is afraid to die should the king fall in battle, but because their love for each other has not yet been fulfilled. Śalya restrains her and comforts her with sweet words and declarations of his undying passion. He pretends to her that he has deliberately misled Nakula since, as she must surely know, he is invincible. In this way Satyawatī's threat to take her life is temporarily averted — but the outcome is ultimately far more tragic. This scene which comprises the left-hand panel of Figure 6.7 has been given a modern interpretation in two mid-twentieth century modern paintings (see Figures 6.8–6.9) by renowned artists Ida Bagus Made Togog (1911–89) and I Wayan Kebeten (1931–). These more recent works attest to the ongoing significance of this loving couple as a cultural symbol for Balinese artists.

FIGURE 6.7

Nakula attends Śalya, who is restraining Satyawatī. I Ketut Gede (LOr 3390, p. 303).

FIGURE 6.8

Śalya restrains Satyawatī. Ida Bagus Made Togog, 1940s. (Private Collection of Batuan, Singapore).

FIGURE 6.9

Śalya restrains Satyawatī. I Wayan Kabetan, 1951. (Private Collection of Batuan, Singapore).

As night falls, Śalya and Satyawatī seek comfort in love-making and fall asleep in each other's arms. There follows one of the most poignant sections in the *kakawin* repertoire when, at daybreak, Śalya slips away silently from their bed-chamber to go into battle (BY 38.11–17; Supomo 1993, pp. 233–34):

> Then while she was asleep, using his arm as a pillow, the bell struck the seventh hour, as if to wake him. The king awoke, but he was worried that the queen, sleeping on his arm, might be awakened too, and he could imagine how she would cling to him, lamenting and weeping.
>
> This was why he moved aside and gently freed his arm from under her. But his outer garment was still beneath her, twisting around her awkwardly, so without regret he swiftly cut it with his kris, and rearranged the remainder of the garment that trailed on the bed, covering her with it.
>
> Grief-stricken, he departed reluctantly, coming back again and again to kiss her. He placed his quid and chewed betel leaves in her hand, and striving after her love, he placed his writing board at her breast like a doll. His tears were the tears of the doll which was crying because it had been left behind.
>
> Its laments, in the form of a poem, had been written on it as it lay sorrowfully on her breast. "Tell your mother that I, your father, have left her secretly. 'He said that he was going into battle, mother, and that he would make every effort to enhance your beauty, for he would be ashamed if Ratih would not pay homage to you as a temple of love.'"
>
> Thus was the short message he wrote on the writing board. Then he put to rights her loosened hairknot, placing *wiraga* flowers in it, and putting back the scattered hair decoration of *campaka* and jasmine flowers, but its radiance, thus restored, seemed to restrain him and prevent him from leaving.
>
> Moreover, her appearance now looked even more enchanting, unearthly and divine, while the lights that glared brightly as if serving her, enhanced her beauty. So, filled with compassion and pity, the king was heartbroken and distracted. His mind was confused, terribly disturbed, as he was torn apart by his passion and love.
>
> Finally he left, all the while glancing back, sighing and murmuring. His deep love for the queen prompted his tears which he brushed aside

> time and again. He walked slowly, as if being pulled back pausing at every step, and he would not have proceeded into battle had he not wished to be faithful to his words.

Śalya's stealthy departure, as detailed in the Bhāratayuddha and later Balinese works such as the Gaguritan Senopati Śalya, appears to have held particular appeal for artists and painters in the late nineteenth century. There are three classical *wayang*-style paintings of this scene from the Van der Tuuk Collection, each the work of a different artist (see Figures 6.10–6.12), but showing similar stylistic effects that position this scene as a familiar, somewhat stereotypical image (Hinzler 1986, p. 35).

FIGURE 6.10

Śalya cuts the cloth binding him to Satyawatī. Artist No 5 (LOr 3390, p. 172).

FIGURE 6.11

Śalya cuts the cloth binding him to Satyawatī. I Made Tlaga (LOr 3390, p. 149).

FIGURE 6.12

Śalya cuts the cloth binding him to Satyawatī.Ida Putu Hema (LOr 3390, p. 104).

The first of these paintings, Figure 6.10, is by Artist No 5 (Hinzler 1986, pp. 22–23), the same artist as the one who painted the scenes in Figures 6.1 and 6.2. Just as in Figure 6.2, the artist has depicted Śalya's servant Sangut, in the bottom left (Hinzler 1986, p. 258). Figure 6.11 is by Ida Made Tlaga, whose work is represented by thirty paintings in the Van der Tuuk Collection. Unusually, he signed the back of all his paintings. He was a famous *dalang* and maker of *wayang* puppets and died around 1924 (Hinzler 1986, pp. 26–30; 231–32). This painting of Śalya and Satyawatī is the only one in which he depicts a Bhāratayuddha theme. In Figure 6.12, Ida Putu Hema from Griya Pratoda in Badung, who appears to have worked for Van der Tuuk in the late 1880s, shows Śalya drawing his *kris* to cut through his own loincloth that is entwined around his beloved wife (Hinzler 1986, pp. 163–64). The text in Balinese script at the bottom reads: "Śalya speaks sweet words to his wife" (*pangupik salya*). The longer text in Balinese script on the top right states: "Śalya draws his *kris* to cut the cloth binding him to Satyawatī that she has twisted around them for fear that he will leave her behind when he goes to fight the Kaurawas [*sic* for Pāṇḍawas]."[1] But duty triumphs over love. There can be no turning back.

Intervention 4. Śalya's Death

All that has been preordained now comes to pass. As the battle reaches its peak (Canto 40), Śalya is finally abandoned. All his allies have been slain or have fled. He now faces Yudhiṣṭhira alone. As Śalya unleashes his Rudraroṣa arrow, which spews forth demon arrows, Krĕṣṇa, the all-knowing incarnation of Wiṣṇu, orders the Pāṇḍawa forces to lay down their weapons since Śalya's arrows are powerless against those who have set aside their arms. Still Yudhiṣṭhira refuses to oppose Śalya who is like his "own father", until even the gods become so alarmed that they cry out (BY 40.10; Supomo 1993, p. 236):

> The battle has taken a wrong turning. How can the powerful Rudraroṣa arrow be destroyed if Yudhiṣṭhira does not wish to kill Śalya.

Yudhiṣṭhira seems to have lost his resolve to annihilate Śalya with his book-arrow in accordance with the course of events that had been foreshadowed at the beginning of hostilities when the Pāṇḍawas set off in procession for the battlefield (BY 9.9; Supomo 1993, p. 176):

> Yudhiṣṭhira, the son of Dharma, accompanied [Dropadī], mounted on a rutting elephant. Completely at ease under a yellow parasol, he held a book bound together with a knot of sparkling jewels. Truly he was the embodiment of God Dharma, for his wish was to placate Śalya and Duryodhana: but if they were intent on fighting, he would transform the book into a thunderbolt weapon.

Finally, Yudhiṣṭhira is persuaded by Krĕṣṇa to set aside his reluctance to fight his kinsman and the Kalimahoṣadha, once nothing more than "a book bound together with a knot of sparkling jewels", is transformed into a blazing lance (BY 42.5, 8; Supomo 1993, pp. 237–38):

> Then [Śalya] was struck down by the excellent weapon in the form of a book which was gleaming and luminous, for it was a staff of jewels and gold. It pierced through his breast, and like a rainbow it drank his blood that gushed forth. Such was its power. Śalya's soul then returned to the abode of the gods.

In this way, Śalya dies a true hero. According to Javanese tradition, "a rainbow with a cup at either end drinks water of the Java Sea and the Indian Ocean then pours it down back as rain" (Supomo 1993, p. 281) and Śalya's life-substance will return to nourish the earth.

There is no trace of this book-weapon in the Sanskrit text where Yudhiṣṭhira instead launches "a spear (*śakti*) which was bright as gold and which had a shaft that was covered in gold and jewels" (Meiland 2005, p. 199). Supomo (1997, p. 231) has proposed that *kalimahoṣadha* means "the great medicine of Kali" (*kali* + *mahā* "great" + *uṣadha* "medicine") and derives from a misunderstanding of the Sanskrit verse through a conflation of the meaning of the word *śakti* "spear" with a second meaning of the same word as "the energy or power of a deity personified as his wife". By association, it thus refers to the goddess Kali, the wife of the supreme deity, Śiwa, in her demonic form. Kalimahoṣadha, or Kalima Usada, is also the title of a Balinese manual on magic and incantations with reference to medicine, as well as the name of a compendium of religious speculation. Because Mpu Sĕḍah refers to the weapon in his section of the poem the misunderstanding cannot be attributed to Mpu Panuluh's personal misreading of the Sanskrit text. Rather, this novel Javanese understanding of the nature of Yudhiṣṭhira's book-weapon must have already entered the Javanese tradition before the composition of the Bhāratayuddha. That similar misreadings (or reinterpretations) of the Sanskrit text occur frequently in the transformation of the first book of the Mahābhārata, the Ādiparwa, into Old Javanese (Creese 1998, pp. 65–75) may be taken as evidence for the possible existence of one of the "missing" *parwa* as the source of this Javanese tradition.

Whatever its origins, the Kalimahoṣadha appears to have been a symbol of considerable potency. In later Javanese traditions dating from the early nineteenth century, the Old Javanese word *kalimahoṣadha* was reinterpreted as *kalimah sahadat*, the Muslim profession of faith. In a legend related in the Sĕrat Cabolang, Sunan Kalijaga encounters Yudhiṣṭhira meditating in the forest of Glagahwangi, where for six hundred years he has sought release from his material body in order to enter heaven. Sunan Kalijaga explains the true meaning of the amulet in the form of a book, given to the Pāṇḍawa king at birth called *kalimasada*. It is, he explains, "the origin of the True Knowledge", given by God to the Prophet. Those who master it achieve peace and die a perfect death. Yudhiṣṭhira, made aware of how to attain his goal, accepts the teachings and becomes a Muslim. On his death, his soul ascends immediately to heaven (Supomo 1997, pp. 231–36). This legend is a testament both to the intrinsic power of textual knowledge and to the enduring legacy of Java's Hindu–Buddhist past four hundred years after the arrival of Islam, but it is, naturally enough, unknown in Bali, where, in the same period, poets and artists drew instead on the original twelfth-century Bhāratayuddha poetic tradition.

In Figure 6.13, also ascribed to I Ketut Gede (Hinzler 1986, pp. 474–75), Yudhiṣṭhira's weapon takes the form of a Balinese *lontar* palm-leaf manuscript inscribed with sacred syllables in Balinese characters. The text above the figures identifies each of them: "Śalya hit by the book-arrow" (*salya kna pustakĕ*); "Yudhiṣṭhira holds the bow" (*yudistira, nggawa langkap*) and "Twalen pays homage" (*twalén ngaturang bakti*). Twalen is Yudhiṣṭhira's companion. It is significant that Twalen pays homage to

FIGURE 6.13

Yudhiṣṭhira shoots Śalya with the Kalimahoṣadha. I Ketut Gede (LOr 3390, p. 304).

Śalya whose blood falls on his head. This act of homage marks Śalya's death iconographically as that of an epic hero.

The Death of Satyawatī

For Mpu Panuluh, however, Śalya's death does not signal the end of his narrative. He turns again to Satyawatī. When she receives news of Śalya's death from an old and trusted servant who has hidden himself under a pile of corpses to escape the slaughter, there is only one course open to her. She sets off immediately to find her beloved husband. As she wearily makes her way around the carnage of the battlefield, she despairs of finding Śalya, and the gods, taking pity on her, show her where he lies. She prostrates herself on his lifeless body, berating him for abandoning her and beseeching him to wait for her "on the swaying bridge to heaven" so that they can be united in love for eternity (BY 44.17–45.2; Supomo 1993, pp. 241–42). She immediately receives the reward for her unwavering love, for Śalya, "bursting with impatience", is indeed waiting for her seated on "an awe-inspiring cloud" (BY 45.10; Supomo 1993, pp. 240–41).

The Śalya-Satyawatī story adds more than a mere romantic interlude to the narrative. Satyawatī is not the first woman to take her life during the course of the war. Indeed, a series of battlefield laments punctuates the narrative of the Bhāratayuddha. The first of these scenes of grief is the lament of the King of Wirāṭa and his queen after the death of their sons (BY 12.1–4), most notably Śweta, who rather than Dhrĕṣṭadyumna as in the Sanskrit text, serves as the Pāṇḍawa's first commander. The second lamentation scene follows the death of Abhimanyu, the son of Arjuna and Subhadra, when his wives, Uttarī and Kṣitisundarī, mourn the loss of their husband (BY 14.3–5). Kṣitisundarī then immolates herself on his funeral pyre (BY 15.4–18). This tale of love and loss, mirroring the fate of Abhimanyu's own parents, has also provided a popular narrative episode for Balinese artists (Vickers 2012, pp. 42–43; 158–59). Kṣitisundarī's death is depicted in Figure 6.14, another painting by Artist No 5 (Hinzler 1986, pp. 229–30). Kṣitisundarī leaps from a tower into the burning pit below and the painting therefore reflects the form of *sati* known to have been practised in Java and Bali in the precolonial period (Creese 2004*a*, pp. 230–44; 2016, pp. 250–54). Finally, comes Hiḍimbī's lament when her son, Ghaṭotkaca, is slain by Karṇa and she chooses to follow him in death (BY 19.13–19).

In Mpu Sĕḍah's section of the Bhāratayuddha, these battlefield lamentations return the action from the liminal, male world of heroic battle to the domestic, female world of human affairs and human pain only briefly. In contrast, Mpu Panuluh affords Satyawatī a central role in his "Death of Śalya" *kakawin* within the *kakawin*. Such carefully elaborated *sati* scenes are characteristic of many later Old Javanese *kakawin* belonging to both the Javanese and Balinese traditions. It is hard to escape the impression that they are included in the story to play precisely the role that their characters claim, namely, to provide

FIGURE 6.14

Kṣitisundarī leaps into Abhimanyu's funeral pyre. Artist No 5 (LOr 3390, p. 147).

a model of appropriate behaviour for loyal wives and maidservants. In expressly extolling Satyawatī as "the one who died faithfully, one who was a worthy example for noble and praiseworthy women" (BY 46.1), Mpu Panuluh firmly cemented Satyawatī herself and the trope of the virtuous and loyal wife not only in Old Javanese *kakawin* poetry, but also as the role model for this ultimate display of loyalty for Balinese royal women on the deaths of princes until at least the mid-nineteenth century (Friederich 1959, pp. 92–99; Creese 2004*a*, pp. 210–30; 2016, pp. 630–40).

The long-standing view of the field (Zoetmulder 1974, p. 279; Supomo 1993, pp. 3–35), including my own (Creese 2004*a*), has always been that these women had no equivalent in Sanskrit tradition, but that they may have been familiar from Javanese oral traditions or the *wayang*.

Nevertheless, as Harry Aveling points out in his chapter in this volume, several generations of Old Javanese scholars have missed the fact that Kṣitisundarī is a well-known figure in South Indian folk traditions, where she is known as Vatsala or Sasirekha. Not only that, but so too is the story of her original abduction by Abhimanyu with the help of his half-*rākṣasa* cousin, Ghaṭotkaca. Mpu Panuluh's later and final *kakawin* work, the Ghaṭotkacāśraya, mirrors these South Indian traditions, later popularized in the 1950s through K. V Reddy's 1957 Telugu film *Maya Bazaar* (Prasad 2016). We must therefore assume that this rather lovely romantic *kakawin*, the prelude to Kṣitisundarī's act of self-immolation told here in the Bhāratayuddha, sprang from a tradition shared between Java and South India. There is ample evidence for early and prolonged contact between South India and the Indonesian archipelago but no serious comparative work has been undertaken on oral and performance traditions. Whether the figure of Satyawatī is similarly linked to South Indian folk tradition remains an open question. A preliminary investigation has failed to find any trace of her partnership with Śalya or of her battlefield death scene in any readily accessible South Indian sources but the possibility cannot be ruled out. There undoubtedly remains much to discover through more detailed comparative research across genres and geographical spaces.

Conclusion

Śalya's death takes place only part way through the narrative contained in the Sanskrit Śalyaparvan. The remaining episodes from the ninth and tenth books of the Sanskrit epic are passed over in quick succession in just ninety-one stanzas (Cantos 46–51) of the Bhāratayuddha. The Old Javanese *kakawin* and Sanskrit epic are broadly in agreement about the course of events as the war comes to an end and its horrific aftermath runs its course. Still to come are the final destruction of the Kaurawas; Bhīma's breaking of Duryodhana's thigh as foretold in the Sabhāparwa; Duryodhana's vow that he will not surrender his life until he has trodden on the heads of the five Pāṇḍawas and their offspring; Aśwatthāmā's revenge and the slaughter of the five Pāṇḍawa princes under cover of darkness; Aśwatthāmā's confrontation with Arjuna; and, finally, when

Aśwatthāmā releases his powerful arrow, the killing of Abhimanyu's son, Parikṣit, in his mother Uttarī's womb, only to be revived again by Krĕṣṇa in order to continue the Pāṇḍawa dynasty. No literary works or paintings depicting these final episodes have yet come to light hinting that, for the Balinese at least, with Śalya's death, the dramatic possibilities of the Bhāratayuddha narrative had been fully explored.

In his Śalyawadha, Mpu Panuluh took the epic frame and recreated its plot lines, characters, relationships and even magical weapons into beautiful poetry. These changes carry the Javanese version of the epic some distance away from its Indian and Sanskrit origins in ways that must reflect local concerns and interests. The popularity and longevity of the Bhāratayuddha in its original *kakawin* form, in Balinese poetic renderings and rewritings as *gaguritan*, in modern Indonesian translations and adaptations, in painting and in the *wayang* and other performance genres is striking. These artistic works attest to the resilience and longevity of these narrative sequences as core components of Mahābhārata mythology and creativity in Java and Bali.

It seems appropriate to end this chapter with one final contemporary work of art, *The death of Salya* by Mangku Mura (see Figure 6.15). This 1981 painting brings together the full cast of characters, the entire Śalyawadha in a single work of art, compelling evidence for the longevity of Mpu Panuluh's creativity. In the bottom panel, reading from left to right, Mangku Mura shows Nakula (bottom left) taking leave of his four brothers, Dropadī, Krĕṣṇa and the servants Twalen and Merdah to visit Śalya. Nakula then travels with his servants until he reaches Śalya's residence where he finds his uncle in a pavilion restraining Satyawatī who has drawn her *kris*. The lovers spend the night together and at dawn Śalya cuts the cloth that binds him to the sleeping Satyawatī and slips silently away (bottom right). The top panel, again reading from left to right, depicts scenes from the battle until Śalya meets his fate (top right) as the Kalimahoṣadha arrow pierces his breast (Vickers 2012, pp. 42–45). This modern painting in classical Balinese style reprises a number of the images already presented above. It is heir to a "Śalyawadha" poetic and artistic tradition stretching back, via nineteenth-century Bali, to the creative imagination of its creator, Mpu Panuluh in the Bhāratayuddha, in far-off twelfth-century Java.

FIGURE 6.15

The death of Salya. Mangku Mura, 1981 (Private Collection).

NOTES

This chapter is dedicated to the memory of Pak Pomo, teacher and mentor, who introduced me to the world of Old Javanese *kakawin* poetry and was the inspiration for my own lifelong journey.

The following individuals and institutions have kindly granted permission to reproduce the images included in this chapter.

Australian Museum, Sydney (Figure 6.5)
Nyoman Gunarsa Museum, Klungkung, Bali (Figure 6.3)
Private Collection of Batuan, Singapore (Figures 6.9 and 6.10)
Private Collection of Sanur (Figure 6.15)
Special Collections, Leiden University Library (Figures 6.1, 6.2, 6.6, 6.7, 6.10, 6.11, 6.12, 6.13 and 6.14)

I would like to thank Peter Worsley and two anonymous reviewers for their helpful suggestions on earlier versions of this chapter. I would also like to thank Stan Florek, Australian Museum, for providing the photograph for Figure 6.5. Special thanks to Adrian Vickers for supplying the photographs of Figures 6.3, 6.4, 6.8, 6.9 and 6.15, and for his ongoing advice on Balinese art.

1. "Prabhu salya, ngunus krĕis jagĕ ngtas wastrĕ, kalilit hantuk ḍéwi satyawaṭṭi, kṛĕṇṇa kalilit takut katinggallin mayuḍda, ngalawan watĕkorawa/prabu Salya ngunus kris jaga ngetas wastra kalilit antuk dewi Satyawati krana kalilit takut katinggalin mayuda nglawan watek Korawa" (*sic* for Pandawa; artist's error in original).

REFERENCES

Aveling, Harry. "Abimanyu Gugur: The Death of Abimanyu in Classical and Modern Indonesian and Malay Literature". This volume, 2018.

Brandes, J.L.A. *Beschrijving der Javaansche, Balineesche en Sasaksche handschriften aangetroffen in de nalatenschap van Dr H.N. van der Tuuk* I. Batavia: Landsdrukkerij, 1901.

Cohen Stuart, A.B. *Brata-joeda: Indisch-Javaansch heldendicht*. Batavia: Lange, 1860. Verhandelingen van het Bataviaasch Genootschap van Kunsten en Wetenschappen 27–28.

Creese, Helen. *Pārthayaṇa. The Journeying of Partha: An Eighteenth-Century Balinese Kakawin*. Leiden: KITLV Press, 1998. Bibliotheca Indonesica 27.

———. *Women of the Kakawin World: Marriage and Sexuality in the Indic Courts of Java and Bali*. Armonk, New York: M.E. Sharpe, 2004*a*.

———. *Guide and Index to the Hooykaas-Ketut Sangka Balinese Manuscript Collection in the Australian National University Library*. 2004*b*. Available at <http://library-admin.anu.edu.au/balinese-manuscript-collection-index/>.

———. "The Balinese Rāmāyaṇa Tradition". In *From Langka Eastwards: The Rāmāyaṇa in the Literature and Visual Arts of Indonesia*, edited by Andrea Acri, Helen Creese, and Arlo Griffiths. Leiden: KITLV Press, 2011. VKI 247, pp. 93–118.

———. *Bali in the Early Nineteenth Century: The Ethnographic Accounts of Pierre Dubois*. Leiden: Brill, 2016. VKI 305.

Forge, Anthony. *Balinese Traditional Paintings*. Sydney: Australian Museum, 1978.

Friederich, R.H.Th. *The Civilization and Culture of Bali*. Calcutta: Susil Gupta, 1959.

Griffith, Helen. "Śalyawadha: The Death of Śalya". Honours thesis. Australian National University, 1976.

Gunning, J.G.H. *Bhārata-yuddha: Oudjavaansch heldendicht*. The Hague: Nijhoff, 1903.

Hinzler, H.I.R. *Catalogue of Balinese Manuscripts in the Library of the University of Leiden and Other Collections in the Netherlands*. Part 2. *Descriptions of the Balinese Drawings from the Van der Tuuk Collection*. Leiden: E.J. Brill/Leiden University Press, 1986. Codices Manuscripti 23.

———. *Catalogue of Balinese Manuscripts in the Library of the University of Leiden and Other Collections in the Netherlands*. Part 1. *Reproductions of the Balinese Drawings from the Van der Tuuk Collection*. Leiden: E.J. Brill/Leiden University Press, 1987. Codices Manuscripti 22.

———. "Balinese Palmleaf Manuscripts". *Bijdragen tot de Taal-, Land en Volkenkunde* 149 (1993): 438–74.

Juynboll, H.H. *Supplement op de catalogus van de Sundaneesche handschriften en catalogus van de Balineesche en Sasaksche handschriften der Leidsche Universiteitsbibliotheek*. Leiden: Brill, 1912.

Kats, J. *De wajang poerwa: Een vorm van Javaans toneel*. Dordrecht, Holland/Cinnaminson, USA: Foris Publications, 1984.

Maxwell, Robyn, Niki van den Heuvel, Melanie Eastburn, and Lucie Folan. *Bali: Island of the Gods*. Canberra: National Gallery of Australia, 2014.

McDonald, Barbara. "Kawi and Kawi Miring: Old Javanese Literature in Eighteenth Century Java". PhD thesis. Australian National University, 1983.

———. *Old Javanese Literature in Eighteenth-Century Java: A Consideration of the Processes of Transmission*. Clayton, Victoria: Monash University, 1986. Centre of Southeast Asian Studies Working Paper 42.

Mededeelingen van de Kirtya Liefrinck-Van der Tuuk, Aflevering 3. Singaraja-Solo: Kirtya Liefrinck-van der Tuuk, 1931.

Meiland, Justin, trans. *Mahābhārata. Book 9 Śalya. Volume 1*. New York University Press/JJC Foundation (The Clay Sanskrit Library), 2005.

Pigeaud, Th.G.Th. *Literature of Java: Catalogue Raisonné of Javanese Manuscripts in the Library of the University of Leiden and Other Public Collections in the Netherlands*. Volume 1. The Hague: Martinus Nijhoff, 1967.

Poerbatjaraka and C. Hooykaas. "Bhārata-Yuddha, vertaald door-". *Djawa* 14 (1934): 1–87.

Prasad, M. Madhava. "Genre Mixing as Creative Fabrication". In *Salaam Bollywood Representations and Interpretations*, edited by Vikrant Kishore, Amit Sarwal and Parichay Patra. London, New York: Routledge, 2016, pp. 46–61.

Raffles, T.S. *The History of Java*. London: Black, Parbury and Allen, 1817. Two volumes.

Soreyana, I Made. "Studi alur dan penokohan Hikyat Pandawa Lima dan Geguritan Baratayuda (suatu pendekatan reseptif)". PhD dissertation, Universitas Gadjah Mada, 1987.

Supomo, S. "On the Old Javanese Wirāṭaparwa". In *Studies in Indo-Asian Art and Culture*, edited by Perala Ratnam. New Delhi: International Academy of Indian Culture, 1972. Śata-Piṭaka Series 95, pp. 261–66.

———. *Bhāratayudha: An Old Javanese Poem and its Indian Sources*. New Delhi: International Academy of Indian Culture/Aditya Prakashan, 1993. Śata-Piṭaka Series 373.

———. "From Śakti to Shahāda: The Quest for New Meanings in a Changing World Order". In *Islam: Essays on Scripture, Thought and Society. A Festschrift in Honour of Anthony H. Johns*, edited by Peter G. Riddell and Tony Street. Leiden: E.J. Brill, 1997, pp. 219–36.

Tuuk, H.N. van der. *Bataksch-Nederduitsch woordenboek*. Amsterdam: Muller, 1861.

———. *Kawi-Balineesch-Nederlandsch woordenboek*. Batavia: Landsdrukkerij, 1897–1912. Four volumes.

Vickers, Adrian. *Balinese Art: Paintings and Drawings of Bali 1800–2010*. Singapore: Tuttle, 2012.

Vickers, Adrian, Steven Hayes, Ian Johnson, Steve White, Wayan Jarrah Sastrawan, James Watson, Ireneusz Golka and Safrina Thristiawati. *The Virtual Museum of Balinese Painting*, 2011. Available at <http://sydney.edu.au/heurist/balipaintings/index.html>.

Zoetmulder, P.J. *Kalangwan: A Survey of Old Javanese Literature*. The Hague: Nijhoff, 1974. KITLV Translation Series 16.

7

THE ILLUSTRATED ASṬABRATA IN PAKUALAMAN MANUSCRIPT ART

Edwin P. Wieringa

The Asṭabrata or "Eight Rules of Life", which refer to the meritorious acts of the eight Hindu deities which the ideal king should emulate, was first introduced in Java through the Old Javanese kakawin Rāmāyaṇa, in which Rāma lectures Wibhīṣaṇa on the status and role of a king. This exposition of ancient Hindu political theory has remained popular in Java until this present day, Islamization notwithstanding. Over time it has even become regarded as a genuinely Javanese theory on leadership, and part of indigenous wayang *philosophy. This chapter takes a closer look at a Yogyakarta version of the Asṭabrata made at the Pakualaman principality, represented in two early twentieth-century illuminated manuscripts with coloured drawings in* wayang *style. These rare and beautiful artefacts are a wonderful example of how the age-old Indic tradition was once redefined in an Islamicate environment. Examining the iconography of the eight deities that embody the ideal royal virtues, the conclusion is drawn that the illustrations seem to offer merely visual diversion. Although the two manuscripts discussed here were produced in a colonial context as gifts to high-ranking Dutch representatives of the colonial regime, the words and images do not seem to suggest a mode of "writing back" to the dominant Dutch ideology.*

Keywords: Asṭabrata, Yogyakarta, Pakualaman, Javanese manuscript art, mirror for princes.

Rāma's Lessons on Leadership and "Javanese Genius"

In 2011, a book on the *astabrata,* also known under such designations as "the eightfold teachings", "the eight ways of life", and "the eight royal virtues", was published in Indonesia, stating in the blurb that Indonesians were nowadays intoxicated by imported theories on leadership that, however, were ill-fitted to local realities.[1] Hence, the author argued that local wisdom from Indonesia's own heritage as presented in the Astabrata is in fact still relevant (Yasasusastra 2011). Strictly speaking, however, the Astabrata is no less foreign-derived, being a concept of ancient Hindu political theory on "the divine qualities that a king was to emulate" (Weatherbee 1994, p. 414). This model of exemplary kingship ultimately goes back to the *kakawin* Rāmāyaṇa, a long Old Javanese narrative poem, supposed to be dating back to the second half of the ninth century or early tenth century, where Rāma in stanzas 51-60 of canto 24 lectures Wibhīṣaṇa on the status and role of a king on the occasion of the latter's ascension to the throne of Lĕngka after the demon-king Rāwaṇa had been killed.[2] For this passage the Old Javanese poet appears to have drawn upon the ancient Sanskrit Manusmṛti ("Laws of Manu"), which specifically deals with "the idea of eight divinities who are embodied in the king and should be his role-models" (Khanna and Saran 1993, p. 240).

Ever since its first introduction to Java, the Astabrata has been so thoroughly incorporated into Javanese tradition that it became accepted as truly autochthonous. After the Islamization, however, the doctrine was slightly accommodated, so that "not gods, but the virtues represented by those gods, are incorporated in the king" (Behrend 1989, p. 179) while the symbolic contents remained basically unaltered. Its lasting importance and popularity can be gleaned, for example, from the fact that Soemarsaid Moertono (1968; reprinted 2002) in his classic study *State and Statecraft in Old Java: A Study of the Later Mataram Period, 16th to 19th Century* uses the Asṭabrata (taken from the mid-eighteenth-century Sĕrat Rama or "Story of Rama") as one of his principal sources.

Pardi Suratno (2006), too, routinely classifies it as one of the great Javanese works on leadership. Local publications in Javanese, e.g. by the bookshop and publisher Sadu-Budi in Surakarta from the 1960s, treat the Asṭabrata as an important Javanese moralistic-didactic work, belonging to the indigenous world of *wayang* (see Figures 7.1 and 7.2).[3]

According to the anthropologist Hughes-Freeland (2008, pp. 112–13), even today, the regalia of the contemporary court of the Yogyakarta Sultan Hamĕngkubuwana X (r. 1989–present) are golden objects, "representing the eight attributes of kingship (*astabrata*) or meditatory images: the goose of purity; the deer of quickness; the cock of bravery; the peacock of dignity; the king dragon of might; the handkerchief of cleanliness; the powder box of benevolence; and the lamp of illumination".[4] The competing court of Surakarta has a similar set of regalia and there, too, the concept of *asṭabrata* is still very much alive. For example, the anthropologist Sri Kuhnt-Saptodewo (2006, p. 114) informs us of a court dance (*bĕḍaya*) performed by eight female dancers in Surakarta, created in the 1980s, in which the octet is supposed to "embody the Javanese wisdom called *astabrata*".

Discussing the originally Hindu *asṭabrata* in a post-Hindu Islamic context problematizes the use of heavily connotative terms such as "Hindu" and "Muslim", questioning the idea that there are discrete "Hindu" and "Muslim" cultural forms which are diametrically opposed to each other, such that the one excludes the other. All too easily the fact of the popularity of the "Hindu" *asṭabrata* could feed into the persistent prejudice that most Javanese are "bad Muslims". In order to place less of an emphasis on Islam "*in the proper, the religious sense*", the historian Marshall Hodgson (1974, p. 59) introduced the neologism "Islamicate" which refers "not directly to the religion, Islam, itself, but to the social and cultural complex historically associated with Islam and the Muslims". In the same vein scholars employ the term "Indic" in order "to move beyond a fixation with bounded categories"; in the latter case "beyond Hindu doctrine or practice" (Gilmartin and Lawrence 2000, p. 2). Richard Foltz (2013, p. xiii) has proposed that "religion/culture is best understood not in terms of essential features, but as a set of possibilities within a recognizable framework, or 'pool'." His approach, attempting to identify "a pool of ideas and behaviours from which

FIGURE 7.1

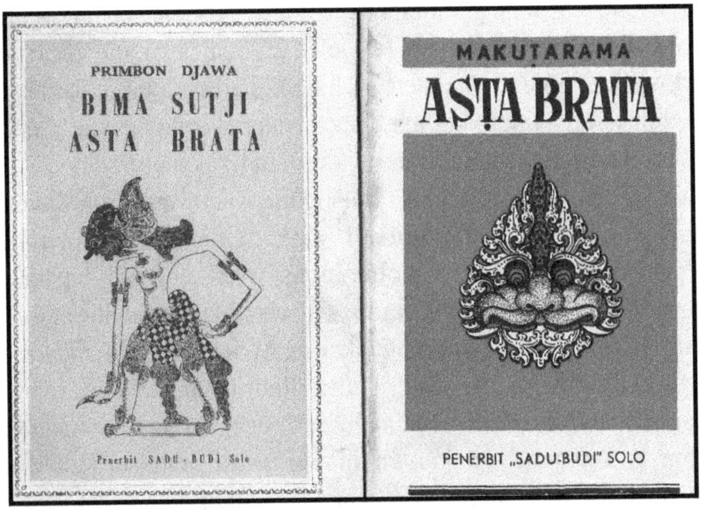

Two Javanese publications of the *Asṭabrata* from the 1960s.
Left: *Primbon Djawa. Bima Sutji, Asta Brata* (Solo: Sadu-Budi, [n.d.]).
Right: *Makuṭa Rama lan Asṭa Brata* (Solo: Sadu-Budi, 1960).

FIGURE 7.2

Javanese *wayang*-style representations of Rāma (*Prabu* or "King" Rama) and Wibhīṣaṇa (Wibisana). Opening pages of the *Makuṭa Rama lan Asṭa Brata* (Solo: Sadu-Budi, 1960).

communities and individuals may draw in constituting their particular worldview", might help us understand the reception and internalization of the *asṭabrata* in Java. Such key characteristics of the ideal king as justice, love, cleverness, piety, etc., which are articulated in the *asṭabrata*, are not exclusively Hindu, but may be considered as to be nearly universal, and hence easily appropriated as Islamic and Javanese.

In this volume's framework of tracing the Rāmāyaṇa and Mahābhārata in Javanese and Malay literature, I wish to discuss the *asṭabrata* as it is represented in a rather voluminous work entitled Sastra Agĕng Adidarma that was originally composed in 1841 under the auspices of Pakualam II (r. 1829–58) in Yogyakarta. At least four manuscripts are known to exist, two in two Yogyakarta libraries and two in two Leiden libraries.[5] A search in published catalogues revealed that the Sastra Agĕng Adidarma is apparently unknown in Surakarta manuscripts.[6] Lavishly illustrated, these beautiful artefacts are wonderful examples of how the age-old Indic tradition was once redefined in an Islamicate environment. The aim of the present chapter is to look into the iconography of the eight deities that embody the ideal royal virtues. The eight impressive *wayang*-style figures are depicted in "the language of the silhouette" (Solomonik 1980), which is particularly rich in detail. However, given the limits of space and ability, I will focus upon those elements that may perhaps be considered to function as a "visual gloss or exegesis of the text" (Karkov 2001, p. 8). The Pakualaman manuscript rendition of the Asṭabrata contains both verbal and visual narratives and what interests me here is the way in which the drawings that serve to "illustrate" the text translate the worded version into the language of the silhouette. Firstly, however, a brief introduction of the sources used is in order to provide some contextual background. For the sake of brevity, I will refer to Leiden University Library Cod. Or. 6388 as MS A, to KITLV Or. 189 as MS B, and to Yogyakarta Pakualaman Library Pi.36 (the source of Suryodilogo 2012) as MS C.

Mirrors for Princes as Presents for Professors

Although the Pakualaman principality boasts a distinct regional style of manuscript embellishment and illumination, little research has been done on it hitherto. Of course, one may easily blame the few specialists (who can be counted on the fingers of both hands at the very most) for their "logocentric" attitude, primarily focusing upon manuscripts as text carriers. However, in this case a more practical reason hampering research is that the main depository of Pakualaman manuscripts, viz. the library held in the Pakualaman principality, still tends to be difficult to gain access to. Official regulations stipulate that its manuscripts are, in principle, not allowed to be reproduced in any form (e.g. microfilm, photograph, digitization).

However, gradually an era of more openness seems to be emerging. A few years ago, a very welcome catalogue of the manuscript collection was published, admirably edited by Sri Ratna Saktimulya (2005), who is herself an expert on Pakualaman manuscript art. Furthermore, in 2012, within the framework of celebrating the 200th foundation year of the principality, the Pakualaman library brought out a book, edited by Saktimulya, Sudibyo and Sumardiyanto, on the court's cultural aspects (architecture, *wayang*, literature, culinary art, etc.), featuring many photographs depicting beautiful manuscript pages.[7] In the same year, the Pakualaman library published another book, this time showcasing the Asṭabrata as contained in the Sĕstradisuhul (Suryodilogo 2012).[8] In fact, this official publication of the Pakualaman, preceded by a foreword by the then ruling Pakualam IX (r. 1998–2015) and suffused with wonderful images and insightful commentaries, inspired me to have a closer look at MSS A and B. The Sĕstradisuhul, which is discussed in Suryodilogo (2012), will be referred to as MS C. Further research is needed to look into the way the Asṭabrata is represented in other works from the Pakualaman such as the Baratayuda, the Pawukon Saha Sĕrat Piwulang, Dasanama Saha Pĕpali, and the Slawatan Langĕn Pradapa (Saktimulya et al. 2012, p. 147; Suryodilogo 2012, p. xi). The fact that the Asṭabrata is included in twelve (Suryodilogo 2012, p. xi) or perhaps even fourteen (Saktimulya et al. 2012, p. 147) manuscripts in the Pakualaman library indicates its high reputation. However, as such research needs to be conducted in the Pakualaman library itself and with no reproductions to work from, few scholars will be able to take up the gauntlet.

My focus upon the two Leiden artefacts is, however, not solely motivated by practical circumstances. Arguably, these two manuscripts share a similar function as ritual objects, having been specifically produced in the Pakualaman scriptorium as gifts for Dutch scholars. Pangeran Arya Natadiraja (1858–1917), son of Pakualam V (r. 1878–1900) and long-time manager of the day-to-day politics of the principality, was the principal person behind both offerings.[9] The first manuscript, kept in Leiden University Library under call number Cod. Or. 6388 (described in Pigeaud 1968, p. 365), was presented by him on 1 September 1900 to Godard (Arend Johannes) Hazeu. The manuscript is identified on a label on the binding in Latin characters as Adidoemastrå.

Born in Amsterdam on 22 August 1870, Hazeu read Indonesian studies in Leiden and in 1897 obtained his PhD on Javanese *wayang* theatre under the guidance of Professor Hendrik Kern who was later to become the second Dutch recipient of a Pakualaman manuscript of the Sastra Agĕng Adidarma (more thereon below). Appointed as lecturer for Javanese at the Gymnasium Willem II in Batavia the following year, Hazeu built a network of contacts in Javanese circles in order to deepen his knowledge of Javanese culture.[10] From 1904 to 1919 he held several high-ranking positions in the colonial hierarchy, where his affectionate feelings for the Indies and especially his sympathy for the Indonesian nationalist cause not only made him into a *rara avis* among his Dutch peers, but increasingly into an outsider. Although he acted as the Advisor for Native and Arab Affairs, his advice increasingly fell on deaf ears with the Governor General.

The Dutch newspaper *Nieuws van den Dag* called him in 1919 a "traitor of his own race", and his courteous behaviour in accordance to Javanese etiquette and his habit of conversing with the "indigenes" in their own language, was mocked as "slimy" (Jaquet 2012). In the same year, another newspaper, *Het Indische Volk*, described him as "not the man of the curse and the fist" (*niet de man van den vloek en de vuist*, cited in Jaquet 2012), thus he was apparently lacking in essential skills of colonial administration. According to the colonial press and Dutch bureaucrats, Hazeu was not only a "meek fool" (*goedige dwaas*), but also a "dangerous enthusiast" (*gevaarlijke dweper*), suffering from "Kromo-mania" (*Kromo* was the Dutch nickname for Javanese commoners (Van den Doel 1994, p. 381; Bosma 1997, p. 268). Disappointed with Dutch rule in the Indies, he finally left for Holland where he was appointed professor of Javanese language and literature at the University of Leiden in 1920. However, already suffering from bad health, he had to resign in 1928, passing away the following year.

From this potted life-story we may gather that MS A probably must have been offered as a token of appreciation to a devoted Dutch student of Javanese culture, perhaps as a birthday present. In contrast to earlier Dutch scholarship, which routinely emphasized foreign roots for almost all things Indonesian, Hazeu's ideas were of a strongly Indonesian-centric nature. His PhD, which purported that *wayang* was an essentially Javanese phenomenon rather than just another Indian borrowing, made a great impression upon early twentieth-century Javanist leaders (Sears 1996, pp. 134–35).

In 1910, another copy of the Sastra Agĕng Adidarma was offered to another Dutch academic, viz. Professor Hendrik Kern (1833–1917), as a present on behalf of the Pakualaman House.[11] Since 1958, this manuscript has been kept under call number Or. 189 in the library of the KITLV in Leiden.[12] An accompanying Dutch letter, by Kern's former student Sosro Kartono (1877–1951), dated 20 July 1910 in Leiden, and co-signed by six other aristocratic Javanese (ex-)students in the Netherlands, states that it was meant as a token of "homage for all you did for our language and history, for our country and people".[13] Johan Hendrik Caspar Kern, born on 4 April 1833 in Purworejo, Central Java, was the first professor of Sanskrit in the Netherlands after he was appointed to the chair in 1865. Covering the broad field of what was then called *Indologie* ("Indology", which primarily covered Indonesian studies), he was a phenomenally productive scholar who wrote on wide-ranging areas encompassing "linguistic and philological studies, ancient Indian astronomy, and Buddhism, as well as many languages, including Sanskrit, Avestan, Old Javanese and those of the Austronesian family" ('t Hart 1989, p. 127). As one biographer put it, "[i]t would take at least five scholars to even begin to evaluate Kern's contribution" (cited in 't Hart 1989, p. 140). In the framework of this volume, it should perhaps be remembered that modern scholarly study of the Old Javanese Rāmāyaṇa begins with Kern's 1900 text edition.[14] Even after his retirement in 1903 Kern kept up his prodigious work rate until his death in 1917.

His Javanese student Raden Mas Panji Sosro Kartono was the brother of the famous Raden Ajĕng Kartini (1879–1904), who had entered Leiden University as a student in 1901, becoming the "first fully-fledged Indonesian university student" (Poeze 1989, p. 253).[15] The "old, authoritative Professor H. Kern felt very sympathetic towards the young Javanese [man]" (Poeze 1989, p. 253) who became his protégé. The six co-signatories of the letter of congratulations to Kern were also members of the Javanese elite living in the Netherlands: the first four, viz. Raden Mas Notok(u)woro, Raden Mas Noto Suroto, Raden Mas Notodiningrat, and Raden Mas Gondowinoto were all sons of Pangeran Notodirodjo (or Natadiraja), i.e. the same person who ten years earlier had presented Hazeu with MS A. The two other men, viz. Raden Mas Brantĕl and Mas Ngabehi Rajiman, were both *dokter jawa*, pursuing further medical studies in Amsterdam. The latter was none other than Radjiman Widijodiningrat (1879–1951), who had received his *dokter jawa* title in 1899 and who in 1909 went to Holland and became a Dutch-trained physician (van Niel 1984, p. 54). Also known as Raden Ngabehi Wediodipoera, he belonged to the "best educated Javanese men of his time" (van Miert 1995, p. 134), who after his return to Java (in 1911) became the court physician in Surakarta and a prominent member of the Javanese aristocratic organisation *Budi Utomo* ("Beautiful Endeavour") (Ricklefs 2001, p. 208).

I should like to point out that although the Asṭabrata constitutes the central concern of my contribution, this part only takes up a few pages in the entire volume of the Sastra Agĕng Adidarma. According to Pigeaud's description of MS B, its entire text, which he calls Adi Darma Sastra (the title page of MS B calls it Sĕrat Aḍidarmasastra), consists of 93 cantos in *tĕmbang macapat* verse, containing "Javanese moralistic reflections, tales and animal fables, i.a. kañcil stories, lessons in strategy (battle-arrays) and statecraft (asṭa brata), genealogical trees" (Pigeaud 1968, p. 830). On the basis of catalogue descriptions of the four Sastra Agĕng Adidarma manuscripts, it seems that Pakualaman library Pi.35 constitutes its most complete version, comprising 96 cantos (Saktimulya 2005, pp. 108–9), whereas MS A is the shortest, lacking e.g. the part on battle-arrays.

Pigeaud (1968, p. 830) mentions that "[a]ccording to outside information, the original was written in 1832." In fact, this "outside information" comes from Petrus Voorhoeve (1899–1996), the well-known cataloguer of Indonesian manuscripts and one-time curator of the KITLV's collection, who in an accompanying Dutch note to MS B (dated 24 May 1958) describes the text as "a collection of several Javanese pieces of information and ethical expositions, some of which are elucidated with stories and fables; copy of a manuscript written in 1832 from the Pakualaman."[16] However, in the text's opening stanza (MS B, p. 1) the date 15 Sapar 1769 (*Anno Javanico*) is provided, signified by the chronogram *trus usiking panḍiteng rat* or when "penetrating (9) were the thoughts (6) of the wise men (7) of the world (1)". This date converts to 7 April 1841 of the Common Era. As the Yogyakarta manuscript Pi.35 also mentions this (Javanese) date, I am inclined to think that Voorhoeve's earlier date may simply be due to a miscalculation on his part.

In his survey of literature and the arts in the Pakualaman principality, Ki Hadjar Dewantara (2003, p. 337) describes what he calls the Sĕrat Ngadidamastra as "an original work" of Pakualam II, "the content of which lies in the area of moral teaching. This cannot be called a short moralistic poem but is quite a large poetical composition of around 200 folio pages." In the introduction to the work itself, however, we learn from the second stanza (MS B, p. 1) that "the name of this book is Sastra Agĕng Adidarma" (*namane sĕrat puniki / Sastra Agĕng Adidarma*). Such a lofty title, which is full of Sanskrit borrowings, is difficult to translate in English. *Sastra Agĕng* could be rendered as "Great Literature", but one should know that the primary role of *sastra* ("writing; literature", derived from Sanskrit *śāstra*, i.e. "any instrument of teaching, especially religious or scientific book") is imparting knowledge, commonly of a religious or philosophical nature (Ras 1986, pp. 251–52). This is also brought out by the term *adi* ("fine, beautiful", borrowed from Sanskrit *ādi* "beginning", taken in the sense of "eminent", see Gonda 1998, p. 449), which is here attached to *darma*, which in New Javanese means "duty, obligation", but is still closely connected to the semantic field of the original Sanskrit word *dharma* (religion, law, and justice).

Although in the same stanza Pakualam II is credited with drafting the composition (*Pakualaman kapinḍo / rengrengira kasariran*), the actual work is said to have been carried out by two of his servants: Raden Panji Jayengminarsa was the "the servant who did the work" (*abdine ingkang garap*) and, according to the third stanza (MS B, p. 1), Raden Panji Harjawinata acted as "the servant who reads" (*abdine kang maos*). How should we interpret this tantalizingly brief information? The same team, with the same division of roles, also created the so-called *Sĕstradisuhul* (mentioned above and our MS C), which was begun on 11 Saban 1775 AJ, or 24 July 1847 CE. The title, which is no less grandiloquent as the previous work, is glossed as follows: *sĕs* is "excellent sense" (*raos ingkang inggil*); *tra* is "true means" (*sarat ingkang nyata*); *adi* is "eminent" (*luwih*, also see above); *suhul* is "perfect meaning" (*kalogatan tutug*) (Saktimulya 1998, p. 10). In her discussion of this text, Saktimulya (1998, p. 13) regards Pakualam II as the *spiritus rector* of the undertaking, viewing him as the "originator and drafter", with Harjawinata reading out Pakualam II's ideas to Jayengminarsa who subsequently put them into writing.

Adopting a less deferential view, however, it is also possible to regard Pakualam II as the commissioner who roughly explained to his servants what he wished to be done.[17] In composing the narrative text in *tĕmbang* verse, Jayengminarsa seems to have been primarily responsible for the text, whereas Harjawinata had a more editorial role. As Bernard Arps (1992, p. 3) informs us, "[a]uthors compose texts in tĕmbang while singing". As texts in *tĕmbang* were intended to be chanted aloud in public gatherings, Harjawinata's task should perhaps be understood here as proofreading. His job, referred to as *maos* in Javanese, in fact not merely means "to read", but rather "to recite, chant, sing (poetry)". Furthermore, in the case of the *Sĕstradisuhul* the text continues: "and there was another servant, Mas Jayadin who often functioned as advisor" (*lawan wontĕn abdi malih / Mas Jayadin kang sring mangka pangosekan*).[18] However, there is not a single word about the artists responsible for the illustrations. The copyists and the illustrators of MSS A and B, too, remain anonymous.

The Iconography of the Eight Deities

Suryodilogo (2012) provides rather detailed descriptions of the eight gods depicted, mentioning physical traits (face and body, including the types of eyes and noses) as well as social features (clothes and ornaments). Of course, the "language of the silhouette" is most important for identifying individual characters in *wayang*, but as the figures of the gods are directly embedded in the text, the reader is not really faced with identification problems. All of the gods are facing left, as their natural place is on the right side of the screen (*kĕlir*), which is "associated with characters of greater power" (Mrázek 2005, p. 107). As all eight figures belong to the highest class of the *baṭara* or deities, they share many characteristics. For example, a long cloak or robe (*jubah*), a shawl (*slendang*) as a "sign of piety and virtue" (Solomonik 1980, p. 492), and shoes (*sĕpatu*) are typical pieces of clothing that belong to the outer appearance of the gods and religious classes (Mellema 1988, p. 28). Gods generally also like to wear the clerical cap (*kĕṭu dewa*), often combined with the diadem (*jamang*) and with the hair ornament or griffin (*garuḍa mungkur*) (Mellema 1988, p. 24). Unsurprisingly, then, we can observe that almost all gods in our manuscripts (see Figures 7.3–7.10) wear most of these class markers, with the notable exception of the figures of the Gods Bayu (see Figure 7.7) and Brama (see Figure 7.9), who are individualized in almost exactly the same way.

Yet there are also quite a few differences between the eight deities that may open up a potential pathway for further research. As *wayang* aficionados well know, the list of bodily and sartorial details could easily be expanded upon. For example, Suryodilogo (2012) does not go into the fact that five of the gods (Indra, Yama, Bayu, Brama, and Baruna) sport a beard under the chin (*wok*), whereas three of them (Surya, Candra, and Wisnu) are completely clean-faced. As research has shown (e.g. Hiltebeitel and Miller 1998), hair is used as "the key signifier or semiotic device" in a variety of Asian cultures (Obeyesekere 1998, p. xii), but in this particular case the meaning of the presence or absence of facial hair remains puzzling. Beards are generally considered powerful symbols of masculinity and especially in the case of Bayu (see Figure 7.7) and Brama (see Figure 7.9) we are dealing with big, hairy, awe-inspiring warriors, but by the same token this cannot imply that the beardless Gods Surya (see Figure 7.5), Candra (see Figure 7.6), and Wisnu (see Figure 7.8) are somehow not “manly”. Another question needing further clarification is why it is that in contrast to Candra and Wisnu, who are also beardless in conventional *wayang* iconography, Surya should be beardless, too, whereas he normally has a full beard (Hardjowirogo 1989, p. 57).

My approach will be to focus upon those differential elements that may be considered to be consequential for the specific quality of a certain god. The search, then, must be for certain unique signifiers that may help us to reveal the key characteristic of an individual god. Suryodilogo (2012) must be praised for his pioneering work in this respect, attempting to pinpoint specific details as defining elements, although I think that his identifications are not always truly discriminating and hence not individual enough. For example, dealing with facial hair, Suryodilogo (2012, p. 71) comments that Candra’s lock of hair at the temple (see Figure 7.6) symbolizes that he is “always in a youthful state”. Of course, this may well be true, but, on the other hand, it is not a unique feature of this god only, because almost all other gods also have this trait, which Suryodilogo (2012), however, does not comment upon. He does not explain the connection between the lock of hair and youth either, but the suggestion seems to lie in its very name, viz. *sinom*, which not only denotes “a fringe of hair worn by girls [*sic*] across the forehead at the hairline”, but also “young shoots; young leaves of the tamarind tree” (Robson and Wibisono 2002, p. 683). The connotation with youth is further evoked by the derivation *sinoman*, which is “an association of unmarried boys and girls” in rural society (Robson and Wibisono 2002, p. 683).

Conversely, in the case of the ear ornament (*sumping*) of the so-called *surengpati* variety, we find that Brama (see Figure 7.9) appears to be the sole deity to wear this decoration, although normally it is worn by most gods (and nearly all of the kings) in traditional *wayang* iconography (Solomonik 1980, p. 488). According to Suryodilogo (2012, p. 72), this element symbolizes that its wearer is “ruthless and resolute” and once again the name is significant here: *surengpati* means “death scorning”, which is indeed in tune with Brama’s character. Unfortunately, however,

Suryodilogo (2012) does not comment on the possible meaning of the ear ornaments worn by the other gods. The gods Indra (see Figure 7.3), Yama (see Figure 7.4), Surya (see Figure 7.5), Candra (see Figure 7.6), and Baruna (see Figure 7.10) all wear ear ornaments of the *waděran* type (i.e. like a *waděr* which is a kind of small freshwater fish), which according to *wayang* lore is found in different classes and therefore not connected with specific titles (Solomonik 1980, p. 489).

However, both Bayu (see Figure 7.7) and Wisnu (see Figure 7.8) have very particular ear ornaments, which should therefore warrant closer scrutiny. Suryodilogo (2012, p. 71) identifies Bayu's ear ornament as *puḍak satěgal* or *panḍan biněṭot*, whereas Wisnu wears the *mangkara* variety (Suryodilogo 2012, p. 71), which is rather remarkable, because both deities in traditional *wayang* iconography wear the *waděran* type (Hardjowirogo 1989, pp. 49 and 51). I must confess to be at a loss as to why Bayu should be connected to the *puḍak* or *panḍan*, i.e. pandanus flower, and although Wisnu is commonly represented in *wayang* iconography with the *mangkara* (lobster) variety, here, too, I am unaware of any specific meaning. The explanation that it would symbolize "greatness, majesty" is so general to be almost useless.[19]

Let us now turn to the illustrations of the eight deities (see Figures 7.3–7.10) and discuss them individually, attempting to look whether the specific "meritorious practices" (*brata*) attributed to them are also visually discernable. The first deity is Indra (see Figure 7.3) and, as expressed in the accompanying text, "it belongs to God Indra's character / to be fond of teaching" (*watěke Běṭara Endra / měmulang karěměnane*, MS C, p. 418, see Suryodilogo 2012, p. 6). In his right hand he holds a book which, according to Suryodilogo (2012, p. 69), indicates this characteristic, but then, four other gods (Yama, Surya, Candra, and Baruna) are likewise pictured with a book. Intriguingly, in MS B a courtier is sitting in front of Indra, in a style reminiscent of a teacher–student relationship, which we also find in MS C, but this is missing in MS A. Suryodilogo (2012, p. 69) remarks that Indra has pulled off his shoes, which in MS C are placed under his throne. As Suryodilogo (2012, p. 69) duly notes, the shoes are class indicators of godly status, but it remains unexplained as to why he should be barefoot here. In MS B we see that the illustrator has sketched the shoes, but apparently the drawing was not quite finished.

FIGURE 7.3

Indra in MS A (left) and MS B (right).

In this respect it is also worth noting that the pages of Indra's book have been left blank. In accordance with traditional *wayang* iconography, MS B shows Indra with closed lips (Hardjowirogo 1989, p. 47), but in MS A we can clearly see his teeth — again a difference perhaps with potential meaning.

Concerning the second deity (see Figure 7.4), the Old Javanese poet (canto 24:54) writes that "Yama's rule is to chastise evil *karma* (deeds)" (*Yamabrata ḍumaṇḍa karmāhala*).[20] The New Javanese rendition rephrases this idea as "Yama's character is unwaveringly wise, destroying the dregs of society" (*Nora pĕgat watĕke Yama wicaksuh / nglinapsuh gĕlahing bumi*, MS C, p. 426, see Suryodilogo 2012, p. 14). The accompanying image (see Figure 7.4) could perhaps be interpreted as that of a judge reading the sentence, but the other illustrations of no less than four gods (Indra, Surya, Candra, and Baruna) likewise show a similar reading posture. According to Suryodilogo (2012, p. 69), Yama is pictured with facial traits expressing resoluteness, boldness,

FIGURE 7.4

Yama in MS A (left) and MS B (right).

and authority. I suppose this is very much in the eye of the beholder, but at least we can say that Yama does not show a very friendly expression on his face. However, this makes Suryodilogo's (2012, p. 69) remark that in certain situations Yama likes to joke around rather hard to imagine. Yama's eyes are *ṭĕlĕngan*, i.e. having purely round pupils (Mellema 1988, p. 18), which Suryodilogo (2012, p. 69) interprets as indicating clear-sightedness. Furthermore, Suryodilogo (2012, p. 69) describes the nose shape as *ḍĕmpok*, i.e. "large and thick with a bump at the end" (Robson and Wibisono 2002, p. 186), but it remains unexplained as to what this physiognomic detail possibly tells us about the inner character. Again we notice the same small differences between the drawings of MS A and B: the deity in MS B does not wear shoes and the pages of his book are blank.

The third deity, Surya (see Figure 7.5), "likes to collect gold and money, / anything of worth, / all which may have a high price" (*rĕmĕn ngumpulkĕn mas picis / apa kang aji-aji / kang kira keh harginipun,*

FIGURE 7.5

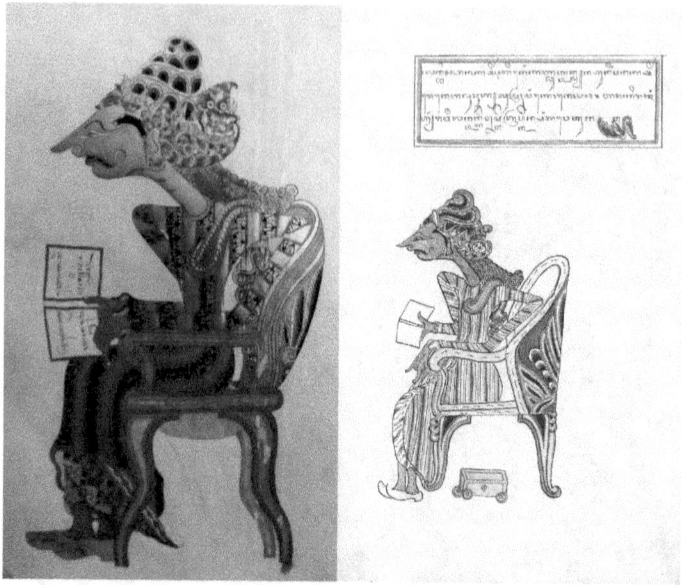

Surya in MS A (left) and MS B (right).

MS C, p. 435, see Suryodilogo 2012, p. 22). In MS B there is a cash box on wheels, which is also shown in MS C, but it is missing in MS A. As Suryodilogo (2012, p. 70) explains, the wheels symbolize the proverbial wisdom that you must keep money moving. This attribute, clearly indicating Surya's connection with money, would seem to be of primary importance in the illustration and one wonders whether its omission in MS A may be due to error. Suryodilogo (2012, p. 70) merely notes the dominance of gold, but in my opinion this colour, too, could be regarded as another hint in the direction of Surya's chief characteristic. Intriguingly, only in MS C Surya has a dagger (*kĕris*) at the front on the waist, which may perhaps point to an important aspect of money, viz. its "power to kill people" (*mateni uwong kuwasa*, MS C, p. 439, see Suryodilogo 2012, p. 439).[21]

The Old Javanese *Rāmāyaṇa* (canto 24:56) states that "[t]he Śaśi (Candra) rule is to gladden the whole world" (*Śaśibrata humarṣukang rāt kabeh*, see Robson 2015, p. 650 and Van der Molen 2015, p. 530;

cf. Santoso [1980], p. 624), admonishing that "[y]our actions should be soft and tender to behold" (*ulahta mṛdu komalā yan katon*, see Robson 2015, p. 650 and Van der Molen 2015, p. 530; cf. Santoso [1980], p. 624). Basically the same message can be found in its New Javanese adaptation, emphasizing that "God Candra is in love / with beauty" (*Yyang Candra kang brangti / maring ing lĕlango*, MS C, p. 444, see Suryodilogo 2012, p. 30). His amorous character is made visible by his reading of a book on sexual pleasure (*asmaragama*) which, according to Suryodilogo (2012, p. 70), shows that Candra likes to teach about love-making (see Figure 7.6). It may take some effort to decipher the text on the pages of Candra's book in MSS B and C, but at least in MS A the last word is clearly *asmaragama* (see Figure 7.6). In the main text, the poet rather elaborately celebrates the joys of heterosexual love, adding an interesting Islam-inspired aside (MS C, p. 446, see Suryodilogo 2012, p. 30):

FIGURE 7.6

Candra in MS A (left) and MS B (right).

Mila wadyane Ywang Candra inggih	Therefore, indeed, of God Candra's followers
meh sĕdaya mawon	almost all
sami wayuh nyĕkawan semahe	have four wives,
sabab idining dewane nĕnggih	as this is in fact permitted by their god.

We can see a protruding hand offering a flowerpot with some (unidentified) flowers in MSS B and C. According to Suryodilogo (2012, p. 70), in the context of love, flowers symbolize beauty and romance, which would thus seem to be an important signifier, and one can only guess as to why it is missing in MS A.

The fifth deity, Bayu (see Figure 7.7), is "always diligent and indefatigable" (*mung taběri nora lěson*, MS C, pp. 450–51, see Suryodilogo 2012, p. 38). It is well-known that "lying down to rest and acting in a lazy way are detested by him" (*lěson ngěsed kang den-sěngiti*, MS C, p. 453, see Suryodilogo 2012, p. 38), because "rigid and solid is the venerable Bayu / comparable to a mountain of steel" (*kaku kukuh sang Bayu iki / lir gunung wěsi pama*, MS C, p. 454, see Suryodilogo 2012, p. 38). Although Suryodilogo (2012, p. 71) provides a rather detailed description of the way the god of the Winds is pictured in the illustration, he does not really go into the relation between the signifiers and the signified. Apart from Bayu's imposing physique in general, an outward sign of his ferocious character is surely his club (*gada*). Another weapon is his razor-sharp thumbnail (*pancanaka*). Benedict Anderson (1996, p. 50) furthermore points to the magical *poleng* loin-cloth, whose checks symbolize "the four super-deities Bråmå, Guru (Shiwa), Wisnu, and Suryå". Bayu has a hairy chest in MS C, which may be regarded as a symbol of masculinity and power, but this is not the case in MS B, whereas in MS A his (hairy) chest is covered by a shawl (*slendang*), which is a general class marker (see above).

As the poet tells us about Wisnu's character, "his mind is only set on worshipping" (*pěnggalihe mung karěm měmuja*, MS C, p. 462, see Suryodilogo 2012, p. 46) and this is very clearly depicted in the illustration (see Figure 7.8). This deity is sitting in front of an incense burner with his hands in a gesture perhaps suggesting praying hands. In MSS B and C the scene takes place in an enclosed place

FIGURE 7.7

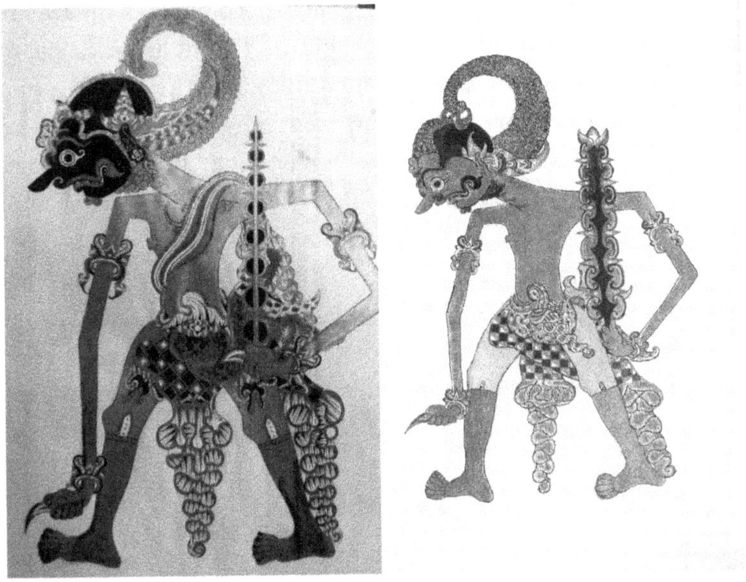

Bayu in MS A (left) and MS B (right).

FIGURE 7.8

Wisnu in MS A (left) and MS B (right).

of worship (*pamujaan*). In contrast to this serenity, the seventh deity, Brama (see Figure 7.9), has many points in common with Bayu (see Figure 7.7), having a comparable physique and outfit as well as carrying weapons (a sword and a dagger). Suryodilogo (2012, p. 72) points to Brama's pink facial colour indicating aggressiveness. It belongs to the symbolic category of "red", generally denoting a violent temper in *wayang* iconography (Mellema 1988, p. 64), which is in accordance to his description as being "hot-tempered" (*panasbaran galih*, MS C, p. 467, see Suryodilogo 2012, p. 54). In fact, Brama is the "god of fire" (Hardjowirogo 1989, p. 52; Sudibyoprono 1991, p. 126). The poem describes how Brama demands complete discipline, not accepting orders not being obeyed, and his military demeanour and stern appearance are

FIGURE 7.9

Brama in MS A (left) and MS B (right).

clearly visible in the illustration. His "bossy" behaviour is emphasized in MS B where he appears to give orders to two subordinates. It is rather remarkable that Brama wears the dagger (*kĕris*) on his back which, to be sure, is in accordance to the normal Javanese way, but not usual for Brama in *wayang* iconography, where he wears it in the front, ready to draw — a further symbol of his hot temper (Hardjowirogo 1989, p. 53).

According to the Old Javanese Rāmāyaṇa (canto 24:59), Baruna possesses a highly effective weapon, a sort of magic noose for ensnaring (*nāgagapāśāngapus*) and hence the king should be aware of the "duty of using chains" in exercising his punishing power.[22] The New Javanese Pakualaman rendition of the Asṭabrata, however, which is written in a "[h]ighly artificial and mannered poetic style" (Pigeaud 1968, p. 830), is not always easy to comprehend, but if I understand the rather highfalutin wording correctly, it is said about Baruna that "his character is to reduce all rudeness" (*watĕkira angglung sanggyaning wĕgig*, MS C, p. 472, see Suryodilogo 2012, p. 62).[23] Two proverbs (*paribasan*) are applied to him, viz. that he is "standing out among the crowd" (*mrojol ing krĕp*) and "way above surface level" (*moncol ngapapak*) (MS C, p. 475, see Suryodilogo 2012, p. 62). According to Suryodilogo (2012, p. 72), Baruna is said to be clever in all things he does, which interpretation could be seen as supported by common explanations of both proverbs.[24] Perhaps this is hinted at by his holding a book, understood to be the source of wisdom. The illustration (see Figure 7.10) does not seem to contain any specific elements revealing this deity's individuality. However, Baruna is none other than Varuṇa, the Vedic god of the waters, who in *wayang* iconography has a fishy body covered with scales (Sudibyoprono 1991, p. 104) and perhaps this aquatic aspect is alluded to in MS A, in which he wears a robe with a motif which is rather reminiscent of fish scales or seashells. By contrast, in both MSS B and C his robe is striped (*lurik*).

In conclusion, the illustrations of the deities seem to offer merely visual diversion, not really prompting distinctive re-readings of the

FIGURE 7.10

Baruna in MS A (left) and MS B (right).

written text. We have seen that there exists a small range of "variant readings" within the pictorial narrative, e.g. the omission of the money box of Surya in MS A or the addition of two servants for Brama in MS B, but at this stage of research it is too premature to comment on the complex question as to whether some of the variants are to be regarded as lacunae or errors. Is there something like a "correct" reading or are we dealing with different interpretations, "much as the minstrel interprets the text in its oral transmission" (Hindman 1994, p. 5)?[25] Only a comparison with other illustrated Asṭabrata manuscripts from the Pakualaman tradition will shed more light upon the artistic transmission of the text and pictures, so that we can more fully grasp what the "canonical standard" was.

Concerning the interpretation of individual manuscripts, MSS A and B hold a special position within Pakualaman manuscript art as they were expressly produced as gifts for non-Javanese recipients. One final point still needs to be discussed here, because I have not yet addressed the proverbial elephant in the room: manuscript production and its colonial context. As the anthropologist Nicholas Thomas (1991, p. xi) notes: "Nearly all the societies which anthropologists made into case studies for exchange theory were or still are colonized, but this context of illiberal domination entered into these accounts, if it was mentioned at all, only as external contingency, never as a fact that needed to be central to analysis." Critical theory and post-colonial criticism have long since exactly done that, focusing upon the power differentials at work in the colonial era and its aftermath.

Javanese Lessons for the Dutch?

Given the context of MSS A and B, manuscripts produced in a colonial context to be presented to high-ranking representatives of the colonial regime, there is a bigger question that presents itself: that of scrutinizing colonialist and anti-colonialist discourse. As postcolonial theorists like to ask, what about "voices of resistance" and testimonies of "agency"? Or as Gayatri Spivak, in a founding text of post-colonialism, phrased it: "Can the subaltern speak?" Are there perhaps indications for a mode of narrative presentation which can be identified as "writing back", "oppositional literature", or "counter-discourse"?[26]

In his article on "Malays toying with Americans", Ian Proudfoot (2000) has pointed to a mid-nineteenth-century case of a Malay scribe who had the audacity to produce a mock manuscript, knowing well that his Western audience was unable to read what he wrote. I myself have argued that another Malay scribe, in 1828, copied a work of religious admonition as a farewell present to his Dutch superior, which not only could be read as a forget-me-not, but also as a final homiletic lesson (Wieringa 1998). As we have seen (above), the illustrated

Asṭabrata forms part of a much larger work, known as Sastra Agĕng Adidarma, a comprehensive compilation of texts belonging to the "Mirror for Princes" genre of literature. Were MSS A and B, containing texts of a moralistic-didactic nature, perhaps intended to teach a lesson or two to their highly learned Dutch recipients about the principles of good governance? Attempting to answer this question would involve a very time-consuming research programme as the manuscripts should not only be read in their entirety, but close attention also would need to be paid to their rich visual language. Had I done so, I would have written a different contribution and most certainly not have had the occasion to attend the conference on "Traces of the Two Great Epics".

Let me close with a remark on why such a search for possible anti-colonialist clues is not without its methodological problems. I am thinking particularly of the temptation to adopt an approach which the Germans aptly call *hineininterpretieren* or "reading too much into" the text and its pictures. For example, browsing the pages of MS B, which dates from the early twentieth century (see above), my eye was drawn to one particular battle array with firing cannons and guns with bayonets, and displaying not only Dutch flags (which, by the way, are ubiquitous in this segment on military strategy), but also what seem to be the "Rising Sun" flag of Japan (see Figure 7.11). In the late nineteenth and early twentieth centuries, Japan built an extensive empire, fighting several significant wars in Asia. Its emerging power on the world stage became clear in the Sino–Japanese War (1894–95) when it defeated the Middle Kingdom, whereas the Russo–Japanese War (1904–5) further greatly enhanced its modern army's prestige after an Asian victory over a Western state. The conflict found great interest in vernacular newspapers in Java in those years and therefore it may perhaps be suggested that we have discovered a lingering trace of this in the illustration. However, upon closer inspection the supposedly Japanese flag with its white banner and red circle is in fact the polar opposite of the flag with the red banner and white circle, and hence, perhaps, just functional and not necessarily Japanese and political at all.

FIGURE 7.11

Battle array with three different flags. MS B, p. 28.

On the other hand, it could be counter-argued that the flag with the red banner and white circle might indicate the Ottoman flag which, properly speaking, should have the crescent moon and a star.[27] Rather puzzlingly in that context, the final illustrated battle array (see Figure 7.12)

FIGURE 7.12

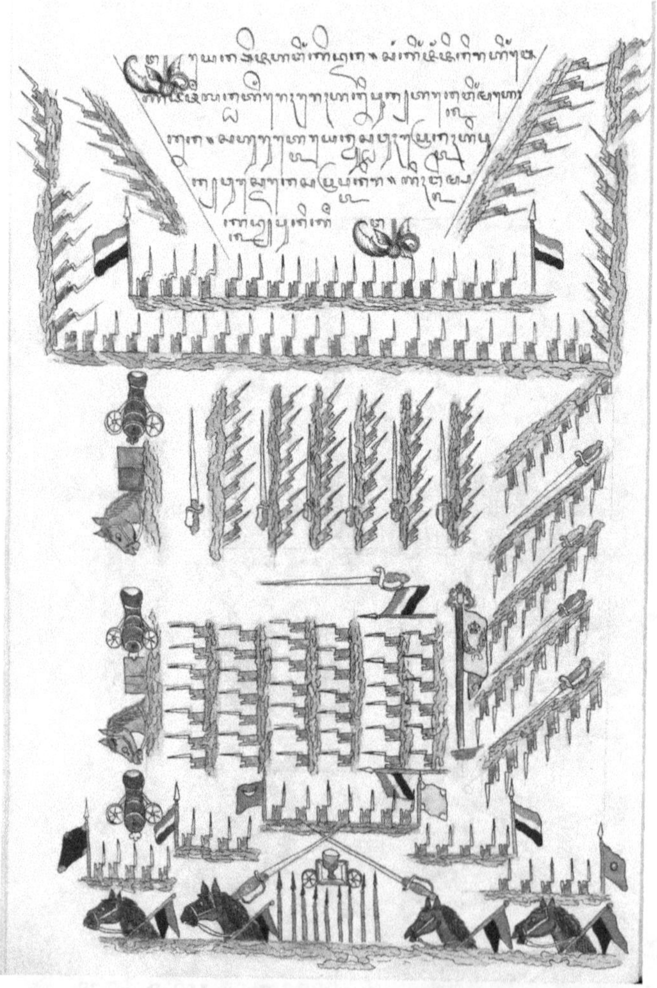

Battle array with the ubiquitous Dutch tricolour and, in the bottom of the drawing, two red flags, viz. one with a white crescent moon lying down and one with a white circle. MS B, p. 37.

features not only a flag with red banner and white circle, but also a flag with red banner and what may be described as a white moon lying down.[28] Another suggestion would be to interpret the flag with the red banner and white circle as referring to the first official Philippine flag of 1897, which depicted a white sun with eight rays and a face in a red field.[29]

However, even should we be dealing with representations of real-world, extra-textual flags (i.e. Dutch, Japanese, and Ottoman or revolutionary Filipino), at the time when MS B was produced, Japan's military victory over Russia was not a source of nationalist inspiration for a struggle against Dutch rule (Rodell 2007, p. 24 and p. 38, n. 9).

In short, then, although there may exist extensive theorizing on the gift, particularly since Marcel Mauss's classic essay, *The Gift*, sometimes a gift is just a gift. Furthermore, sometimes a cigar is just a cigar.

NOTES

As always, the library staff at the University Library of Leiden and the KITLV ensured that my research of the manuscripts in their collections could be done smoothly. The KITLV very quickly provided me with digital reproductions from MS B, whereas Leiden University Library kindly allowed me to take photographs of MS A myself. As ever so often, I gratefully thank Mrs Katherine Maye-Saidi, MA for taking on the chore of proofreading.

1. The term (Sanskrit and Old Javanese *aṣṭabrata*; New Javanese *asṭabrata*; Indonesian *astabrata*) consists of two (Sanskrit) words, viz. *aṣṭa* which denotes "eight", whereas *brata/vrata* has a number of related meanings: "a religious act of devotion", "a vow, promise, resolve", "an observance, practice", "mode of life, course of conduct", "a rule, law", "sacrifice" or "an act, a deed, work". See Khanna and Saran (1993), p. 242, n. 15. In New Javanese *asṭabrata* is glossed as *laku wolu* ("eight courses of conduct, practices, rules"), see Gericke and Roorda (1901), volume I, p. 99.
2. For an English translation, see Santoso ([1980]), pp. 623–25. Recently, a new edition has become available, viz. Van der Molen (2015) together with Robson (2015). Rāma's lecture can be found in Van der Molen (2015), pp. 529–31 and Robson (2015), pp. 649–51. Ando (2003) and Satyavrat (2003) were not available to me at the time of writing.

3. For its incorporation into *wayang* philosophy, see also Herusatoto (2008), pp. 140–45 where the *asṭabrata* are said to be symbolized by *wanita* (woman), *garwa* (wife), *wisma* (house), *turangga* (horse), *curiga* (kris, dagger), *kukila* (bird), *waranggana* (interpreted here as *ronggeng* or dancing-girl), and *pradangga* (gamelan ensemble).
4. Hughes-Freeland (2008), pp. 112–13 bases this information on a publication by K.P.H. Brongtodiningrat, which was not available to me at the time of writing, but in another publication this Yogyakarta aristocrat mentions the existence of nine *ampilan* (royal insignia carried in procession in front of the ruler), emphasizing the symbolic importance of the number nine. See Brongtodiningrat (1978), pp. 17–19. Haryanto (2013), p. 92, too, opines that the regalia are nine in number, supposedly symbolizing the "completeness" of a ruler's character. To increase confusion, an official coffee table book on life in the Yogyakarta palace compound, prefaced by the ruling Sultan, states that the regalia consist of ten items, adding the money box symbolizing generosity (also the attribute of the third deity, Surya, see below) and the cuspidor (*kecohan*), symbolizing the decision-making process, see Soeratno et al. (2004), pp. 132–33. For a similar set at the Surakarta *kraton*, see e.g. Jessup (1990), p. 169 (with eight items); and Miksic et al. (2004), p. 283 (with nine items). However, an in-depth discussion of this matter is beyond the scope of this chapter.
5. One manuscript is held in the princely library of the Pakualaman (former call number 0012; new call number 0012/PP/73; described in Girardet et al. 1983, p. 761 under code number 58530; described in Saktimulya 2005, pp. 108–9 under code number Pi.35). A second manuscript is kept in the Widyabudaya library of the Yogyakarta royal palace, but seems to be a rather young copy, produced perhaps in 1928 (call number C 57; described in Girardet et al. 1983, p. 678 under code number 44100; described in Lindsay et al. 1994, pp. 192–93 under code number W.295). The Leiden manuscripts are Cod. Or. 6388 of Leiden University Library (Pigeaud 1968, p. 365) and Or. 189 of the KITLV (Pigeaud 1968, p. 830). Furthermore, there is a text called Adidamasastra Pĕṭikan (Girardet et al. 1983, p. 740 under code number 54100) or Kyai Adidamastra [sic] (Saktimulya 2005, p. 88 under code number Pi.14), which was written during the reign of Pakualam V (1878–1900) and kept in the princely library of the Pakualaman (former call number 0031; new call number 0031/PP/73), but its relationship to the Sastra Agĕng Adidarma is still unclear.
6. However, according to Saktimulya et al. (2012), p. 147, during the reign of Pakualam III (1858–64), the Pakualaman version of the Asṭabrata was once

copied for the Surakarta palace of the Mangkunagaran. The only candidate for this is the manuscript shelved as P 35 in the Mangkunagaran palace which, however, according to Florida (2000, p. 188 under project number MN 294C.23), was copied in Yogyakarta in "ca. 1816".

7. The chapter on literature was written by Nyi M.W. Sestrorini, a pen name of S.R. Saktimulya.
8. Call number 008/PP/73. Described in Saktimulya (2005), pp. 109–10. K.B.P.H. Prabu Suryodilogo (on 7 January 2016 inaugurated as Pakualam X), the oldest son of Pakualam IX, is formally named as the author of the book on the asṭabrata, but Sri Ratna Saktimulya and Sudibyo, both lecturers at the Gadjah Mada University in Yogyakarta, acted as the editors. Saktimulya had earlier written an (unpublished) postgraduate thesis on the function of illuminated frontispieces in the Sĕstradisuhul (Saktimulya 1998) and her signature is clearly recognizable in the book on the Asṭabrata.
9. A brief biography is provided by Karels (2010), pp. 26, 31–34.
10. For a short biography of Hazeu, see Jaquet (2012).
11. The title page reads (in Javanese script): Sĕrat Aḍidarmasastra. Tanḍa katrĕsnan sangking Kangjĕng Gusti Pangeran Adipati Arya Prabu Suryadilaga ḍumatĕng ingkang saudara professor ḍoktor H. Keren, 6 April 1910 ("Sĕrat Aḍidarmasastra. Token of affection from His Highness Pangeran Adipati Arya Prabu Suryadilaga to Mister Professor Doctor H. Kern, 6 April 1910").
12. It has also been made available for inspection in black and white photographs on microfiche (Or. 189 mf).
13. The Dutch text reads: "[...] hulde te betuigen voor al wat u gedaan heeft voor onze taal en geschiedenis, voor ons land en volk."
14. Its significance can be gauged from the fact that it was recently made available again by the Romanized edition by Van der Molen (2015).
15. Returning to Java in 1925, Sosro Kartono would quickly gain a reputation for himself as a spiritual guide and latter-day guru. Aksan (1997) describes his "wisdom and conduct" (*ilmu dan laku*). For an obituary, see Purbopranoto (1973).
16. The Dutch text reads: "[...] een verzameling van allerlei Javaanse wetenswaardigheden en zedekundige uiteenzettingen, sommige met verhalen en fabels toegelicht; afschrift van een in 1832 geschreven handschrift uit de Pakoealaman." For an obituary of Voorhoeve, see Teeuw and Uhlenbeck (1997).
17. Intriguingly, a booklet from the Pakualaman museum, which lists the impressive cultural achievements of Pakualam I until Pakualam VIII, does not mention the Sastra Agĕng Adidarma and the Sĕstradisuhul at all, see Anonymous [n.d.].

18. See Saktimulya (1998), pp. 12–13. The word *pangosekan* is explained as "someone who helps to sharpen the brain, oracle, walking encyclopaedia" in Gericke and Roorda (1901), volume I, p. 467 under *kosek*.
19. See e.g. Jandra (1991), p. 266, explaining it as "*keagungan*".
20. See Van der Molen (2015), p. 530 and Robson (2015), p. 650.
21. Another possibility, suggested by an anonymous reviewer, is that the dagger in front could perhaps be understood as linked to the need to defend money.
22. This is how Zoetmulder and Robson (1982), p. 1320 interpret the term *pāśabrata*. See also Santoso ([1980]), p. 625. The new translation by Robson (2015), p. 650 reads as follows: "Lord Baruṇa holds in his hand a weapon / That is highly poisonous, the snake-snare that binds; / You should adopt the snare rule, / And you should tie up the host of evildoers. //"
23. Suryodilogo (2012), p. 63 arrives at a completely different translation. I interpret *angglung* as a variant of *angglong* in the meaning of "reduced to a small amount", see Robson and Wibisono (2002), p. 43 and Gericke and Roorda (1901), I, p. 224. The crux is *wĕgig* which may mean "clever", but also "bold" and "rude" (the latter meaning marked as dialectal or non-standard), see Robson and Wibisono (2002), p. 805. Pigeaud (1938), p. 616 also provides these meanings, but adds that "bold" should be understood as "brazen, shameless". Poerwadarminta (1939), p. 660 also mentions "koerang adjar", i.e. "rude, impolite, impertinent, uncultured, etc."
24. The first proverb ("*mrojol ing akĕrĕp*") can be found in Darmasoetjipta (1985), p. 120, Mardiwarsito (1992), p. 102 and Suwarno (1999), p. 210; the second ("*punjul ing apapak*") in Darmasoetjipta (1985), p. 161, Mardiwarsito (1992), p. 136 and Suwarno (1999), p. 295.
25. According to an anonymous reviewer who draws attention to the case of the iconographic conventions of Balinese Kamasan paintings, the detailed differences between illustrations may not be due to any systematic difference in the iconographic conventions employed by the illustrators but due entirely to "the quirks of style" of individual painters.
26. In a recent handbook of postcolonial studies (Rothberg 2013), p. 368 it is stated that "[i]f most postcolonial critics have moved away from this seemingly 'reactive' mode of 'writing back', it remains an important part of the genealogy of postcolonial studies and an important dimension of postcolonial literatures."
27. On perceptions of the Ottoman Empire in related traditional Malay literature, see the recent monograph of Braginsky (2015).
28. The same flags also appear in another battle array known as *supit urang* or "shrimp claw". See MS B, p. 22.
29. A suggestion by Adrian Vickers to the author, 25 April 2014.

REFERENCES

Aksan. *Ilmu dan laku Drs. RMP. Sosrokartono*. Surabaya: Citra Jaya Murti, 1997. First published, 1985.

Anderson, Benedict. *Mythology and the Tolerance of the Javanese*. New York: Cornell University, 1996. First published, 1965.

Ando, Mitsuru. "The Aṣṭabrata in the Old Javanese Rāmāyaṇa". In *Sanskrit in Southeast Asia: The Harmonizing Factor of Cultures*, edited by Chirapat Prapandvidya. Bangkok: Sanskrit Studies Centre, Silpakorn University, 2003, pp. 189–95.

Anonymous. *Selayang pandang penguasa pradja Paku Alaman*. Yogyakarta: Bebadan-Museum Puro Paku Alaman, [n.d.].

Arps, Bernard. *Tembang in Two Traditions: Performance and Interpretation of Javanese Literature*. London: SOAS, 1992.

Behrend, Timothy. "Kraton and Cosmos in Traditional Java". *Archipel* 37 (1989): 173–87.

Bosma, Ulbe. *Karel Zaalberg: Journalist en strijder voor de Indo*. Leiden: KITLV Uitgeverij, 1997. VKI 175.

Braginsky, Vladimir. *The Turkic-Turkish Theme in Traditional Malay Literature: Imagining the Other to Empower the Self*. Leiden: Brill, 2015. VKI 301.

Brongtodiningrat. *Arti kraton Yogyakarta*. Yogyakarta: Museum Kraton Yogyakarta, 1978.

Darmasoetjipta, F.S. *Kamus peribahasa Jawa*. Yogyakarta: Kanisius, 1985.

Dewantara, Ki Hadjar. "The Practice of Literature and the Arts in the Pakualam Family". In *The Kraton: Selected Essays on Javanese Courts*, edited by Stuart Robson. Leiden: KITLV Press, 2003. Translation Series 28, pp. 331–44.

Doel, H.W. van den. *De stille kracht: Het Europese binnenlands bestuur op Java en Madoera, 1808–1942*. Amsterdam: Bert Bakker, 1994.

Florida, Nancy K. *Javanese Literature in Surakarta Manuscripts*. Volume 2: *Manuscripts of the Mangkunagaran Palace*. New York: Cornell University, 2000.

Foltz, Richard. *Religions of Iran: From Prehistory to the Present*. London: Oneworld, 2013.

Gericke, J.F.C. and T. Roorda. *Javaansch-Nederlandsch handwoordenboek*. Amsterdam: Müller; Leiden: Brill, 1901. Two vols. Fourth edition.

Gilmartin, David and Bruce Lawrence. "Introduction". In *Beyond Turk and Hindu: Rethinking Religious Identities in Islamicate South Asia*, edited by David Gilmartin and Bruce Lawrence. Gainesville: The University of Florida Press, 2000, pp. 1–20.

Girardet, Nikolaus with the assistance of Suzan Piper and Soetanto. *Descriptive Catalogue of the Javanese Manuscripts and Printed Books in the Main Libraries of Surakarta and Yogyakarta*. Wiesbaden: Steiner, 1983. Schriftenreihe des Südasien-Instituts der Universität Heidelberg; Band 30.

Gonda, J. *Sanskrit in Indonesia*. New Delhi: International Academy of Indian Culture and Aditya Prakashan, 1998. Śata-Piṭaka Series, Indo-Asian literatures, volume 99. First published, 1973.

Hardjowirogo. *Sejarah wayang purwa*. Jakarta: Balai Pustaka, 1989. First published, 1949. BP 1698.

Hart, Hanna 't. "Imagine Leiden without Kern". In *Leiden Oriental Connections 1850–1940*, edited by Willem Otterspeer. Leiden: Brill, 1989, pp. 126–40.

Haryanto, Sindung. *Dunia simbol orang Jawa*. Yogyakarta: Kepel Press, 2013.

Herusatoto, Budiono. *Simbolisme Jawa*. Yogyakarta: Ombak, 2008.

Hiltebeitel, Alf and Barbara D. Miller. *Hair: Its Power and Meaning in Asian Cultures*. New York: State University of New York Press, 1998.

Hindman, Sandra. *Sealed in Parchment: Rereadings of Knighthood in the Illuminated Manuscripts of Chrétien de Troyes*. Chicago and London: University of Chicago Press, 1994.

Hodgson, Marshall G.S. *The Venture of Islam: Conscience and History in a World Civilization*. Volume One: *The Classical Age of Islam*. Chicago and London: University of Chicago Press, 1974.

Hughes-Freeland, Felicia. *Embodied Communities: Dance Tradition and Change in Java*. New York and Oxford: Berghahn Books, 2008.

Jandra, M. *Perangkat, alat-alat dan pakaian serta makna simbolis upacara keagamaan di lingkungan keraton Yogyakarta*. Jakarta: Departemen Pendidikan dan Kebudayaan, 1991.

Jaquet, F.G.P. "Hazeu, Godard Arend Johannes (1870–1929)". *Biografisch woordenboek van Nederland*, 2012. Available at <http://www.historici.nl/Onderzoek/Projecten/BWN/lemmata/bwn2/hazue> (accessed 12 November 2013).

Jessup, Helen Ibbitson. *Court Arts of Indonesia*. New York: The Asia Society Galleries and Harry N. Abrams, 1990.

Karels, René. *Mijn aardse leven vol moeite en strijd. Raden Mas Noto Soeroto, Javaan, dichter, politicus 1888–1951*. Leiden: KITLV Uitgeverij, 2010. Boekerij 'Oost en West'.

Karkov, Catherine E. *Text and Picture in Anglo-Saxon England: Narrative Strategies in the Junius 11 Manuscript*. Cambridge: Cambridge University Press, 2001.

Khanna, Vinod and Malini Saran. "The *Rāmāyaṇa* Kakawin: A Product of Sanskrit Scholarship and Independent Literary Genius". *BKI* 149 (1993): 226–49.

Kuhnt-Saptodewo, Sri. *Getanzte Geschichte: Tanz, Religion und Geschichte auf Java*. Münster and Wien: Lit, 2006. Veröffentlichungen zum Archiv für Völkerkunde; Band 11.

Lindsay, Jennifer, Soetanto and Alan Feinstein. *Katalog induk naskah-naskah Nusantara*. Jilid 2: *Kraton Yogyakarta*. Jakarta: Yayasan Obor Indonesia, 1994.

Mardiwarsito, L. *Peribahasa dan saloka bahasa Jawa*. Jakarta: Balai Pustaka, 1992. BP 3436.

Mellema, R.L. *Wayang Puppets: Carving, Colouring and Symbolism*. Amsterdam: Royal Tropical Institute, 1988. First edition, 1954.

Miert, Hans van. *Een koel hoofd en een warm hart: Nationalisme, Javanisme en jeugdbeweging in Nederland-Indië, 1918–1930*. Amsterdam: De Bataafsche Leeuw, 1995.

Miksic, John et al., eds. *Karaton Surakarta*. Surakarta: Yayasan Pawiyatan Kabudayan Karaton Surakarta, 2004.

Moertono, Soemarsaid. *State and Statecraft in Old Java: A Study of the Later Mataram Period, 16th to 19th Century*. Ithaca, New York: Cornell University, 2002. First edition, 1968.

Molen, Willem van der. *H. Kern Rāmāyaṇa: The Story of Rāma and Sītā in Old Javanese. Romanized edition*. Tokyo: Tokyo University of Foreign Studies, 2015. Javanese Studies 1.

Mrázek, Jan. *Phenomenology of a Puppet Theatre: Contemplations on the Art of Javanese Wayang Kulit*. Leiden: KITLV Press, 2005. VKI 230.

Niel, Robert van. *The Emergence of the Modern Indonesian Elite*. Dordrecht and Cinnaminson: Foris, 1984. KITLV, Reprints on Indonesia. First published, 1960.

Obeyesekere, Gananath. "Foreword". In *Hair: Its Power and Meaning in Asian Cultures*, edited by Alf Hiltebeitel and Barbara D. Miller. New York: State University of New York Press, 1998, pp. xi–xiv.

Pigeaud, Th. *Javaans-Nederlands handwoordenboek*. Groningen and Batavia: Wolters, 1938.

———. *Literature of Java*. Volume II. *Descriptive Lists of Javanese Manuscripts*. The Hague: Nijhoff, 1968.

Poerwadarminta, W.J.S. *Baoesastra Djawa*. Groningen and Batavia: Wolters, 1939.

Poeze, Harry A. "Indonesians at Leiden University". In *Leiden Oriental Connections 1850–1940*, edited by Willem Otterspeer. Leiden: Brill, 1989, pp. 250–79.

Proudfoot, Ian. "Malays Toying with Americans: The Rare Voices of Malay Scribes in Two Houghton Library Manuscripts". *Harvard Library Bulletin* 11 (2000): 54–69.

Purbopranoto, Koentjoro. "Ter nagedachtenis van Drs. R.M.P. Sosro Kartono". *BKI* 129 (1973): 287–301.

Ras, J.J. "The *Babad Tanah Jawi* and its Reliability: Questions of Content, Structure and Function". In *Cultural Contact and Textual Interpretation*, edited by C.D. Grijns and S.O. Robson. Dordrecht and Cinnaminson: Foris, 1986. VKI 115, pp. 246–73.

Ricklefs, M.C. *A History of Modern Indonesia since c. 1200*. Houndmills: Palgrave, 2001. Third edition.

Robson, Stuart. *The Old Javanese Rāmāyaṇa: A New English Translation with an Introduction and Notes*. Tokyo: Tokyo University of Foreign Studies, 2015. Javanese Studies 2.

Robson, Stuart and Singgih Wibisono. *Javanese–English Dictionary*. Singapore: Periplus, 2002.

Rodell, Paul A. "Southeast Asian Nationalism and the Russo–Japanese War: Reexamining Assumptions". *Southeast Review of Asian Studies* 29 (2007): 20–40.

Rothberg, Michael. "Remembering Back: Cultural Memory, Colonial Legacies, and Postcolonial Studies". In *The Oxford Handbook of Postcolonial Studies*, edited by Graham Huggan. Oxford: Oxford University Press, 2013.

Saktimulya, Sri Ratna. "Fungsi wêdana rênggan dalam Sêstradisuhul". Yogyakarta: Universitas Gadjah Mada, 1998. Unpublished, S-2 thesis.

———. *Katalog naskah-naskah perpustakaan pura Pakualaman*. Jakarta: Yayasan Obor Indonesia and The Toyota Foundation, 2005.

Saktimulya, S.R., Sudibyo and B. Sumardiyanto. *Warnasari sistem budaya kadipaten Pakualaman Yogyakarta*. Jakarta: Trah Pakualaman Hudyana, Eka Tjipta Foundation and Perpustakaan Pura Pakualaman, 2012.

Santoso, Soewito. *Ramayana Kakawin*. Volume 3. Singapore: Institute of Southeast Asian Studies; New Delhi: International Academy of Indian Culture, [1980]. Śata-Piṭaka Series, Indo-Asian literatures, volume 251.

Satyavrat, Usha. "Astabrata Tradition in Indonesia: Its Sanskrit Connection". *Sanskrit in Southeast Asia: The Harmonizing Factor of Cultures*. Bangkok: Sanskrit Studies Centre, Silpakorn University, 2003, pp. 510–13.

Sears, Laurie J. *Shadows of Empire: Colonial Discourse and Javanese Tales*. Durham and London: Duke University Press, 1996.

Soeratno, Chamamah et al., eds. *Kraton Jogja: The History and Cultural Heritage*. Jakarta: Karaton Ngayogyakarta Hadiningrat and Indonesia Marketing Association, 2004.

Solomonik, I.N. "Wayang Purwa Puppets: The Language of the Silhouette". *BKI* 136 (1980): 482–97.

Sudibyoprono, R. Rio. *Ensiklopedi wayang purwa*. Jakarta: Balai Pustaka, 1991. BP 3127.

Suratno, Pardi. *Sang pemimpin menurut Asthabrata, Wulang Reh, Tripama, Dasa Darma Raja*. Yogyakarta: Adiwacana, 2006.

Suryodilogo. *Ajaran kepemimpinan Asthabrata kadipaten Pakualaman*. Yogyakarta: Perpustakaan Pura Pakualaman, 2012.

Suwarno, Peter. *Dictionary of Javanese Proverbs and Idiomatic Expressions*. Yogyakarta: Gadjah Mada University Press, 1999.

Teeuw, A. and E.M. Uhlenbeck. "In Memoriam Dr. Petrus Voorhoeve". *BKI* 153 (1997): 311–17.

Thomas, Nicholas. *Entangled Objects: Exchange, Material Culture, and Colonialism in the Pacific*. Cambridge, MA: Harvard University Press, 1991.

Weatherbee, D.E. "The Aṣṭabrata, Saptadewawṛtti, and Nāgarakṛtāgama VII:1–2". *BKI* 150 (1994): 414–16.

Wieringa, E.P. "A Last Admonition to P.P. Roorda van Eysinga in 1828: Haji Zainal Abidin's Syair Alif-Ba-Ta". *BKI* 154 (1998): 116–28.

Yasasusastra, J. Syahban. *Asta Brata: 8 unsur alam symbol kepemimpinan*. Yogyakarta: Pustaka Mahardika, 2011.

Zoetmulder, P.J., with the collaboration of S.O. Robson. *Old Javanese–English Dictionary*. 's-Gravenhage: Nijhoff, 1982. Two vols.

INDEX

Note: Page numbers followed by "n" denote endnotes.

A

Abdul Rahman Kaeh, 100, 132n2. *See also* Hikayat Misa Taman Jayeng Kusuma (HMTJK)
Abhimanyu Wiwaha, 37–38, 41
Abimanyu's death, 2, 30, 31
  "Adi Parwa", 32–33
  in Bharatayuddha, 37–41
  in Hikayat Pandawa Lima, 41–45
  Indian background to tales, 32–37
  ksatriya-dharma, 36
  "Nostalgia", 45–49
  "sipping the Absolute Essence", 48
  unfair fight, 34–35
Abhimanyuvadha Parwa, 33
Adi Darma Sastra, 188, 209n11
"Adi Parwa", 32–33, 37
Agastya, 13
Al-Ghazali, 46
Angling Darma, 23
Anoman (Hanuman), 15, 81, 113, 126
Arjuna, 12, 35, 41–42, 48, 50, 52n4
  Abhimanyu son of, 31, 32
  Indra's selection of, 105
  and Karṇa, 151
  Niwatakawaca's death, 106
  Pasupati (magic arrow), 105
Arjunawijaya, 13
Arjunawiwaha, 18, 105, 108
Astabrata, 4, 11, 181, 207n1
  Hazeu's ideas, 186–87
  iconography of eight deities. *See* eight deities, *wayang* iconography of
  Javanese lessons for Dutch, 203–7
  Javanese publications of, 182, 183
  Kern's contribution, 186–88
  KITLV's collection, 187, 189, 207
  Pakualaman principality, 184, 185, 189
  Pakualaman rendition of, 184–85, 201, 208n6
  in post-Hindu Islamic context, 182
  Rāma lessons on leadership, 181–84
  Sastra Agĕng Adidarma, 184, 186–89, 204
  Sĕstradisuhul, 185, 190

Aśwatthāmā, Śalya and confrontation between, 150–58
Atala, 8

B

Babad Brahmana, 15
babon (original) manuscript, 17
Bakir, Muhammad, 129
Baladewa, 43, 120, 121
Bali, 5, 11, 14, 22, 23
Balinese Kamasan paintings, 210n25
Balinese language
  Bhāratayuddha in, 144
  gaguritan in, 145, 149
barit ketik, 132n2
Baruna, 193, 210n22
  effective weapon, 201
  wayang iconography, 201, 202
Bayu, 47, 71, 191, 200
  ear ornaments, 193
  symbol of masculinity and power, 198
  wayang iconography, 198, 199
Begawan Narawuji, 73, 74, 77, 90n19
Begawan Tawaruji, 73, 77, 90n19
Belado, 67, 75
Berma Raja, 126, 127
Betara Durga, 101
Betara Guru, 68, 72, 73, 82, 83, 105, 110, 113
Betara Indera Naya, 73, 100
  descent to earth, 104–6
  Betara Kala, 100, 101, 103, 105–7, 110, 115–16, 123, 129
  Betara Kangsa Dewa, 117, 118–22, 127
  Bhagavad Gita, 9, 12, 36, 49, 53n14
  Bharatayuddha/Bhāratayuddha, 50–51, 78, 79, 138, 154, 158
  on Aśwatthāmā, 152
  authorship of, 140
  battle depicted in, 139
  central narrative of, 138
  composition, 38
  death of Abimanyu in, 37–41
  erotic overtones of, 42
  fratricidal violence story, 31
  Gaguritan Bharatayuddha, 145
  Kidung Bratayuda, 144–45
  Mpu Panuluh, 141–43, 150, 152
  Mpu Panuluh's section of, 146
  Mpu Sĕḍah, 142
  in Old Javanese literature, 139
  painting corpus, 150
  reframing, 143–46
  Śalyawadha section of, 143
  tradition in Bali, 140
  Van der Tuuk Collections, 147
Bhaṭṭikāvya (BhK), 8–9, 13, 24
"Bhisma Parwa", 33, 138
Bhomāntaka ("Bhoma's Death"), 78, 112, 114, 133n15
"Bima Purified" (Bima Suci), 62, 63
Bima's quest, 3
  Cod. Or. 3240, 65, 66, 67, 72
  Cod. Or. 3377, 65
  Destarata, 69
  distressed mother exclaims, 67
  Drona's betrayal of, 68
  episode of, 68, 78
  kawitra water, 81, 82
  with *kesaktian*, 81
  Narawuji teaches, 74
  Pandawas and Korawas, 68–69
  in Raffles Malay 21, 78
  Rama Widara, 69
  Sangkuni, 69
  story of, 65, 66, 67
  stretch of dialogue, 73
Bisma, 47, 52n7

"blemish and misfortune" (*mala petaka*), 80, 82
Boma, and Samba, 111–14
Book of the Devil (*mengaji dari Kitab Syaitan*), 130
Braginsky, Vladimir, 8, 53n12, 59, 78, 81, 82, 114, 128
Brakel, L., 31, 79
Brama, 112, 191, 202
  ear ornament, 192
  wayang iconography, 200–1
Brihadbala, 34
Brongtodiningrat, K.P.H., 208n4
"Burning of Kama, The", 108

C

"*Cakra Anggar*" formation, 41–42
cakra-vyuha, 34, 50
Candi Panataran (Palah), 14
Candra, 192
  wayang iconography, 196–98
Carang Kembar Kusuma, 124, 126
Carey, William, 18
"*cerita yang mengerikan ini*", 31
Counterfeiters of 1925, The (Gide), 128

D

'*dalang*', 110–11, 113, 129
Dalang Mangku Jaya, 110, 111
Dalang Sungging Anom, 110–12, 113, 125
Danarto, 31, 48, 51, 55n30
  abangan environment, 46
  on human beings, 47
  life history, 45–46
  "Nostalgia", 46–49
  pantheistic worldview, 49
  short stories, 46
Death of Salya, The, 142, 150, 172, 175, 176
Derma Dewa, 112
Derma Dewi, 112, 113
Destarata, 69
Dewa Ruci, 62, 77, 81–82
Dewi Derma Dewi, 118–20
Dewi Januwati, 111, 112, 127
Dewi Mandurati, 100, 101
Dewi Segerba, 106–7, 108, 109
Dhand, Arti, 33
Dharmeśwara, 138
Drauni-Asvataman, 34
Draupadi, 36
Dritarastra, 31, 35, 36
Drona, 34, 39, 41, 42, 66–76
"Drona Parwa", 33, 38, 50, 51n3
Dronabhisheka Parwa, 33
Droṇaparvan, 138
Dropadi, 39, 146, 175
Dursasana, 34
Duryodana, 34, 42, 66–76, 151, 153
Dutch, Javanese lessons for, 203–7
Dwijendratattwa, 15

E

eight deities, *wayang* iconography of, 191, 201–3
  Baruna, 201, 202
  Bayu, 198, 199
  Brama, 200–1
  Candra, 196–98
  Indra, 193–94
  "language of the silhouette", 184, 191
  Surya, 195–96
  Wisnu, 198, 199
  Yama, 194–95
Endang Kusuma Jiwa, 115–16
Engelenberg, A.J.N., 23
enspherement, notion of, 93n45

F

Foltz, Richard, 182
"the formula Water Destruction" *(aji Jala Sengara)*, 74

G
Gagelang, *gambuh*-performance in, 114–22
Gaguritan Bharatayuddha, 144, 145
Gaguritan Senapati Śalya, 145, 146, 149, 165
gambuh-performance
  in Gagelang, 114–22
  in Tambak Kencana, 122–27
Ghatotkaca, 39, 41, 42, 52n9, 148, 149, 174
Ghatotkacha-vadha Parwa, 33
Gide, André, 128
Gift, The (Mauss), 207
Gonda, J., 64, 65
Gunti, 71, 76

H
Hang Jebat, 44–45
Hanuman. *See* Anoman (Hanuman)
Hariśraya A, 16
Hariśraya B, 16
Hariwangśa, 120, 141
Hayam Wuruk, 18
Hazeu, Godard Arend Johannes, 186–87
Heritage of Traditional Malay Literature, The (Braginsky), 8
Het Indische Volk, 186
Hidimbi, 38–39, 52n9
hikayat, 8, 41, 50, 51, 87, 88, 100, 111, 127
Hikayat Andaken Penurat, 59
Hikayat Cekel Wanengpati, 129–30
Hikayat Galuh Digantung, 59
Hikayat Hang Tuah, 44, 45, 59, 85
Hikayat Misa Taman Jayeng Kusuma (HMTJK), 100–1
  Betara Indera Naya's descent to earth, 104–6
  fictionality and creative amplification, 127–31
  gambuh-performance. *See* *gambuh*-performance
  narrative of, 101–3
  as Panji romance, 103–4
  Raden Galuh Candra Kirana, 106–10, 131
  Raden Inu Kertapati, 106–10, 131
  wayang kulit purwa performance, 110–14
Hikayat Pandawa Jaya, 78, 79
Hikayat Pandawa Lima, 31, 55n39, 59, 121
  copyist of, 51
  death of Abimanyu in, 41–45
Hikayat Panji Kuda Semirang, 105, 109, 133n18
Hikayat Sang Boma, 78, 112, 114, 127–28
Hikayat Seri Rama, 13, 23, 81, 91n33, 126, 127, 130
Hindu and Muslim cultural forms, 182
Hindu-Buddhist antecedents, 83
"Hindu-Javanese", 10, 23
Hindu-Javanese gods, 130
Hinzler, H.I.R., 146–48
History of Java, The (Raffles), 139
History of Malay Literature, A (Winstedt), 60
Hodgson, Marshall, 182
Hooykaas, C., 8, 60, 66
Hookyaas-Ketut Sangka (HKS) Collection, 144
Hughes-Freeland, Felicia, 182, 208n4
Hyang Manon, 80
Hyang Widi, 80

I
I Ketut Gede of Singaraja, 148, 149, 158–61, 170, 171

I Wayan Kebeten (1931–), 161, 163
iconographic representations, of Śalyawadha, 146–50
Ida Bagus Made Togog (1911–89), 161, 162
Ida Made Tlaga of Sanur, 149, 166, 168
Ida Putu Hema of Badung, 149, 167, 168
Ida Wau Rauh, 15
ilmu, 84
"Indic", 182
"Indology", 187
Indra, 105, 108
  wayang iconography, 193–94
Ing Tegal Amlagung, 72
"Islamicate", 182

J
javanaiserie, 84–88. *See also* Malay culture, javanaiserie in
  characteristics, 85
  common strategy, 87
  cultural meanings of, 87
  element of, 86
  hikayat, 87, 88
  javanesque style, 86
  Malay, 85, 87
"Javanese Genius", 181–84
Javanese tradition manuscripts, 17
Jayabhaya, 38, 138, 140, 141
Jayadrata, 33, 34, 39, 42, 43, 50
Jayadratha-vadha Parwa, 33
Jayajatra, 48
Jungmann, Josef, 8
Juynboll, H.H., 22, 63

K
kakawin, 9, 10, 13, 14, 20, 23, 111, 114, 121, 138–40
  "death of Śalya", 172
  literature, 141
  repertoire, 164
  tradition, 146
Kakawin Arjunawiwaha. *See* Arjunawiwaha
Kakawin Bharatayuddha/Bhāratayuddha. *See* Bharatayuddha/Bhāratayuddha
Kakawin Bhomantaka ("Bhoma's Death"). *See* Bhomāntaka ("Bhoma's Death")
Kakawin Krishnandaka. *See* KrishnandakaKakawin Rāmāyaṇa (Old Javanese), 181, 196, 201. *See also* "The Rāmāyaṇa Kakawin: A Product of Sanskrit Scholarship and Independent Literary Genius"
Kakawin Smaradahana. *See* Smaradahana
Kalamisani, 105
Kalayawanantaka, 120
kalimah sahadat, 170
kalimahoṣada, 169–71, 175
kalimasada, 170
Kama and Ratih, 108–9
Karna, 34, 42, 43, 150–2, 155
Karṇaparvan, 138
Kats, J., 19
Kaurawas/Kurawa, 34, 39, 48, 66, 68–69, 138, 143, 146, 150, 153, 158
kāvya ("artificial court epic"), 9
kawi miring, 17, 139
kawitra water, 70, 72, 73, 81, 82
Kebu Sendubama (Semar), 115, 116
kekayaan Dewata Mulia Raya, 80
Kelana Anom Perwira, 114, 116
Kelana Merta Jiwa, 103, 117–19
Kelana Panji Kayangan, 117–19
Kelana Prabu Desa, 117, 118
Ken Segerba Ningrat (RGCK), 102, 115–16, 122

Kern, Hendrik, 186–88
kesaktian (magical power), 69, 74, 81, 84
Khanna, Vinod, 8, 9
Ki Hadjar Dewantara, 189
Kidung Bratayuda, 144–45, 149
Kieven, Lydia, 15
kingship, institution of, 12
Klokke, Marijke J., 15
Korawas. *See* Kaurawas/Kurawa
Kripa, 34
Krishna, 12, 37, 48, 49, 50
Krishna-Dwaipayana (Ganguli), 35
Krishnamurti, 46
Krishnandaka, 120
Krishnawijaya ("Krishna's Victory"), 120
Kritavarman, 34
"Kromomania", 186
ksatriya-dharma, 2, 12, 36
Kṣitisundarī, death of, 172–74
Kuda Kerta Negara, 111, 117
Kuhnt-Saptodewo, Sri, 182

L

Laksamana Kumara, 42
"language of the silhouette", 184, 191
Lara Danta, 123, 124
Lara Gading, 123, 124, 125
Lasem, *wayang kulit purwa* performance in, 108, 110–14
Leadbeater, C.W., 46
Leiden manuscripts, 185–86, 208n5
Leiden University Library, 15–16, 26, 63, 65, 145, 186
Lombok, 16, 22, 23
LOr 3240, 65, 66, 67, 72
LOr 3377, 65
LOr 3390, 146, 148
LOr 3814, 145
LOr 3924, 145

M

macapat verse-forms, 22, 24, 25, 139, 144, 145
Madurese Rama, 23
Majapahit period, 13, 14, 15, 18, 23
Malay Concordance Project, 84
Malay culture, javanaiserie in
  characters, 59
  fifteenth and sixteenth centuries, 59
  Hikayat Hang Tuah, 59
  influence, 61
  language, 59
  literature and performance, 59, 60
  Malay language, 61
  mid-fifteenth century, 62
  Nawaruci, 61–65
  protagonists, 59
  Raffles Malay 21. *See* Raffles Malay 21
  renditions, 63, 65
  Sejarah Melayu, 59
  traditional communities in, 83
Malayo-Javanese literature, 59
"Malays toying with Americans" (Proudfoot), 203
Mangaspati, 41, 43
Mangku Mura (1920–99), 157, 175, 176
Manusmṛti, 9, 11
Marrison, Geoffrey E., 23
Marshman, Joshua, 18
Martawangsa, 68, 76
Mauss, Marcel, 207
McDonald, Barbara, 17, 20–21
McGrath, Kevin, 39
memanjangkan, 129
mempe(r)dayakan, 80
Merapi-Merbabu manuscript collection, 18

Milner, A.C., 44
Misa Edan Sira Panji Jayeng Kusuma, 102–3, 114, 116
Misa Kusuma Yuda, 117, 122, 123
Misa Merga Asmara, 117, 122, 123
Moertono, Soemarsaid, 181
Mpu Kanwa, 105, 108
Mpu Panuluh, 38, 52n9, 140, 141–43, 172, 174
  Bhāratayuddha, 150, 152, 175
  epic narrative by, 158
  longevity of, 175
  Śalya's death, 171
  Śalyawadha, 175
  personal contribution, 144
  personal misreading, 170
Mpu Sĕḍah, 138, 140, 142, 145, 169–70, 172

N

Nakula, 143, 144, 148, 158–61
"*nama*", 44
National Library of Indonesia, 65
"Nawaruci", 61–65
  Bima Suci, 62
  Dewa Ruci, 62
  Malay rendition, 63
  mid-fifteenth century, 62
  Old Javanese version, 63, 64, 76
  Poerbatjaraka, 63–64
  Prijohoetomo, 77
  teachings, 63
Nieuws van den Dag, 186
Nila Utama (Tillotama), 108, 110, 112
Nirartha, 15
Niwatakawaca, 106
"Nostalgia", 2, 31, 45–49

O

Old Javanese, 5, 6
  academic study of, 6
  author, 9
  kakawin, 138, 144, 150, 172, 173
  kalimahoṣadha, 170
  language in Balinese script, 147
  literature, 6, 139, 140
  parwa, 138
Old Javanese Rāmāyaṇa (OJR), 8, 9, 196, 201
  babon (original), 17
  in Bali, 16
  in Java, 16–17
  in Lombok, 16
  jarwa (explanatory) text, 17, 24
  precise dating of, 9–10
  recopied textual history, 14
  thought-world, 10–13
  transmission process, 17
Ottoman flag, 206
Overbeck, H., 60, 61, 85
Over Maleise Literatuur (Hooykaas), 60

P

'pāśabrata', 210n22
Pakualam II, 184, 189, 190
Pakualaman library, 184, 185, 209n17
Pakualaman principality, 184, 185, 189
Pakubuwana IV, 17
Pandawas, 34, 39, 76, 77, 138, 151. *See* also Panji (prince)
  kalimasada, 170
  and Korawas, 68–69
  narratives, 59, 60
  Rama Widara and Gunti, 76
Pangeran Arya Natadiraja, 186
Pangeran Tambak Kencana, 103, 123–25, 127
Panji (prince), 59
  and Pandawa narratives, 59, 60, 85
  See also Sira Panji (RIK)

Panji Jayalengkara, 23
Panji romance, Hikayat Misa Taman Jayeng Kusuma, 100, 103–4
pantheism *(wahdat al-wujud)*, 46
Parameśwara, 11
Parikan Bharatayuddha, 144
Pariksit, 33, 50, 175
parwa, 138
'*pasemon*', 107, 115, 124, 134n37
Pasupati (magic arrow), 105–6
-pe(r)dayakan, 82
Peletz, Michael G., 83, 84
Philippine flag of 1897, 207
Pigeaud, Th.G.Th., 17, 18, 19–20, 21, 22, 26n8
Poerbatjaraka, 19, 26n4, 63–65, 74, 77
"Popular Rama Tales" (Pigeaud), 22
postcolonial studies, 210n26
Prabu Anom, 102–3, 123–25
Prambanan (Loro Jonggrang), 12–13
Prihatmi, Rahayu, 46
Prijohoetomo, 77
Proudfoot, Ian, 203

R

Raden Asmara Agung, 110
Raden Galuh Candra Kirana (RGCK), 101–3, 106–10, 131
Raden Gunung Sari, 110, 117, 125
Raden Inu Kertapati (RIK), 100, 101–3, 106–10, 131
Raden Kangsa, 121
Raden Kembar Dahang, 110–13
Raden Ngabehi Wediodipoera, 188
Raden Panji Harjawinata, 190
Raden Panji Jayengminarsa, 190
Raden Ratna Langoe, 115–16, 117
Radjiman Widijodiningrat, 188
Raffles, Thomas Stamford, 139
Raffles Malay 21, 66–68, 72, 73, 74, 78, 83, 84, 89n7, 89n9
Rāma, 10, 11, 24
  divine nature of, 12
  as incarnation of Wiṣṇu, 12
  Javanese *wayang*-style representation of, 183
  lessons on leadership, 181–84
  Madurese version of, 18
Rama Jarwa, 17
Rama Kawi, 17
Rama Kling (Kĕling), 22
Rama Widara, 69, 71, 76
"The Rāmāyaṇa Kakawin: A Product of Sanskrit Scholarship and Independent Literary Genius", 8
Ratih, Kama and, 108–9
reincarnation, metaphysics of, 47
religiosity, 79–84
Ricklefs, M.C., 21
"Rising Sun" flag of Japan, 204
ruat, 83
Rubinstein, R., 15
Russo–Japanese War (1904–5), 204
Rāwaṇa, 10, 11, 13, 126, 127

S

Sabhāparwa, 158, 174
Sadewa, 42, 71, 75, 76
sakti, 84
Saktimulya, Sri Ratna, 185, 209n8
Sakula, 42, 71, 75, 76
Salim, Agus, 46
Śalya/Śalyawadha, 38, 39, 140, 142, 143
  and Aśwatthāmā, 150–58
  in Bali, 143–46
  and Bhīṣma, 148
  of Bhāratayuddha, 143
  death, 168–71

Gaguritan Senapati, 145, 146, 149, 165
iconographic representations of, 146–50
and Karṇa, 151, 155
Nakula's embassy to, 158–60
narrative interventions, 144
and Satyawatī, 143, 149, 160–68
Śalyaparvan, 138, 143
Samba, Boma and, 111–14
Sang Seta Jaman, 42
Sang Setyaki, 42
Sanggarbambu ("Bamboo Monastery"), 45
Sangkuni, 66, 68–75
Saran, Malini, 8, 9
Sarkar, H.B., 8
Sastra Agĕng Adidarma, 184, 186–89, 204
Satyawatī, 38, 39, 140, 143, 160–68
death of, 171–74
Sauptikaparvan, 138, 143, 158
Sejarah Melayu, 59, 130
Semar, 42, 67, 75, 101, 115. *See also* Kebu Sendubama (Semar)
Sembadra, 48
Serat al-Mustakim, 130
serat kandha, 78–79, 91n29
serat kandhaning ringgit purwa, 78
serat purwa, 78
Serat Rama, 2, 18, 19, 20, 21, 24
Seta (Sweta), 47
Si Kuncang, 45
Sino–Japanese War (1894–95), 204
Sira Panji (RIK), 114–17, 122
Sita Dewi, 10, 11, 24, 81, 126–27
Siti Sundari, 38, 40, 41, 48, 50, 52n9
Sosro Kartono, 187, 188
Spivak, Gayatri, 203
Sĕrat Ngadidamastra, 189
Sĕstradisuhul, 185, 190
Smaradahana, 108
State and Statecraft in Old Java: A Study of the Later Mataram Period, 16th to 19th Century (Moertono), 181
Stutterheim, W., 12
Subadra, 31, 36, 37, 52n4
sudahlah ruat mala petakaku, 72
Sugandhika, 39
Sunan Kalijaga, 170
Sunan Pakubuwana VII, 18
Supomo, S., 38, 39, 40, 137, 139, 144, 169
Suprabha, 106, 107, 108
Surakarta, 17, 19, 20, 22, 24, 64, 182, 184
Suratno, Pardi, 182
'*surengpati*', 192
Surya, 192, 193, 202
wayang iconography, 195–96
Sweeney, P.L., 60, 61, 84
syair, 8, 110
Syair Buah-Buahan, 129
Syair Ken Tambuhan, 103–4, 107, 110

T

Tambak Kencana, *gambuh*-performance in, 122–27
Tantri, 23
"tantrism", 41
Teeuw, A., 7, 23, 25
foreign texts importance, 8
literary history, 7, 12, 23
tembang macapat, 18, 19
'*tĕmbang*' texts, 190
Tillotama, 106, 108
"Translation, Transformation and Indonesian Literary History" (Teeuw), 7
Treaty of Giyanti, 20

Trijaṭā, 24
Tunjung Maya, 128
Tunjung Sari, 113, 128
Tuntunan Salat, 46

U
Udyogaparvan, 138
Uhlenbeck, E.M., 6
Utari, 36, 37, 38, 40, 41, 48, 50
Uttarakāṇḍa, 13, 16

V
Van der Tuuk, H.N., 63, 65, 79, 145
  Bhāratayuddha paintings, 147
  collection of paintings, 146–47, 154, 165
  LOr 3390, 146
  LOr 3814, 145
  LOr 3924, 145
  LOr 4129, 145
  pivotal role, 149
Vatsala/Sasirekha, 174
Visual Museum Collection, 150
Vālmīki Rāmāyaṇa, 8–9, 13, 18
Vodička, F., 8
Voorhoeve, Petrus, 189
Vyasa (Lal), final assurance to Yudistira, 35–36

W
"The War of the Bhāratas", 138
wayang, 40, 42, 50, 53n11, 77
  iconography, of eight deities. *See* eight deities, *wayang* iconography of
  Javanese-style, 67
  mythology, 63, 68
  theatre, 20, 25, 26n5
wayang Jawa, 87
wayang kulit purwa, 99, 108, 110–14, 130
wayang-style paintings, 147, 165
Wibhīṣaṇa, 11, 183
Winstedt, Richard, 59, 60, 68
Winter, C.F., 18, 19
"Wirata Parwa", 13, 33, 37
Wiryamartana, 18
Wisnu, 12, 168, 192
  ear ornaments, 193
  wayang iconography, 198, 199
worldmaking, 86, 88n2

Y
Yama, *wayang* iconography, 193, 194–95
Yangyang Kusuma, 108
Yasadipura, 18, 19, 64, 108
Yogyakarta, 20, 45, 182
  libraries, 184, 208n4
Yudistira/Yudhiṣṭhira, 41, 42, 75, 151, 169
  book-weapon, 143, 170
  orders Nakula to visit Śalya, 159
  persuaded by Krĕṣṇa, 169
  pleads with Abimanyu, 34
  refuses to oppose Śalya, 168
  shoots Śalya with kalimahoṣadha, 171
  Vyasa's final assurance to, 35–36

Z
Zoetmulder, P.J., 9, 26n2, 37, 40, 139, 142

NALANDA-SRIWIJAYA SERIES

1. *Nagapattinam to Suvarnadwipa: Reflections on the Chola Naval Expeditions to Southeast Asia*, edited by Hermann Kulke, K. Kesavapany and Vijay Sakhuja
2. *Preserving Cultural Identity through Education: The Schools of the Chinese Community in Calcutta, India*, by Zhang Xing
3. *Early Interactions between South and Southeast Asia: Reflections on Cross- Cultural Exchange*, edited by Pierre-Yves Manguin, A. Mani and Geoff Wade
4. *Hardships and Downfall of Buddhism in India*, by Giovanni Verardi
5. *Portuguese and Luso-Asian Legacies in Southeast Asia, 1511–2011, vol. 1: The Making of the Luso-Asian World: Intricacies of Engagement*, edited by Laura Jarnagin
6. *Anthony Reid and the Study of the Southeast Asian Past*, edited by Geoff Wade and Li Tana
7. *Portuguese and Luso-Asian Legacies in Southeast Asia, 1511–2011, vol. 2: Culture and Identity in the Luso-Asian World*, edited by Laura Jarnagin
8. *Sino–Malay Trade and Diplomacy from the Tenth through the Fourteenth Century*, by Derek Heng
9. *Tradition and Archaeology: Early Maritime Contacts in the Indian Ocean*, edited by Himanshu Prabha Ray and Jean-Francois Salles

10. *Civilizations in Embrace: The Spread of Ideas and the Transformation of Power; India and Southeast Asia in the Classical Age*, by Amitav Acharya
11. *India and China: Interactions through Buddhism and Diplomacy — A Collection of Essays by Professor Prabodh Chandra Bagchi*, compiled by Bangwei Wang and Tansen Sen
12. *Of Palm Wine, Women and War: The Mongolian Naval Expedition to Java in the 13th Century*, by David Bade
13. *Literary Migrations: Traditional Chinese Fiction in Asia (17th–20th Centuries)*, edited by Claudine Salmon
14. *Offshore Asia: Maritime Interactions in Eastern Asia before Steamships*, edited by Fujita Kayoko, Momoki Shiro and Anthony Reid
15. *Buddhism and Islam on the Silk Road*, by Johan Elverskog
16. *The Tongking Gulf through History*, edited by Nola Cooke, Li Tana and James A. Anderson
17. *The Royal Hunt in Eurasian History*, by Thomas T. Allsen
18. *Ethnic Identity in Tang China*, by Marc S. Abramson
19. *Eurasian Influences on Yuan China*, edited by Morris Rossabi
20. *The Sea, Identity and History: From the Bay of Bengal to the South China Sea*, edited by Satish Chandra and Himanshu Prabha Ray
21. *Early Southeast Asia Viewed from India: An Anthology of Articles from the Journal of the Greater India Society*, edited by Kwa Chong-Guan
22. *Asia Redux: Conceptualizing a Region for Our Times*, edited by Prasenjit Duara
23. *Buddhism across Asia: Networks of Material, Intellectual and Cultural Exchange, vol. 1*, edited by Tansen Sen
24. *Trails of Bronze Drums across Early Southeast Asia: Exchange Routes and Connected Cultural Spheres*, by Ambra Calo

25. *Buddhist Dynamics in Premodern and Early Modern Southeast Asia*, edited by Christian Lammerts
26. *Imperial China and Its Southern Neighbours*, edited by Victor H. Mair and Liam Kelley
27. *China and Beyond in the Mediaeval Period: Cultural Crossings and Inter- Regional Connections*, edited by Dorothy C. Wong and Gustav Heldt
28. *A 14th Century Malay Code of Laws: The Nitisarasamuccaya*, by Uli Kozok
29. *Esoteric Buddhism in Mediaeval Maritime Asia: Networks of Masters, Texts, Icons*, edited by Andrea Acri
30. *Indian and Chinese Immigrant Communities: Comparative Perspectives*, edited by Jayati Bhattacharya and Coonoor Kripalani
31. *Spirits and Ships: Cultural Transfers in Early Monsoon Asia*, edited by Andrea Acri, Roger Blench and Alexandra Landmann
32. *Bagan and the World: Early Myanmar and Its Global Connections*, edited by Goh Geok Yian, John N. Miksic and Michael Aung-Thwin
33. *Records, Recoveries, Remnants and Inter-Asian Interconnections: Decoding Cultural Heritage*, edited by Anjana Sharma
34. *Traces of the Ramayana and Mahabharata in Javanese and Malay Literature*, edited by Ding Choo Ming and Willem van der Molen

www.ingramcontent.com/pod-product-compliance
Lightning Source LLC
Chambersburg PA
CBHW052036300426
44117CB00012B/1848